RAILWAYS
&
THE RAJ

How the Age of Steam
Transformed India

CHRISTIAN
WOLMAR

Atlantic Books
London

First published in hardback in Great Britain in 2017 by Atlantic Books,
an imprint of Atlantic Books Ltd.

This paperback edition first published in Great Britain in 2018
by Atlantic Books.

10 9 8 7 6 5 4 3 2 1

A CIP catalogue record for this book is available
from the British Library.

E-book ISBN: 978-1-78239-766-3
Paperback ISBN: 978-1-78239-767-0

Designed by Carrdesignstudio.com

Printed and bound in Great Britain by Clays Ltd, Elcograf S.p.A.

Map artwork by Keith Chaffer

Atlantic Books
An imprint of Atlantic Books Ltd
Ormond House
26–27 Boswell Street
London WC1N 3JZ

www.atlantic-books.co.uk

Dedicated to Deborah Maby who has put up with me in good times and bad, and is the best possible travel and life companion.

CONTENTS

ILLUSTRATIONS

SECTION ONE

Lord Dalhousie (*Hulton Archive / Getty Images*)

Alice Tredwell (*The Institution of Mechanical Engineers*)

Inauguration of the East Indian Railway to Burdwan, 1855
  (© *Illustrated London News Ltd/Mary Evans*)

Construction of the railway through the ghats (*The Institution of
  Mechanical Engineers / Mary Evans*)

Reversing station (*Hulton Archive / Getty Images*)

Empress Bridge (*De Agostini / Biblioteca Ambrosiana / Getty Images*)

Bridge collapse, 1863 (*British Library Board. All Rights Reserved /
  Bridgeman Images*)

Lahore station (© *Corbis / Getty Images*)

Victoria Station (*SSPL / Getty Images*)

Bengal–Nagpur Railway worksite, 1890 (*DeGolyer Library, Central
  University Libraries, Southern Methodist University*)

Darjeeling Himalayan Railway (© *Hulton–Deutsch Collection / Corbis /
  Getty Images*)

Khyber Pass Railway (*Peter Jordan / Alamy Stock Photo*)

Rawalpindi station, 1910 (*Mary Evans / Grenville Collins Postcard
  Collection*)

Cotton bales being loaded at Akola station in Maharastra, *c.* 1930
  (*SSPL / Getty Images*)

Victoria Station booking hall, *c.* 1930 (*SSPL / Getty Images*)

Gandhi (*Dinodia Photos / Getty Images*)

Nationalist protesters blockading the railway, 1945 (*Universal History Archive / UIG via Getty Images*)

Indian refugees during the Partition of India and Pakistan, 1947 (*Bettman / Getty Images*)

SECTION TWO

Indian State Railways posters (*Swim Ink 2, LLC / Corbis / Getty Images*)

Indian Railways logo (*india view / Alamy Stock Photo*)

Indian railway scenes from the 1980s by Chris Gammell (*Courtesy of Bernard Gambrill and Roy Dension*)

Locomotive on the Konkan railway (*Dinodia Photos / Alamy Stock Photo*)

Nilgiri Mountain Railway (*IndiaPictures / UIG via Getty Images*)

Mumbai commuter line (*Pal Pillai / AFP / Getty Images*)

Accident at Kasara near Mumbai, September 2012 (*Mahendra Parikha / Hindustan Times via Getty Images*)

Cement bags being transported (*Prashanth Vishwanathan / Bloomberg via Getty Images*)

Hawkers at Agra station (*Robert Nickelsberg / Photonica World / Getty Images*)

Crowded train in New Delhi (*Manan Vatsyayana / AFP / Getty Images*)

Protesters at Borivli station (*Prasad Gori / Hindustan Times via Getty Images*)

Commuters at Chennai station (*Alexander Mazurkevich / Shutterstock.com*)

Rush hour outside Sealdah station in Kolkata (*Steve Raymer / National Geographic Creative / Bridgeman Images*)

Pictures of the author's trip round India, February 2016 (*Courtesy of Deborah Mabey*)

MAPS

(NB: Place names on maps refer to the contemporary versions.)

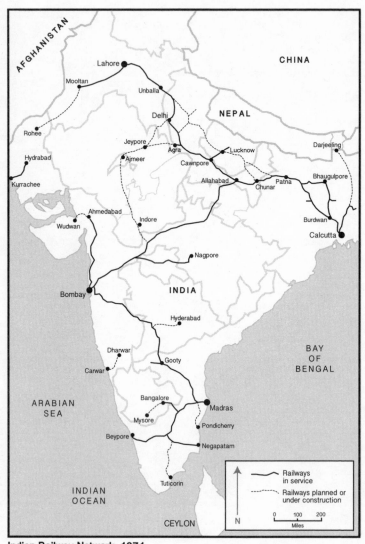

Indian Railway Network, 1871

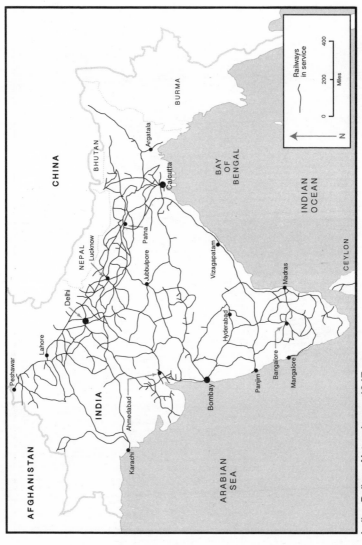

Indian Railway Network, pre-1947

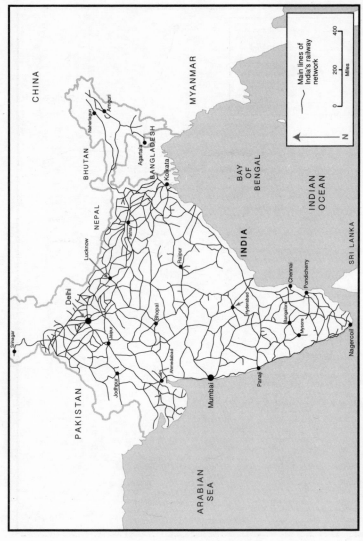

Indian Railway Network, 2017

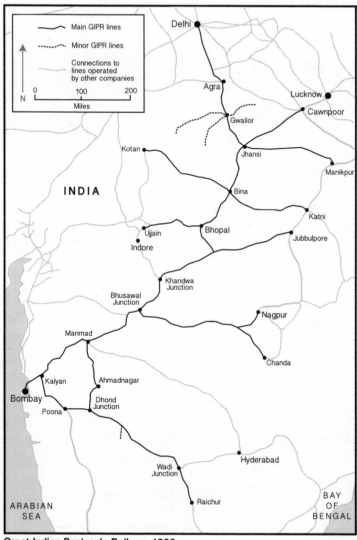

Great Indian Peninsula Railway, 1909

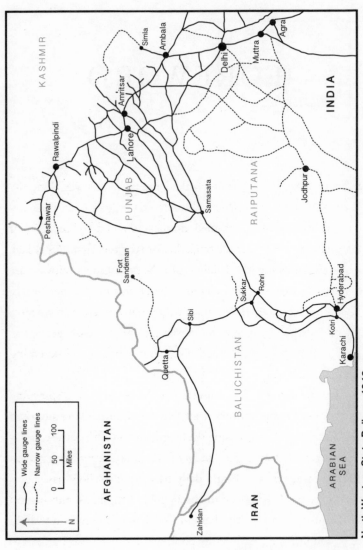

North Western State Railway, 1942

FOREWORD

Since India's first train clanked and puffed its way along the 21-mile track from Bombay to Thane in 1853, Indian Railways has captivated writers, charmed filmmakers, and fired the bellies of historians eager to trace the tracks back to the very first sleeper laid. Lovingly known as the Lifeline of a Nation, India's railways are the arteries that keep the country's heart beating. So much more than a simple method of transport, the railways are a microcosm of Indian society, carrying more than 25 million passengers every day, blasting through cities, crawling up mountains and skimming along coasts.

To write about India's railways is a challenge as vast, sprawling and complex as the network itself, which I discovered in 2010 when I spent five months travelling the length and breadth of the country to research my travelogue, *Around India in 80 Trains*. As a British Indian I was reminded on a daily basis by my fellow passengers that these trains had been the brainchild of the Brits, but to wind in the history and politics behind the birth of the railways would have doubled the length of my book, and I knew it was best left to accomplished railway experts, like Christian Wolmar, to accept the gargantuan task.

The horrors of empire are left blank in the history books of British schools, and the trope 'but we gave you the railways!' is swift to emerge in discussions on legacies of the British Raj. Ignoring the fact that many countries developed a railway system without the devastation of colonization, apologists for empire remain blinkered to the British motivation. As India marks seventy years of Independence, this much-needed history seeks to demolish a number of infuriating myths. Wolmar expounds, with aplomb, how the building of the railways was hardly an act of benevolence towards the Indian people, more a fast-track plan to govern more efficiently, facilitate the plunder of loot, and line their pockets at the expense of the Indian taxpayer who footed the bill for the railways' construction. But we also discover how Indians learnt to harness the railways and weaponize them against the very people who had put them in place.

Eschewing the dryness of other books on the subject, Wolmar's historical detail is pumped with colour and life. He recounts how the first trains were viewed by some as an 'iron demon' driven by magic and powered by children and young couples buried under the sleepers to provide sustenance for the 'fire chariot'. We travel deep into the mountainous ghats where 6,000 daily explosions often sent workers tumbling into the ravines below, watch troops being evacuated during the Second World War, and gain a fly-on-the-wall look at Gandhi's relationship with the railways. Tracing the evolution of Indian Railways, Wolmar rightly caps off his exploration of their role in today's modern age by buying a ticket to ride along the Konkan Railway, the missing link that the British were too frightened to attempt building. Flanked by the Western Ghats and the Arabian Sea, this 460-mile feat of engineering excellence was left in the hands of Indian railway workers who completed construction of the line in 1998. And if we're ever to trust a writer on India's railways, it should be one who isn't afraid to sit in the open doorway of a moving train, chai in hand, watching the country roll past in all its glory.

Monisha Rajesh, author of *Around India in 80 Trains*

INTRODUCTION

A s with several of my railway histories, *Railways & the Raj* is an attempt to set out a complex story in a clear and simple way, which few other authors have attempted. There are surprisingly few books about Indian railway history and none have covered the story of their creation, their influence and their enduring legacy in one volume. *Railways & the Raj* is consequently an overview of a railway system that merits far more study and analysis than it receives. I have tried to touch on all the major events and the various ways in which the railway has been important for the subcontinent, but inevitably much has been left out.

India is a vast nation and it has seen huge political transformation since the advent of the railways, changing from a country controlled by a company to being Britain's most important colony and eventually an independent state. In the process, India has lost parts of its territory, which left me with something of a dilemma over what to include and what to leave out. My compromise has been to include the story of railways now in Pakistan and Bangladesh while they were part of India, but to mention them only briefly in the sections about post-Independence India.

I have offered brief explanations of general historical background because the story of the railways is so strongly intertwined with the history of the country. Indeed, while railways played a key part in the history of nations covered by my other books, such as those on American railroads or the Transsiberian, few people could challenge the notion that India is the nation where the railways have been most influential in historical terms. But, after being so bound up with India for more than a year during the course of writing this book, I may be biased.

Many place names have officially changed since Independence, however, I have used the contemporary version throughout the book in order to fit in with the events being described. Therefore, for events up to Independence, old versions of names are used, while new ones are only used after the change had been made (which happened at different times for various places). For example, Bombay is referred to until the book reaches the mid-1990s, when its name was changed to Mumbai, which it is called thereafter, and that is reflected in the index. Some names have been changed merely to reflect the use of Indian English, or sometimes to reflect the local language, and in these cases the more modern spelling has usually been used everywhere in the book. When states are referred to, the modern names have been used throughout because they have been added to help the reader locate the town or city on a modern map. Therefore, Karnataka is used rather than Mysore, and Tamil Nadu rather than Madras State. This process is still taking place: for example, the state of Odisha has been known as Orissa only since 2011. Apologies for any inconsistencies.

Muslims were largely known as Mahommedans in the nineteenth century and again there were numerous possible spellings.

There are a few linguistic and cultural oddities, too. India uses two numerical terms that are unique to the subcontinent: a 'lakh' is 100,000 and a 'crore' 10 million – consequently 'million' is rarely used. The currency is now just rupees, which presently hover around 90 to the pound, and there are 100 paise to the rupee. The old rupee actually had 16 annas, each anna being further divided into 12 pies – thus there were 192 pies in a rupee until India decimalized in 1957.

Another possible area of confusion is over who ran India. In the nineteenth century, India was ruled by a Governor-General appointed by the British government, but the title became Viceroy and Governor-General from 1858, usually shortened to Viceroy.

✳

The structure of the book is largely chronological, though when a few themes are covered, there is inevitably a bit of jumping about. *Railways & the Raj* is something of a primer which I hope will inspire readers to travel on Indian trains. That is an unforgettable experience and the railway journey my partner, Deborah Maby, and I took in early 2016 was very helpful in providing the backdrop. Consequently, the book ends with a description of the first section of our trip partly written by her. Despite the recent surge in road construction and the introduction of low-cost airlines, the very heavily used railways remain the backbone of the Indian transport system.

Train travel in India is not an easy experience, even for the Westerner with ample funds, but do not be put off. First, you have to book the journey, which can be done online via the Indian Railways website; this, however, is full of confusing information and unnecessary complications. Moreover, Indian websites are quite often unobtainable, in my experience, as it takes a long time to connect.

In London, there is a special agency which deals with Indian Railways and can work out the route for you – so a bow to Shankar at S. D. Enterprises in Wembley, who sold me the India railpasses, a real bargain at just £147 for twenty-one days of second-class AC travel (just double that for first-class AC), but also, crucially, booked all the trains, which is the tough bit.

When you get to India, even if you have not booked online, you need to confirm by entering the PNR – Passenger Number Registration – for each leg of the journey into the system before you travel, a process that is made more tedious by having to relog on to the site every time by filling in a Captcha form. That, however, is the easy bit. The information about your coach and berth number only becomes available on the website a few hours before departure, although it is sometimes posted up at the station on old-fashioned computer paper an hour or so before the train leaves. But not always. At Kolkata, despite queuing for half an hour and only reaching the ticket office by barging my way to the front, which is the sole way to get there in India, the woman behind the counter refused to accept my PNR number, even when I pushed it through to her on a piece of paper. It was only when a couple of fellow travellers loudly complained that she eventually entered the number in her computer and provided the carriage and berth number. There was no apology. Otherwise it would have been guesswork to find the right carriage on a train that was half a kilometre long.

Just to add to the complexity, the various zones of Indian Railways differ in their approach over food provision. On some trains there are endless chains of seemingly officially sanctioned sellers, offering almost as varied a selection of food and drink as their counterparts on the platform. The best is the chai seller who for a few rupees will pour out a small cup of chai, a tiny sugary milky brew that in some parts of the country is heavily spiced with masala. On other trains, there is nothing on offer. The long-distance trains usually, but not always, provide meals to passengers in first and second class, consisting of a byriani, for 75 rupees, or rice with a selection of moderately spicy dishes for 120. It is always edible and sometimes delicious, depending on the skill of the pantry chef.

On other trains, there are no sellers or even meals provided and the only opportunity for sustenance is to buy food from the platform traders, who, despite serving a Westerner who clearly had more money than they would ever have, never attempted to cheat me. The main problem is change, as handing over a 100-rupee note causes consternation, and a 500-rupee note – made illegal since my trip – was impossible to offload on the platform.

Sanitary conditions, too, can be inconsistent. On the train between Chennai and Kolkata, there was, again, a steady stream of cleaners who would either sweep or spray disinfectant which they wiped up with a filthy mop, ensuring its effect was negligible. On others, there would only be a fellow occasionally dropping in to empty the bucket used as a dustbin, or, quite possibly, no one would turn up at all.

Despite all this, for the most part the trains deliver you on time – and certainly, given their cheapness, on budget – and in one piece, as their safety record has improved immeasurably in recent years. The key is, as those overused slogans suggest, to keep calm and enjoy the journey. Things may indeed go wrong, but the experience, in a world that has become all too predictable and over-conscious of risk, is what matters. So this book may be a history of Indian railways, but it is also an injunction to go there and enjoy the ride. There is no better way to see India, and there is no better country in the world to explore. Few are disappointed.

ACKNOWLEDGEMENTS

MY THANKS TO Rajendra Aklekar for showing me Mumbai's stations and helping in many other ways, including reading the draft; Bernard Gambrill and Peter Lewis for reading the draft; Rupert Brennan Brown (once); Ian Kerr; Ram Chandra Acharya; David Elworthy; Roy Denison; and James Nightingale at Atlantic Books, my faithful publishers. A special thanks to Paul Waters at the British Overseas Railways Historical Trust (which, incidentally, needs bigger premises) for allowing me to use the library extensively and opening it up for me several times. And of course to my partner, Deborah Maby, who makes the lonely days writing worthwhile. Apologies to anyone left out and of course all errors are my responsibility. If you find any mistakes or blatant omissions, do not hesitate to contact me via my website, www.christianwolmar. co.uk, and do follow me on Twitter @christianwolmar

Christian Wolmar
April 2017

ONE

A RAILWAY
FOR INDIA

THE BRITISH NEVER really conquered India. But the railways did. Remarkably, the British takeover of India was a commercial operation, carried out by the East India Company in conjunction, at various times, with the British government and its army.

The East India Company first arrived in India as early as 1600 but was for much of its first century what it said on the tin, a trading company interested in profit principally from cloth and spices, and later in a wider variety of produce such as silk, tea and opium. Gradually, though, the Company became something more: an overt weapon of imperialism. By the mid-eighteenth century, 'company' troops were fighting the French for control of India and over the next decades, through a mixture of treaties with local maharajahs and wars against both local and European opponents, the Company ruled over large swathes of its territory. There were, however, still large chunks, such as Hyderabad and parts of the vast Deccan plain, that were under the control of local maharajahs, and Portugal and France still had coastal interests.

By the second quarter of the nineteenth century, while railways were being built in many countries across the world, the East India Company was in full control of the subcontinent but was not particularly keen to join the party. After the almost simultaneous opening in 1830 of the world's first major railways in England and in the USA, a few progressive Indian business people had suggested creating a network in India. There were a couple of local initiatives that are sometimes claimed to be the first lines in India, but they were in reality more akin to the wagon ways that had long existed in the UK to transport minerals from mines to the nearest waterway than fully fledged railways. In 1836, work started on a short line near Madras at Chintadripet to transport granite for roadbuilding, and it opened, as the five-mile-long Red Hill Rail Road, the following year. Although the traction was mostly provided by animals hauling the wagons and, on the return trip of the empties, by a combination of gravity and a sail, one or possibly two or three very crude 'rotary' steam locomotives were apparently deployed for a while, but details, as with all these early schemes, remain sketchy. The promoter, Captain Arthur Cotton, sought to be allowed to carry passengers on the line but was refused permission by the Madras authorities. However, there is a report that on one journey, in August 1838, twenty-one passengers in four carriages were hauled by one of these locomotives, thus, if true, preceding by fifteen years the opening of the Bombay–Thana line, the usual date given by historians as the subcontinent's inaugural passenger journey.

There were other early initiatives, such as a line on a dam project at Rajamundry in Andhra Pradesh, where wagons were hauled by men on tracks, greatly helping the movement of heavy stone. A few years later, an extensive network, stretching more than ten miles, was created to assist the construction of the Solani aqueduct in Uttaranchal in northern India. That line also appears to have seen the first extensive use of a steam locomotive in India, a large six-wheeled standard-gauge engine imported from Leeds. Assembled in situ from parts sent from Britain and carried overland to the site, it was named *Thomason* in honour of the lieutenant-governor of the North-Western Provinces and was reckoned to be able to haul 200 tons at a speed of 4 mph. There are doubts over its fate and even its precise manufacture, but the generally accepted version is that, after only nine months in service, 'it disintegrated in a boiler explosion', which, apparently, was 'to the delight of the construction workers who had viewed it more as a hindrance than a help'.[1]

However, none of these early uses of railway technology had any long-term significance in terms of the development of the subcontinent's rail network. Nor did the odd attempt by Indians to push for the construction of railways, such as the suggestion, in 1844, of a Bengali merchant, Dwarkanath Tagore, who offered to fund a third of the capital of a line linking Calcutta north-west to the Burdwan coalfields. There were other expressions of interest by Indian industrialists, but nothing came of any of these schemes.

It was pressure from merchants in Britain that persuaded the British government to consider the introduction of railways in India. The Governor-General of India from 1844 to 1848, Lord Hardinge, who in effect ruled the nation, suggested that the East India Company should support initiatives by railway promoters to build an east–west line across India. He was clear about the compelling reasons for wanting to see the line built as, in his opinion, 'on military considerations alone, the grant of one million sterling ... may be contributed to the great line when completed from Calcutta to Delhi, and a pecuniary saving be effected by a diminution of military establishments'.[2] Hardinge's argument that facilitating rapid transport between major cities would permit a reduction in the number of troops required to be kept in barracks was the first articulation of a line of thinking that would play a key role in the early history of India's rail network. Supporting the ability of the military to remain in control of the country was always a useful extra line of reasoning to deploy in favour of the railways and, indeed, this military rationale was to play a key role in the development of Indian railways. The military imperative was not, however, the initial stimulus for the railways' introduction, nor a major component of their ultimate raison d'être.

The East India Company, whose power was beginning to wane in the face of a more detailed oversight of the subcontinent by the British government, was initially opposed to the building of railways. Its board, known as the Court of Directors, set out a series of reasons why railways and India were not compatible in a letter to the Governor-General. It was a comprehensive list which included weather-related phenomena such as the 'periodical rains and inundations' and 'violent winds', the hostile nature of the flora and fauna, the fact that it would be impossible to fence in the railway and the difficulty in attracting 'competent contractors and trustworthy engineers'. The killer point seemed to be, in the eyes of the London-based board, the effect of the 'vertical sun', though they did not explain precisely what they meant by that.[3] In reality it was a bureaucratic response designed to avoid doing something in the face of pressure from the government. One key aspect of disagreement was that the government realized the promoters would require a guarantee on their rate of return, an inducement the East India Company vehemently opposed.

The Company's resistance proved to be to no avail. The forces pushing for the railways were far greater than those arraigned against them. The key supporters included the powerful textile manufacturers, who were anxious to source cotton in India and sell the finished product to its people. Alongside them were the shipping interests, who were not only keen to carry the increased trade between the two nations that would result from the development of a rail network, but also, specifically, to supply their relatively new steamships with coal from the mines of western Bengal, which could be brought to the port of Calcutta by rail, allowing them to refuel on the way to points further east. The vision outlined by the supporters and railway promoters was indeed alluring, holding out 'the prospect of vast and opulent India becoming, once opened up by railways, a fabulous supply house of cotton and wheat and a huge consumer of textile and other manufactured products of Britain'.[4] This powerful combination of business interests held much influence in the British parliament and ultimately forced the East India Company begrudgingly to accept the inevitability of railways coming to India.

However, the initial plan for the railways seemed to take into account the Company's misgivings by covering only two sections of line, totalling a mere 142 miles. The idea was that the two lines would be 'experimental' because of the doubts over the viability of railways in India, and, therefore, if they failed or proved technically impossible, the plan could be discontinued without substantial investment. This was pretty timid stuff since by the time the go-ahead was given in 1849, the railway age across the world was in full swing, with most major countries having developed networks and the UK already boasting a system that would soon top 5,000 miles. Modest as it was, the scheme would still ensure India would be a pioneer, by building the first system in Asia.

The primitive nature of India's transport network was another factor that made railways attractive. There was a system of crude roads, but travel on them was notoriously slow, especially as oxen and buffalo, far more suited to the climate than horses, were used to haul the carts that carried both people and agricultural produce. There was one exception, which interestingly later led to an experiment in running steam trains on roads rather than rails. This was the Grand Trunk Road, which opened in 1839 between Calcutta and Delhi, and was extended to Peshawar (now in Pakistan) twenty years later. For its time, it was a very good, well-surfaced and wide road, so much so that in the early 1870s a mechanically minded army officer, Rookes Crompton (who later founded the Crompton company, which made light bulbs), decided to try to run steam vehicles along it. Crompton, stationed at Nowshera on the Grand Trunk Road near Peshawar, brought over steam engines from Edinburgh to run on the road in an effort to speed up transport. Bullock carts travelled at the glacial pace of only 2 mph, slower than walking pace, and the army feared this was not fast enough for troops. The high standard of the trunk road and the sluggishness of the carts persuaded the Governor-General, Lord Mayo, to fund the experiment. With the first engine, *The Primer*, Crompton embarked on a journey of thirty miles from Umballa to Kalka in the Punjab but encountered various difficulties, such as the vehicles being too heavy for the bridges and the shortage of coal (wood provided insufficient power). He persevered with two other engines which he had tested back in the UK, but again technical problems with crankshafts and the high cost of the solid rubber tyres led to the abandonment of the scheme, though Crompton claimed that the 'train' could haul nineteen vehicles and a load of forty tons, and climb up to as much as a 1 in 18 gradient at speeds of 5 mph or more. It was, though, never going to be reliable enough, and, instead, a rail line was soon built connecting Umballa and Kalka with Delhi.

Interestingly, similar experiments had taken place in the UK and France before the railways won out, as they did in India. However, it was inconceivable that the road network could be the solution to nineteenth-century India's transport needs. Much of the network was far older than the Grand Trunk Road, having been built under the Mughal Empire, and it had fallen into neglect after its collapse in the late eighteenth century. The terrible condition of the roads was a catalyst for the development of the railways, both for commercial and for military purposes.

The lack of cheap transport made the export of many commodities uneconomic as the costs were too high in relation to their value and there was considerable spoilage, given the crude nature of the carts. There were the odd exceptions, such as Bengali rice, which could be exported thanks to cheap river transport. Indian cloth, a product expensive enough to be transported over long distances, was also sold extensively abroad (until the British imposed tariffs to protect its mills). However, for the most part, the absence of cheap and reliable transport meant that many regions were effectively cut off and unable to trade, greatly limiting the size of potential markets and consequently restricting the potential economic development of the subcontinent.

It is easy to be cynical about the altruistic reasons often cited at the time for the encouragement of railways in India, but selflessness was a genuine force in Victorian administration. Many supporters of the iron road saw the railways as a civilizing influence, one that would, to put it bluntly, make India a bit more like us. These arguments cannot simply be dismissed as merely masking imperialism under a cloak of altruism, since the case for railways was made by numerous prominent Victorians and accorded with their wider view of Britain's role in the world. Lord Dalhousie, who succeeded Hardinge as Governor-General, himself put it succinctly: 'They [the railways] will lead to some similar progress in social improvement that has marked the introduction of improved communication in various Kingdoms of the Western World.'[5] Or as, twenty years later, Grant Duff, an official in the India Office during Gladstone's government, argued: 'If we are not in India to civilize and raise India, we had better leave it as soon as we can and wind up our affairs.'[6]

The railways also had a great champion who was to be crucial to their introduction. In the history of railway development in every country of the world, there is invariably a pioneering figure who can be characterized as the father of the railways (they are all men). In the case of India, it is undoubtedly Lord Dalhousie who merits this title. He took over as Governor-General in 1848 and was, according to the historian John Keay, 'a modernising and imperious workaholic'[7] who routinely worked sixteen- or even eighteen-hour days. He was a firm advocate of Britain's imperial role, believing that extending it wherever possible would be good for India. During his eight-year tenure, several princely states were taken under Britain's wing thanks to his clever policy of assuming control over any state where a ruler had died without having a son who could inherit the title. Dalhousie had already been involved in the railway industry back in the UK as President of the Board of Trade – the ministry responsible at the time for the railways – in Robert Peel's government during the collapse of the railway mania in 1845. Dalhousie's voracious appetite for work was not wasted, and he was one of those politicians who could master both the big picture and the smallest detail. When he accepted the role of Governor-General of India, he made it clear that he alone would determine policy in the subcontinent, independent of party politics back home, and consequently much of the shape, policies and practices of Indian railways today are a result of the ideas he set out in two renowned 'minutes' written in 1850 and 1853 respectively to the East India Company's Court of Directors.

These are extraordinary and extensive documents, written personally in long hand with the second one running to 216 pages and penned with an eye to future historians. Dalhousie did what the British government had never done at home and planned a network of railways, setting out in some detail the order in which they should be built. He cited political and commercial reasons for their construction, and dismissed the long list of objections cited by the Court. There were no insuperable engineering problems, he argued, though he accepted the main difficulty was the fording of India's vast rivers. He did not attempt to disguise the fact that there were good commercial reasons for the establishment of railways, which would open up coalfields and other sources of minerals for exploitation. Dalhousie pointed out how much time would be saved if there were a line linking Calcutta with Bombay, obviating the need for the long sea voyage through the Palk strait between Ceylon and India. Since his relentless expansion of British control over India necessitated the occasional war, Dalhousie did not omit the military imperative, repeating the notion that the railways would ensure the security of British rule more cheaply. In sum, railways 'would encourage enterprise, multiply production, facilitate the discovery of latent resources, increase national wealth and encourage "progress in social improvement"'.[8]

What was there not to like? Well, there was the fact that this was a nakedly imperial project that not only would later attract the wrath of nationalists but which also limited the usefulness of the railways to the country in which they were being built. As Ian J. Kerr, the most productive historian of Indian railways, summed it up, 'The interests of the Indians were incidental although, as represented in the writings of Dalhousie and many Britons, the progressive consequences for India of the railroads was a self-evident truth.'[9] In other words, the benefits of railways for the subcontinent may have been incidental, but they were nevertheless substantial.

There was, however, the issue of how these lines would be built. Already promoters in Britain had created railway companies with the intention of constructing lines in India, and they had put forward numerous competing schemes. It was a cut-throat business, and the various interests were not averse to criticizing each other's plans, which did little to help the overall cause of the Indian railways, and partly explains why so little progress was made in the 1840s.

The Government of India was in no position to carry out the work itself, and, in any case, such a direct involvement of government went completely against the prevailing UK ideology of the time. The private sector had to be involved, but the way that the railways had developed in Britain, through a system of promoters petitioning Parliament, was clearly unsuitable in the Indian context. There was no question of companies coming forward to suggest where lines were to be constructed. Dalhousie and his successors had drawn lines on the map where they wanted to see routes built and that was how the outline of the system was determined, though they may have been influenced, at times, by earlier maps put forward by private interests.

However, attracting private companies to what was, as the Court of Directors had intimated, a pretty risky enterprise, required a substantial inducement. While direct subsidy was out of the question in Victorian Britain, it was clear that no railways would be built unless the private companies were given a deal that satisfied their investors. For much of the 1840s, negotiations between government and the private companies were stuck over the precise financial arrangements and the degree of risk that the investors would have to bear. The only way of breaking the deadlock was for the government to provide a guaranteed rate of return. The government had initially sought to limit the level to 3 per cent but the companies held out for more, and the eventual figure agreed in March 1849 was 5 per cent, a very healthy level at a time when interest rates were 3 per cent, and consequently the arrangement guaranteed sufficient investment funds would become available.

This generosity on the part of the British government was not all it seemed. While the investment funds would come almost entirely from Britain, the risk was borne by Indian, not British, taxpayers, who would be required to meet any shortfall between the rate of profit from operating the railways and the 5 per cent guarantee. While there is disagreement over how much this would eventually cost the Indian people, Ian J. Kerr reckons 'the revenues of the Government of India were tapped for some £50 million to meet the guarantee'.[10] Moreover, the railways, or rather the railway companies, enjoyed other benefits too, such as not having to pay for the land or for the legal costs of acquiring it, something that proved a heavy burden for British railway companies. The guarantee ensured that British investors came forward in large numbers. These were not capitalists in search of a quick buck but, rather, ordinary people with a bit of money to set aside and earn a steady rate of return. According to one researcher, 'the middle classes predominated – widows, barristers, clergymen, spinsters, bankers and retired army officers'.[11] Both sides were happy. The railway companies got their funding at relatively low rates of interest, while the British bourgeoisie found a safe place for their money.

Dalhousie set out the plans in great detail, even ruling on the question of gauge, the distance between the two rails. At the time, across the world, there was no consensus on what this should be. The size varied between 7ft 0¼in and 3ft 3⅜in (or, rather, metre gauge), with many variants in between. Indeed, there were several countries where no common gauge had emerged triumphant and in Britain itself railways were being built with two very different gauges: the 7ft 0¼in favoured by Brunel's Great Western Railway, and 4ft 8½in that prevailed elsewhere. Indeed, the latter was already becoming known as 'standard gauge' for it was widely used in Europe – though with exceptions such as Spain and Russia – and was becoming dominant in the USA.

The promoters of Indian lines had pressed for standard gauge and that was the basis of the initial agreement between the government and the companies signed in 1849. However, Dalhousie favoured a 6ft gauge, feeling that the particular conditions of India, with its mountainous terrain requiring steep gradients and its high winds, needed the stability of a wider gauge. After much debate, a compromise was reached in London with the adoption of a 5ft 6in gauge, and later many lines in remote or mountainous parts of India used metre gauge (3ft 3⅜in). In a far-sighted move, which was to make increasing the capacity of the system much easier in later years, the major trunk network was built to specifications for double tracks, with wider and stronger bridges, even when initially only a single track was laid.

Dalhousie's second minute set out in precise detail the routes of the initial trunk network. He based his selection on three criteria: the political and commercial advantages of the routes, the ease of construction in the face of engineering challenges, and their potential as a main line connecting various branches. His plan envisaged connecting the principal cities and extending across most of the subcontinent. There was to be a 1,500-mile line across the top of India from Calcutta along the Ganges valley to Allahabad and then to Delhi, through the Punjab to Lahore (in what is now Pakistan). Two lines would stretch out of Bombay, one linking up with the Calcutta–Delhi line, the other eastwards to Poona and onwards. Madras, too, would have a couple of lines stretching out from it, and, of course, the idea was that all routes should be connected at a later stage. All of these lines would eventually be built.

By the time Dalhousie's second minute was despatched in April 1853, work had already started on the first two 'experimental' lines. They were a rather random choice: a short 21-mile-long suburban line stretching from the centre of Bombay to Thana, and a 100-mile-long main line from Howrah, the other side of the Hooghly River from Calcutta, since the crossing was initially deemed to be too difficult and expensive. It was intended to reach Burdwan in order to transport the coal from the Raniganj coalfields through to the port of Calcutta. While deemed experimental, there was little doubt that these two railways would be the forerunners of what was to become a major national network as set out by Dalhousie.

The promoter of the Bombay line was the Great Indian Peninsula Railway, whose grand name rather contrasted with the modest nature of its inaugural railway. The company, formed in London in 1843, had long focused on linking Bombay with its outlying districts as its principal investors included a strong cohort of Liverpool cotton manufacturers who were keen to find new sources of raw materials. It was their involvement which proved to be decisive in establishing that the first line should run from Bombay into its hinterland, where the cotton grew. Despite its large production of cotton, India exported very little because of the poor internal transport system dominated by bullock carts, which were unreliable, particularly at times of drought and famine, resulting in ships often being kept waiting at ports for produce that never arrived. A promotional pamphlet published by the British cotton merchants, *Railways for Bombay*, argued that the Americans, who were flooding the British market with their cotton, did so thanks to their extensive railway network. Creating a rail network in India would not only solve the problem of internal transport but also free the British market of dependence on the potentially unreliable supply from America.

The initial protagonist for the Great Indian Peninsula Railway was one of those amateur enthusiasts who litter the history of early railways. John Chapman was a carriage manufacturer who had rather grander ideas about designing a flying machine, but soon gave up on the plan. He had been a successful manufacturer of knitting machinery for export to the Continent until he ran afoul of British export controls designed to limit foreign acquisition of machinery that could threaten the domestic industry. He was a kind of James Dyson of his time and was to play a key role in turning the dream of Indian railways into reality. Chapman wrote a pamphlet on the need for better transport for cotton and brought together a group of promoters to create the Great Indian Peninsula Railway company. He was motivated enough to take himself to Bombay to undertake a survey of potential routes, but initially chose an alignment that involved passing through already populated areas. As Rajendra Aklekar puts it, 'The plan would have changed the Bombay we know today, if the arrangement had worked.'[12] Instead, the route from Bombay to Thana, a significant town described by Marco Polo, who visited in 1290, as a 'great kingdom' with a substantial port, was selected and incorporated into legislation passed in the British Parliament.

Once the agreement between the government and the companies over the guaranteed rate of return had been made, the Great Indian Peninsula Railway, keen to get started, appointed James Berkley as 'chief resident engineer', and despatched him to Bombay. He was widely recommended, especially by Robert Stephenson, who had built the London & Birmingham Railway and had appointed Berkley as engineer on a couple of railways in the Midlands. On Berkley's arrival in February 1850, he wasted no time in rolling up his sleeves, and work started on the line between Bombay and Thana at the end of October that year, with a British contractor, Faviell & Fowler, in charge. The Bombay terminus was to be at Bori Bunder, the site today of India's grandest railway station, Victoria Terminus (now officially known as Chhatrapati Shivaji Terminus, although Bombay residents, especially taxi drivers, still call it 'VT').

The scale of the enterprise, even for such a relatively short line, can be judged by the fact that Faviell & Fowler took on nearly 10,000 workers to undertake the task. And, inevitably, the cultural differences that were to dog much railway construction on the subcontinent appeared almost immediately. As Aklekar puts it in his history of the line, this first engagement between British rail engineers and 'native' workers 'led to a giant clash of cultures, with British engineers trying to extract their money's worth, and the workers, in truth, demanding respect for their ways and religious practices'.[13] One of the firm's partners, Henry Fowler, complained in a letter to England about how difficult it was to persuade the workers to start work at six in the morning rather than the customary eight: 'It is the most difficult thing to alter the existing system as almost every custom the natives have is founded on absurd but invincible prejudices – generally of religious character.'[14]

Just to complicate matters further for the British contractors, there were the multifarious divisions and sub-divisions into castes whose members refused to work with those of another caste and at times even tried to prevent others from working at all. Fowler was to learn the hard way that Europeans (the word 'European' was used widely and was effectively synonymous with 'British' or 'white') were pariahs. He wrote how one particularly hot day on site he made the mistake of grabbing a worker's water pot only to see 'the innocent vessel ... immediately doomed to destruction as the fact of my touching it had defiled it'.[15] Such incidents could lead to walkouts by groups of men, angered at a slight or by an insensitive overseer. Poor Fowler never acclimatized to India and illness soon forced him back to the UK, where he died in 1854 at the tender age of just thirty-four, leaving the hardier Faviell in sole charge.

The difficulties Faviell faced were unprecedented and he had to learn on the job while in the full glare of the curiosity of local people and the attention of the British rulers. He had tried to recruit British labour, but the men failed to adapt either to the climate or to the culture, and, with only meagre wages on offer, the lucky ones who did not succumb to illness soon returned home. Native labour was cheap and abundant, except during the rice harvest, when many workers returned to their smallholdings, thereby creating a temporary shortage.

The contractors were under pressure to keep costs down. The East India Company remained sceptical of the advantages of the railway and had watched developments in the UK, where many schemes foundered with investors losing their money, with horror. Before work started, they had warned the Government of India to watch the pennies and drew its attention to a 'great error committed by Railway Companies in Europe in the hope that you will studiously avoid a similar error', which was that 'large sums of money ... have been most unnecessarily and extravagantly expended in ornamental works, especially those connected with the stations and offices of the Company'.[16]

There were other novel challenges such as the local wildlife, particularly snakes, with at least two local species capable of delivering fatal bites. The greatest difficulty, however, was the topography of the route. By a strange coincidence, the first line crossed between two islands through the same type of wetland that Britain's first major railway, the Liverpool & Manchester, had encountered more than twenty years previously in the swamps of Chat Moss. George Stephenson, the pioneering engineer of that inaugural line, had developed a radical solution to the problem by creating a kind of 'floating embankment' on a bed of plants, faggots of wood, rubble and tar. This time, it was his son, Robert, who, as consulting engineer to the Great Indian Peninsula Railway, devised a similarly ingenious solution. As Aklekar reports, 'mattresses were made from mangrove trees and spread across the mud, then soil was placed on top to press the mattress; another mattress was superimposed and more soil placed until a sturdy bed emerged, sufficient for solid road and tracks.'[17] Another technological challenge was getting the gauge right. Curves pose particular challenges for railway builders and ensuring the workers used the right equipment to maintain the 5ft 6in separation was no easy task, and in the early days after opening there were numerous train derailments as a result.

Beyond the swamps, the railway crossed open countryside with attractive views of the Thana River and the Ghats (the mountains that would, as outlined in the next chapter, be a major obstacle to extensions of the line). Despite the difficulties created by both the topography and the weather, progress was steady and, by mid-1852, a mere two years from the start of work, part of the line was opened for the use of construction traffic. The big technical challenge was, of course, finding suitable locomotives to power the trains. In this respect, India, by starting to build railways rather late in relation to many other nations, could take advantage of technological developments in locomotive design, which had proceeded rapidly in the two decades since the opening of the Liverpool & Manchester line.

One of the key innovations of the Liverpool & Manchester which marked it out as the world's first modern railway was that it was powered entirely by steam engines. There had been some debate in India, prior to the creation of the Great Indian Peninsula Railway, on whether horses should be used to haul the trains. In fact, a man called Clark had promoted an idea for a railway on a similar alignment to Thana that would have used steam locomotives for passenger trains and horses for goods traffic. Interestingly, he calculated that while this would only have required ten locomotives for passengers, 334 horses would be needed to haul the goods wagons, which suggests that it was simple economics that dictated the use of steam engines as much as speed and practicality.

The first locomotive for the Thana line, built by the foundry of E. B. Wilson in Leeds, arrived with much fanfare. In one of those complications that so often feature in history, as mentioned above, it was not actually the first steam locomotive to run in India, but its predecessor had made little impact and had long been forgotten. The momentous nature of the locomotive's arrival was demonstrated by the huge attention it attracted when, after being craned off the ship, it was pulled along roads filled with thousands of sightseers by a couple of hundred men drafted in for the task. Its initial home was Byculla, in what is now south Mumbai, where a shunting yard had been created for the steam engines. Officially named *Lord Falkland* after the Bombay governor of the time, the engine undertook its initial test shunting runs, watched by crowds of curious onlookers, which triggered debates in the local newspapers on what to call this extraordinary invention that was captivating – and at times scaring – the local population. There were suggestions that it should be called 'Ag-boat', the name given to steam vessels that had started becoming a regular sight at the port of Bombay, but this was rejected in favour of 'fire chariot', a far better description.

Test runs began in February 1852 and not surprisingly caused something of, as Aklekar puts it, 'a cultural shock'. There had been much speculation in Britain when the railways appeared about the damage that could be done to farm animals – they would be turned black – or to people – who would not be able to breathe because of the speed – and it was only familiarity which eventually allayed these fears. In India, which, unlike the UK, did not have the factories and chimney stacks that had sprung up during the Industrial Revolution, the surprise at seeing this behemoth in action was far greater and led to much wilder speculation about the functioning of the engine. For some, it was seen as an ungodly, even evil, invention that earned it the name of 'iron demon' ('lokhandi rakshash' in Marathi). The engine appeared to be driven by magical powers, and there was widespread and understandable incomprehension that it could move so fast without any obvious power source. The most potentially damaging rumour was that the authorities 'had to bury children and young couples under the rail sleepers to "power" the rail engine; British sepoys [soldiers], therefore, were perpetually looking for and catching hold of young couples and children on the streets'[18] to provide the sustenance for the engines. There were warnings, too, that those foolhardy enough to travel on the railway would find their lifespan dramatically decreased since, as Aklekar explains, 'if one reached one's destination so much faster, one was bound to speed up life and age'.[19]

There were numerous test runs before the official opening of the line, which helped to allay these fears and make the new technology more familiar to local people. The line was completed on time and, miraculously, under budget. The opening on 16 April 1853 was seen as an event of national, indeed international, significance. The 400 invited guests, who included royalty as well as rich local merchants and 'zamindars' (landowners), were treated to a rapid ride down the twenty-one-mile line from Bori Bunder to Thana, hauled by three locomotives alliteratively called (according to legend but not officially recorded) Sindh, Sultan and Sahib, all from the Vulcan Foundry in Newton-le-Willows near Liverpool, in which Robert Stephenson was a partner. The guests travelled in fourteen fairly primitive carriages that had just four wheels each – making for a bumpy ride – and which had also been shipped from England, but there were no mishaps. All those test runs had proved their worth. There was, though, a notable absentee. Lord Falkland, the governor of Bombay, did not turn up to the ceremony, preferring to remain in the cool of the local hill station, despite the fact that the inaugural locomotive had been named after him. Perhaps he was peeved that it was not on duty on that historic day.

Along the track, every vantage point on rooftops and hillocks was taken and some of the locals, according to the *Overland Telegraph and Courier*, reported that 'the natives salaamed [bowed to] the omnipotence of the steam engine as it passed'.[20] Others saw the engine as a god and applied the tilak, the red mark of the Hindus, to the smoke stacks of the locomotives, left food and money on the footplate, and laid flowers on the tracks.

It was not only locals who turned out to watch. The *Illustrated London News*, which reported on what it saw correctly as an event that 'would be remembered far longer than the recent battles which had brought India into the British Empire',[21] found there were visitors from as far afield as East Africa, Afghanistan and the Persian Gulf. It was, in other words, recognized as a world-changing event. Even with a stop halfway for the engines to fill their water tanks, it took less than an hour for the pioneering train to cover the route, despite the fact that sightseers slowed its progress by spilling on to the tracks, a phenomenon that survives to this day (and, shockingly, currently causes ten deaths per day in the Bombay area alone).

The blessings must have proved effective. Passengers flocked to the line, with more than 4,000 per day travelling on the railway by the end of the year (today it carries that number on just one of its overcrowded trains). Not everyone, of course, welcomed its arrival. As ever with a new invention, there were losers. The most obvious were the bullock cart owners, who, at risk of losing both their passenger and freight business, picked a fight with the railway and launched a price war. They started charging a fixed rate from the agricultural areas to Bombay, rather than setting a cheaper fare for the shorter ride to the railhead, and, for a while, their clever manoeuvre took considerable business away from the railway. Eventually, however, as the new line expanded further into the hinterland, the advantages of rail travel proved decisive in winning over traffic. As Aklekar puts it, 'as the benefits of easy, clean and swift transport became obvious, both rumours and objections vanished'.

The *Bombay Quarterly Review* was contemptuous of the doubts widely expressed during the construction period on whether 'natives' would use the railway and about predictions that the trains would run empty: 'So erroneous were the prognostications of the failure of passenger traffic, that the natives, down even to the lowest orders, immediately availed themselves of the new mode of conveyance.' The journal went on to recount that 'a poor, ragged, companionless girl, and ticket in hand ... [took] her place in a third class carriage with all the independence of a commercial traveller'.[22]

The fares had been set reasonably cheap, ranging from 4 rupees 4 annas for first class to 8 annas 6 pies for third class (or just 3 pies per mile) for the thirty-three-mile journey from Bori Bunder to Kalyan. The line had been extended to Kalyan, a further twelve miles, in 1854, and with every new addition there were the inevitable celebrations: 'Each official opening was marked by an appropriate ceremony with various festivities, banquets, speeches and toasts, plus the necessary train ride in the foreshadowing of a ritual that was to be repeated throughout the century in various parts of India as more and more lines opened, great bridges completed, long tunnels excavated or precipitous inclines surmounted.'[23] These events played a crucial role in encouraging local people to appreciate the railway, and the provision of a free inaugural ride for the local dignitaries was a clever way of winning the influential elite over to the 'fire chariot'.

The much grander line of the East Indian Railway Company stretching east from Howrah should have been the first to operate in India, given it was perceived at the time as being of far greater importance than its suburban counterpart in Bombay (which today, of course, carries hundreds of millions of people annually). However, the Great Indian Peninsula Railway had been much cannier than its counterpart in the east at winning over local opinion by holding a series of public meetings to raise interest and reduce antagonism towards the messy construction process. By contrast, opposition to the East India's project had delayed the start of work, and a series of quite bizarre and unlikely mishaps caused further setbacks.

The East Indian Railway had its origins in the visit to India of its founder, Macdonald Stephenson, who in the early 1840s travelled with three assistants from London to survey the route of a potential railway from Calcutta, then the capital of India, to Delhi via Mirzapur. He returned home to form the company, having drawn up an outline route to attract investors. The East Indian Railway won the right to build the second of Dalhousie's two experimental lines, a 121-mile track in West Bengal between Howrah and Burdwan, which would be the start of the branch to the large Raniganj coalfields that would provide much of the income for the railway. As with the Great Indian Peninsula, investors in the East Indian were guaranteed the generous 5 per cent rate of return, which would be paid by the Government of India if revenues were insufficient.

Work started in January 1851 and although, in general, the terrain was easier than that encountered on the Thana route, the difficulties were more typical of those that would be encountered by other railways in India. The decision to start on the western side of the Hooghly River was a recognition that India's vast rivers, which flowed rapidly at monsoon time – or, for those in the north, during the snow melt – but were mere trickles the rest of the time, posed a major obstacle for the railways. The rivers have notoriously wide flood plains to accommodate the exceptional storm water of the rainy season, which means the bridges fording them must not only be very long, but also built with piers to withstand the brief period when they are raging torrents, full of debris and running fast enough to scour out even quite substantial foundations. There were, as we see in the next chapter, several mishaps resulting from a failure to understand this fundamental requirement. The rivers, too, had the mischievous habit of altering their course from year to year, with the result that 'more than once, engineers have discovered that the river has shifted before their bridge is finished'.[24] The rivers caused all sorts of difficulties and required not only bridges but numerous culverts, revetments and embankments. In terms of topography, however, the East Indian had it easy because the land was flat, as demonstrated by the fact that even after it had extended through to Delhi, there was only one tunnel on its 1,340 miles of track, which was just a modest 300 yards long.

Various other difficulties beset the East Indian Railway, leading to delays in the full opening of the line. First, a dispute with Chandernagar, a territory still governed by the French on the route of the railway, had to be resolved. Then in one of the great classic errors of early railway history, the cause of much mirth, the locomotive intended to haul the first train was taken to Australia due, apparently, to a clerical error. To compound the railway's problems, the coaches suffered an even worse fate as the ship carrying them from England sank on the voyage. Their replacements were Indian built, the first produced on the subcontinent, but sadly were not to be the genesis of a domestic industry, as for the next century rolling stock and locomotives came predominantly from the UK. If it had not been for the twin mishaps suffered by the rolling stock intended for Howrah, the inaugural service would have been on the East Indian Railway, which was, after all, a far more significant line than the suburban route served by the Great Indian Peninsula Railway.

The line was opened in stages which ensured an immediate stream of revenue for the railway company. On 15 August 1854, sixteen months after the opening of the Thana line, the first train ran on the twenty-three-mile section, between Howrah and the town of Hooghly. As with its predecessor, it was an instant success and it took under four months for the total passenger numbers carried to reach 100,000, with standing quickly becoming the norm in third class. Over the next few months the whole 121-mile section was opened.

The pretence that this was an experimental line was soon forgotten and the contract for expansion of the line to Delhi, which had always been Dalhousie's plan, was already signed a few weeks before the first train ran from Howrah. There was now nothing to stop the iron horse or, rather, the fire chariot, from conquering India.

TWO

BUILDING
FOR INDIA

T HE DIFFICULTIES FACED by Faviell in Bombay and his counterparts on the East Indian Railway would be repeated on other
pioneering railways, though gradually the British engineers and
their Indian workforces would learn from errors on the inaugural
lines. Some of the other early lines, however, faced obstacles that
were far greater than those encountered by the initial two railways
in terms of the topography, as mountain ranges had to be crossed
and huge rivers forded.

The decision to continue with Dalhousie's vision of creating a
nationwide network was effectively made by default. The 'experimental lines' had, despite their name, been a way of getting
the process of building a network started, given that railway
construction was taking off in so many other countries of the
world. First, though, the contracts had to be allocated and signed.
It was initially unclear whether the generous arrangements of the
guarantee by the government of a 5 per cent return for investors
would become the norm. However, Dalhousie was aware that the
Government of India did not have the resources to build railways

and that the guarantee was necessary in order to attract investors from the UK. Influenced by the fact that the railways in France were being built under a similar guarantee system, and were, in fact, paying out a better rate of return to investors than their British counterparts, Dalhousie had recommended in his second minute that the guarantee system should be applied to all future railways at the rate of 4.5 or 5 per cent, depending on the prevailing bank rate.

It was in fact a very modern and successful arrangement which would be known today as a Public–Private Partnership. The Government of India provided the land (for free) while the companies supplied capital and labour. This arrangement was in sharp contrast to the process of railway construction in the UK at the time, whereby the private companies had total control of their railways other than having to conform to basic safety rules and provide a cheap daily train on every route. In India, the private companies built the lines and ran them, but were closely supervised at every stage by the Indian government, which was able to intervene in virtually every aspect apart from selection of staff. Each company had a government-appointed director on its board who was able to veto any decisions that ran counter to the Government of India's policy. Consequently, as J. N. Westwood, the author of a short history of Indian railways, summarizes it, 'the Government approved or specified the routes, set standards of construction ... approved the amount and type of rolling stock, approved passenger and freight tariffs, determined train services, supervised expenditure and maintenance standards, and checked the accounts ...'[1]

That is quite a list. The railways were, in effect, controlled by government while the railway companies, which had ninety-nine-year leases (with possible break points at twenty-five or fifty years), were more like the franchisees in the current British system than genuine independent organizations. One illustration of the intertwined relationship between government and the companies was that in years when the companies made profits greater than the 5 per cent rate of return, the surplus was shared equally between the two parties. Therefore, right from the beginning, in contrast to the situation back in the UK, 'the detailed involvement of government was one of the distinctive features of railway building and railway operation in India'.[2] Moreover, as the railways expanded and the need for them became more apparent, the Government of India exercised ever greater control over all aspects of railway activity. Since the government itself was at times a mere conduit for London's requirements, there 'were few opportunities for the ruled to influence the formulation and execution of railway policy'.[3] In short, London determined railway policy. Inevitably an extensive, and indeed expensive, bureaucracy grew up to service and police the arrangements needed to manage such huge contracts. The British government was involved at every level in great detail: 'Decisions made in London or Calcutta affected the conduct of work at a given construction site from the number of people employed to the tools used or to the degree of danger involved.'[4]

The growth of the railways coincided with the takeover by the Crown, in 1858, of the administration of the subcontinent from the East India Company and of the expansion of the civil service and its bureaucracy, which grew up largely as a way of extracting tax from the Indian people. Now, the railways gave it another important function, overseeing the expenditure of millions of pounds of investors' money that was backed by government guarantee. The railways, in other words, can claim responsibility for creating a large part of the infamous Indian bureaucratic system.

Once the arrangements for the guaranteed rate of return were in place, there was no shortage of investors and something of a mini-construction boom soon took hold across the subcontinent. The first railway in the south was soon under way. The Madras Railway Company had been formed in London as early as July 1845 with the idea of building a line from Madras to Arcot. After much delay over contracts and financing, construction began in June 1853 and the first sixty-four miles of line, built on easy terrain, opened in 1856 and stretched from coast to coast five years later. By then, work was also well underway on the first tracks laid by the Great Southern Railway between the east-coast port of Negapatam and the prosperous inland centre of Trichinopoly. The seventy-eight-mile line opened in 1862 and would later connect with the Madras Railway.

Other large companies emerged to build the lines set out in Dalhousie's plan in the Punjab (the Sind, Punjab & Delhi Railway, which emerged from four separate undertakings) and northwards from Bombay (the Bombay, Baroda & Central India Railway). As we saw in the last chapter, the line to Thana was extended to Kalyan, and then work started on extending it to Poona.

Overall, eight companies, all created by UK investors, built lines in this first period of Indian railway construction and all benefited from the guarantee system which gave investors a generous rate of return. Their first task on any project was to find contractors. While some, such as the Great Indian Peninsula Railway, chose big British contractors, others, like the Madras Railway, effectively did the work in-house by employing their own engineers. There were problems with both systems. The big British firms tended to charge excessively and make too much use of unsuitable labour from the UK, while the local contractors tended to be undercapitalized. Big British contractors like Thomas Brassey's company, the most celebrated in the business, which had worked extensively in European countries as far apart as Spain and Norway, were courted but were not always willing to undertake the work in such unfamiliar surroundings. Brassey had refused the contract to build the initial section of the East Indian Railway but later won several others, such as the 112 miles between Calcutta and Kushtia (now in Bangladesh) for the East Bengal Railway and parts of the Delhi and East Indian railways. Despite having three illustrious partners for the Kushtia line contract, including Sir Joseph Paxton, the designer of the Crystal Palace for the 1851 Great Exhibition, Brassey lost money on the contract because it was a fixed-price deal and costs, notably for labour, proved to be higher than expected.

In contrast, rather than allocating the work to a single big contractor, the East Indian Railway divided up its route into short sections and granted them to small local and British contractors. However, most got into difficulties because the sheer scale of the task was beyond them, given that they were undercapitalized and the company refused to help them out. They were hampered, too, by external events such as the slow delivery of material from England, labour shortages and the failure of the government to obtain the land quickly enough for them to begin work on time.

The most challenging of these early contracts was undoubtedly the extension towards Poona by the Great Indian Peninsula Railway. The railway's promoters had always envisaged extending the line eastwards but this involved the challenge of crossing the Western Ghats, the mountain range running inland parallel to much of India's west coast. Scaling these mountains with a railway had long been seen as a major, possibly insuperable, barrier in connecting Bombay with the Deccan plateau and the rest of India. The concerns about the difficulty were not misplaced and, indeed, scaling the ghats was, according to Ian J. Kerr, 'among the greatest feats of 19th century engineering',[5] quite an accolade given the fact that around 500,000 miles of track were built worldwide in the 1800s.

The assumption had always been for the railway to go over both the Thal and Bhor Ghats, but in 1854 a suggestion was made to Dalhousie that going through the Taptee valley would be easier. Dalhousie instructed the railway company to investigate the options and Berkley undertook an enquiry on the government's behalf. He found that taking the valley route would require around 150 miles of extra railway, which would mean journeys would be at least five hours longer for passengers. Going through the ghats, therefore, would not only permit a faster journey time, but would be cheaper to build, despite the difficulties. Berkley, ever the optimist, was confident that he had found a route through the Bhor Ghat which was shorter and involved less-steep gradients than previous suggestions. He and his team produced some 3,000 drawings and sketches for their survey that would form the basis of the eventual route.

There was much debate over the alignment, with the government initially rejecting Berkley's route in favour of an alternative called 'the cork screw line', which had the advantage of only requiring a gradient of 1 in 60 rather than 1 in 37, a major difference for the rather underpowered locomotives of the period. However, this alternative line would have required far more tunnelling, tighter curves and three extra miles of railway, and consequently was opposed by the railway company. Eventually the matter was referred to Robert Stephenson back in London and he adjudicated in favour of Berkley's alignment.

The challenge of building the railway over the ghats was on a completely different scale to anything previously encountered in India, and, with the exception of the Alpine routes, anywhere in the world. Although, at 2,000 feet, the railway reached a far more modest height than its European counterparts in the Alps, the sheer difficulty of construction was far greater given the local conditions, the heat and the problems of accessing the site. There were considerable distances to overcome, too, as the Thal Ghat required a railway of nine miles, and the climb over the Bhor was far longer at fifteen miles.

The task of crossing these mountains presented particular difficulties due to the lack of water and prevalence of disease, as well as the challenging climate. In a lecture given after the successful completion of the line, Berkley recounted how water was always short – except in the rainy season, when its very abundance caused problems: 'The small springs [near the railway] … were not sufficient even to afford drinking water for the work people in the hot season.'[6] Consequently, teams of carts hauled by bullocks – up to 1,500 were needed in the heat of the summer – were in constant use, bringing up water for the workforce. Berkley later devised a clever scheme to store water from the monsoon period by damming up one of the tunnels before the start of the rains to use as a reservoir.

The most perilous part of the construction process on both ghats was blasting the rock, with, at times, up to 6,000 explosions daily, and there were frequent accidents as a result of flying rock, often because of inadequate warnings and the carelessness of the workers. On some of the cliff faces, there were no footholds and a particularly perilous task was for a man to be lowered on ropes to drill the holes and insert the explosive. It was not uncommon for these workers to lose their foothold and tumble to their deaths in the ravine below, or for the men to fail to haul up the poor fellow dangling below in time to avoid the explosion, leading to the inevitable result. These accidents, according to a contractor's agent, 'had the effect of deterring his fellows altogether, from working for days',[7] but nevertheless little was done to establish even the most basic health and safety rules.

Falling rocks, slips and cave-ins were also an ever-present danger, but those worksite accidents were actually the least of the risks faced by the workforce. It was cholera and other diseases which exacted a terrible toll. The sheer size of the workforce, together with the high casualty rate, ensured the railway had an unprecedented number of deaths for such a project. As soon as work started in 1856, 10,000 people were taken on at the Bhor Ghat alone and this reached a peak of 42,000 in January 1861, more than were ever employed on, for example, the Suez Canal, constructed almost simultaneously. Kerr estimates that if numbers working on the Thal and Bhor Ghats, as well as the sections of line leading up to them, are taken into account, the total workforce may have reached a remarkable 100,000 at its peak. The difficulty of recruiting such an enormous number of workers was compounded by the fact that the great majority were sent home during the four months of the wet season when conditions made most work, other than tunnelling, impossible to undertake.

Not surprisingly, having such a vast army of temporary workers 'bred violence and lawlessness'[8] as the mix of low-caste Indians, often from very deprived backgrounds, and a bunch of rather unprepossessing and nakedly racist European overseers proved to be toxic. The few permanent inhabitants of the ghats, like residents anywhere near railway construction sites, were wary of the huge influx of temporary workers and frequently complained to the railway company about thefts and violence.

As mentioned in the previous chapter, the attempts to recruit large numbers of experienced British navvies were soon abandoned as the men could not cope with the tropical climate. While a few stayed on as overseers, and experienced engineers were brought over from Britain, the number of Europeans on the railway worksites represented a tiny proportion of the total workforce. One estimate is that at the height of the 1860s boom when, typically, a quarter of a million men were building around 1,000 miles of line throughout India, a mere 500 British engineers were organizing and supervising the work.

Recruiting and mobilizing the massive workforce was in itself a considerable task, since public undertakings on this scale were virtually unknown on the subcontinent (apart from the odd palace or temple). As there was insufficient labour locally, messengers were sent out to distant towns, some travelling as far as Lucknow more than 800 miles away, to recruit workers through local gangers. Interestingly, Berkley, in his lecture, noted that 'low caste natives who eat flesh and drink spirits' were the best for the heavy labouring tasks, while 'the higher castes were better at the skilled jobs such as bricklaying, carpentry or masonry'.[9] The workforce was by no means only male. On the contrary, the men tended to bring along their wives and children, as any family member above the age of ten would be taken on.

The death rate from disease on the ghats project was greater than on subsequent projects because of the primitive conditions, the hostile environment of the jungle and the absence of any concern from the British about the fate of the Indian workers. Cholera was particularly rife because of the shortage of safe water due to the lack of any form of sanitation in the vast workcamps which sprang up alongside the railway (cholera is water-borne, as the British surgeon John Snow established in 1849). The insanitary conditions, with people living in cramped conditions, led to the rapid transmission of other fatal diseases such as 'jungle fever', which was usually malaria; as Kerr puts it, 'when it did not kill people, it disabled them', leading to shortages in the workforce.[10] One outbreak of cholera alone in 1860 is reckoned to have killed 25 per cent of the workforce, perhaps some 7,000 people, while 25,000 deaths, the best estimate of the overall toll for the eight-year project, would, if accurate, make it the deadliest railway project ever undertaken anywhere in the world.

Disease did not discriminate between locals and the British. A particularly severe epidemic of cholera in the spring of 1860 killed a quarter of the British overseers and a notable early casualty was the British contractor Solomon Tredwell. The contract for the Bhor Ghat had initially been given to Faviell, who had built the Bombay–Thana line, but he had developed a poor reputation as a 'conceited and obstinate man ... who treated people under him as dogs or inferior beings',[11] paying his workers low wages and providing them with inadequate housing. This terrible treatment was to be his undoing. There was a complicated arrangement of contractors and sub-contractors and Faviell's failure to pay the sub-contractors meant they, in turn, could not pay their workers. In January 1859, a series of simmering disputes over the slow payment of wages broke out into a full-scale riot and the small European force of managers went to the camps in an attempt to quell the protest and arrest the ringleaders. However, they were beaten back with sticks and stones, and one European, who had become separated from the main party, was shot dead, though the culprit was never found. This outbreak of violence was no surprise to British government officials, who had visited the site before the riot and reported that the treatment of the labourers was shameful. Following the outbreak of violence, a senior official reported: 'It is evident that the labourers have been most grossly abused in the matter of their wages.'[12]

Faviell's contract was therefore rescinded and passed on to Tredwell, who had a good reputation in the UK. However, poor Tredwell died in November 1859, a mere month after his arrival, from dysentery acquired on the site. Remarkably, his wife, Alice, took over the contract and with the help of two British engineers, who had worked on previous contracts, managed to see the project through.

The callousness of the British towards the deaths in the workforce, while not remarkable by contemporary standards, appears deeply shocking today. Berkley reported the casualty rate in a rather matter-of-fact tone, suggesting that its worst aspect was the delay caused to the project. In his lecture, he bemoaned the fact that while 'the fine [dry] season of eight months is favourable for Indian railway operations', it was also the time when 'fatal epidemics, such as cholera and fever' break out and that the labourers who 'are generally of such feeble constitution, and so badly provided with shelter and clothing speedily succumb to those diseases and *the benefits of the fine weather are, thereby, temporarily lost* [my italics]'.[13]

This was Victorian 'morality' at its worst. It would have been wrong, according to the strictures of the time, to pay the labourers any more than was absolutely necessary because that would affect profitability, which was sacrosanct. Berkley justified the low wages by the fact that 'the effective work of almost every individual labourer in India falls short of the result obtained in England'.[14] The low pay and poor housing, which Berkley seems to have realized contributed to the high death rate, were the direct result of the company's policy, but he was unable or unwilling to make this obvious connection.

Despite the parsimony exhibited towards the workforce, there was both enormous wastage due to imperial arrogance, which meant so much was supplied from Britain despite local material being available, and considerable extravagance on the part of companies because the guaranteed high rate of return was almost an incentive for them to overspend. As Anthony Burton, author of *The Railway Empire*, reports, 'the belief that Europe knows best was to lead to absurdities'.[15] Imperialism had its blind spots. Although there were plenty of local sources of good useable wood, not enough effort was made to exploit it. Any hardwood forests such as teak near railway sites were quickly cut down, but the lack of efficient transport meant that further supplies were difficult to obtain. Attempts to treat soft jungle timber with various chemicals proved ineffective, as did experiments with cast iron, which is too brittle, with the result that, for much of the early Indian railway construction period, sleepers were sent from the UK, a remarkably inefficient and expensive way of sourcing a cheap and heavy material. This proved to be a continuous burden on the railway companies because the humid weather meant that sleepers tended to last only seven years.

The high cost of transporting bricks, however, meant they were produced locally. Those made by locals using traditional methods were deemed unsuitable because, according to a contemporary writer, 'a native takes any clay that happens to be at hand, digs it, wets it, kneads it with his feet for a short time and then moulds the brick on the ground'. Such bricks, he complained, 'are badly tempered, badly shaped and are, besides, usually cracked and badly burnt'.[16] The bricks made under European supervision were deemed to be of good quality, though on some worksites, notably in Bengal, there was no suitable material to hand and therefore wrought-iron girders were used to support bridges.

Similarly, despite the plentiful supply of local building materials, booking halls and engine sheds were shipped in kit form to be assembled in India and were not always constructed from the appropriate materials. Burton points out that metal was used for constructing the stations and asks, witheringly: 'Could anyone have seriously believed that an iron building was appropriate for a waiting room in the blistering heat of an Indian summer?'[17]

Berkley was cannier as he realized that many Indian methods of work were more appropriate for the climate and the available skills. In particular, the insubstantial-looking bamboo scaffolding, still a feature of construction sites in Asia, proved to be cheaper than systems imported from Europe and just as safe. The 'coolies', as Berkley called them, who carried building materials balanced on bamboo poles, were far more adept at carrying weights than their British counterparts. The British engineers found they were not always right in imposing their methods and instead could learn from the traditions of a culture which, after all, had built the Taj Mahal, which was completed in 1653.

One amusing episode concerned the introduction of wheel-barrows. It was thought that they would speed up the building process, but attempts to replace traditional head baskets were quickly abandoned following the experience of one British engineer who 'having exhausted his morning energy in the fond endeavour to restrain a gang of coolies from using the objectionable basket had the mortification, on making his evening tour of inspection, to find them carrying the wheelbarrows on their heads'.[18] The head baskets were, in fact, often carried by women and children, and the British, finding this distasteful (though, remember, this was a period when underage chimney sweeps were still the norm in Britain), tried unsuccessfully to put a stop to it. However, given the low wages, many families needed to work as a team, with the husband breaking up the stones and the women and children carting them away on their heads, in order to make enough to pay for food and their basic shelters. It was a learning experience on both sides, as Kerr recounts: 'The lessons the British learned from the Bhor Ghat extended well beyond civil engineering and they were applied well beyond the ghat construction.'[19]

The work to complete the route through the Bhor Ghat took eight years. The bare statistics of the achievement illustrate the scale of the task but fail to do justice to it. The project required twenty-five tunnels, the blasting out of 54 million square feet of rock (who counted that?), the erection of eight viaducts supported by arches and the construction of a series of embankments, some of which were sixty feet high and had side slopes that were 300 feet long. The most unusual feature of the railway through the ghats was the system devised by Berkley to build the line up the hill. Instead of constructing a continuous steep line, he carved out a reversing section at a bend near the summit. So the train had to be driven – slowly – into the dead end, whose buffer stop was the only, and wholly inadequate, shield between the tracks and the precipice. Then the guard would get out to change the points, enabling the train to continue its climb. It was slow and cumbersome, but effective, and the method survived well into the second half of the twentieth century, when additional tunnels were built allowing trains to climb up more quickly. The method was, though, later copied successfully on several railways in South America. Not only was construction costly in terms of lives, but it was also very expensive in financial terms. The cost of the line was £70,000 per mile, nearly four times the normal average in India and around one and a half times the average in Britain, where, of course, wages were far higher.

The completion of the Bhor Ghat incline was marked with a more than usually lavish ceremony at Khandala, near the crest of the incline, by the Governor of Bombay, Sir Bartle Frere, who lauded the work of the 'English engineers',[20] while rather forgetting, until the last, that it was Indian labour that had created this almost miraculous railway. His enthusiastic speech reveals how the creation of the Indian railway system was perceived by the Victorian upper classes as a kind of massive do-gooding exercise that would transform Indian society for the better.

Frere spent several minutes praising the achievements of the various British engineers who took part in the construction and gave a special mention to Mrs Tredwell for carrying on the work of her late husband. When, finally, towards the end, Frere addressed the contribution of the 'Indian Cooly', he suggested that the railway and the money it brought from the UK offered an unparalleled opportunity to the Indian underclass. Previously, he said, 'the privilege of labour was in general restricted to particular spots and nothing like the power of taking his labour to the best market practically existed'. Now, he said, thanks to the advent of the railway, 'for the first time in history, the Indian Cooly finds that he has in his power of labour a valuable possession which … will give to him and his family something better than mere subsistence'.

He was, in effect, talking about the dawn of the age of consumerism. He explained that when the railway work finished and the labourer returned to his 'remote Deccan or Konkan village', he would 'work far harder, and acquire new and more civilized wants, in proportion to the high wages he receives', gathering 'a new feeling of self-respect and independence', and become a 'better and more loyal subject' as a result. The railway, in other words, was the catalyst for India to become a modern, civilized nation of petty capitalists and consumers.

Apart from the ghats, the greatest obstacle faced by the railways were the vast Indian rivers which took considerable expertise and huge amounts of capital and labour to bridge, and presented the greatest danger not only to construction teams but potentially also to passengers.

Bridges were the major enterprise on the railway. It took up to five years to build a large one and 'small towns housing many thousands of workers and their families grew up close to the bridge sites'.[21] There were numerous skills to be learnt in both civil engineering and water management before the bridges could be regarded with confidence. The key was laying the foundations deeply enough to withstand the scouring effect of water moving at extremely high speeds at peak flow. The foundations of the piers and abutments had to be built in holes – called wells – dug into the riverbed. The work was obviously carried out in the dry season but, even then, coffer dams were needed to keep the wells from being inundated.

The traditional method of digging out the smaller wells was remarkably primitive. A man would descend into the well and, after loosening the sand and stones at the bottom with his feet, would dive down to collect the material in a basket and hand it to his companion at the edge. The men would regularly swap roles and by using this crude technique would be able to dig out a well stretching to a maximum of fourteen feet deep. Deeper wells, however, would require more sophisticated and consequently expensive methods.

Major rivers such as the Ganga (Ganges) or the Brahmaputra would require wells of up to fifty feet in order to ensure the bridges' safety. By the end of the century, novel techniques such as using divers – who often ruined their health as the effect of the 'bends', the result of rapid depressurization, was not known – connected to an air supply and steam-powered dredges, but in the early days primitive methods inevitably led to many collapses as the wells were simply not dug deep enough.

The foundations for the intermediate supports or piers had to be totally secure to protect them from the effect of scouring by the fast-flowing water. The slightest flaw in the foundation would easily be found by the water and lead to the weakening and possible collapse of the bridge support.

As Samuel Power, the engineer of the Soane Bridge (now in Bihar), the most difficult river crossing in the early stages of the East Indian Railway, lamented, 'nothing is more trying of the patience than the passage from the sand into the clay … although the curb shoes [the outer bulwark for the protection of the piers] may appear to be touching the clay at almost every point of its circumference, the sand will force its way through some small crevices and nearly fill the well again and again'.[22] It was a slow but effective learning process which eventually led to a safe network of bridges on the Indian rail system.

The Soane Bridge was particularly challenging because it had to ford a river that stretched three miles across at times of flood, and finding the best crossing point was a matter of considerable debate and controversy. Initially, the East Indian Railway considered running tracks across the river during the dry season, with a small bridge over what was essentially a stream, and then operating a ferry service in the wet season in order to avoid the massive and expensive task of building the bridge. However, the cumbersome, costly and indeed potentially dangerous nature of such an enterprise convinced the company that a fixed crossing was essential, and a site involving a bridge of just under a mile long was eventually found. After considering a brick arched viaduct, the railway decided to opt for a wrought-iron lattice-work superstructure supported on brickwork piers. The bridge required twenty-eight sections of identical 150-foot-long girders which, when assembled, had to be manhandled onto the piers. This became the preferred method of fording rivers, which was to the great benefit of British engineering companies, who invariably supplied the ironwork (and the steel that was used later). The iron was transported in kit form, with great difficulty if there was not yet a suitable railway between the port and the worksite, and assembled at the river. Hundreds of railway bridges across India were built in this way and many survive today.

The amazing engineering skills required to build these remarkable bridges eventually attracted the attention of the UK press. In 1887, Rudyard Kipling, then an unknown reporter on the *Civil and Military Gazette*, an Anglo-Indian newspaper, described the construction of a bridge similar to the one over the Soane, the Kaisar-i-Hind (Empress of India), across the Sutlej River at Ferozepur in the Punjab. The bridge was almost exactly the same length as the Soane, requiring twenty-seven sections of ironwork, some of which had already been fitted onto the piers by the time he arrived. In the best contemporary description of Indian railway building, Kipling recalls how he was appalled by the crowds and the noise of the scene. The road leading to the bridge 'was filled with bullock carts and *ekkas* [one-horse carriages] and foot passengers all streaming riverwards to where a cloud of dust rose like the smoke of an engagement [battle]'. At the site, he found a 'royal mess' of various temporary railway tracks being used to transport material: 'lines of every gauge – two-foot, metre and broad – rioted over the face of the pure, white sand, between huge dredger-buckets, stored baulks of timber, chupper-built [thatched] villages, piled heaps of warm red concrete-blocks, portable engines and circular saws'.

It was the riveters who left the greatest impression on Kipling, both because of the noise they created and the speed at which they worked. Where the spans had already been set out, he found:

a few hundred workmen hard at work riveting. The clamour is startling, even a hundred yards away from the Bridge; but standing at the mouth of the huge iron-plated tunnel, it is absolutely deafening. The flooring quivers beneath the hammer-strokes; the roof of corrugated iron nearly half an inch thick which will form the floor of the cart-road, casts back the tumult redoubled; and it bounds and rebounds against the lattice-work at the side. Riveters are paid by the job, not by time. Consequently they work like devils; and the very look of their toil, even in the bright sunshine, is devilish. Pale flames from the fires for the red hot rivets, spurt out from all parts of the black iron-work where men hang and cluster like bees; while in the darker corners the fires throw up luridly the half nude figures of the rivetters, each man a study for a painter as he bends above the fire-pot, or, crouching on the slung-supports, sends the rivet home with a jet of red sparks from under the hammer-head.[23]

Kipling used this experience in a work of fiction, 'The Bridge Builders', published a few years later. It was not the ironwork that Kipling watched being installed which tended to fail but, rather, as described above, the piers' supports, which were eaten away by the fast-flowing water. As an example, the Bombay, Baroda & Central India Railway was perhaps unfortunate in the number of incidents that the bridge crossing the Nerbudda River suffered, but its tribulations were typical of the difficulty of getting to grips with the uniquely Indian conditions. Started in 1857, the bridge was damaged by flooding twice during construction, but after opening for traffic in July 1861 it then, according to Kerr, 'suffered from flood damage in 1864, 1865 and 1867, and lost three piers in a heavy flood in August 1868'.[24] Similar damage was caused to three bridges on the Sind, Punjab and Delhi Railway in a major flood in 1871, including the collapse of a bridge over the Beas River, which resulted in a passenger train plunging into the water below.

The most spectacular early failure, the collapse of the Mhow-ke-Mullee viaduct on the Bhor Ghat on 19 July 1867, however, did not result in any casualties thanks to the alertness of a railwayman and the good fortune that two trains scheduled to cross the bridge were far enough away to be halted. The viaduct had been inspected in the early morning and a train passed safely at 6.50 a.m. when, an hour later, an Indian fireman who was on the lookout on a goods train saw the bridge had begun to collapse into the river. He warned the driver and, as the train stopped, the two men watched the rest of the bridge tumble into the water. The fireman quickly crossed the river to warn an approaching goods train of the collapse, thus averting a disaster.

The bridge had been built in brick and masonry and there were strong suspicions that the foundations had been skimped as a result of poor workmanship or corruption, or both, as well as a lack of supervision. Its replacement was another of the Meccano bridges of ironwork prefabricated in the UK, which was carrying trains by the following summer; a remarkable achievement of which the Great Indian Peninsula Railway was exceedingly proud in its reports back to shareholders.

Major collapses like the one at Mhow-ke-Mullee exposed the extent to which the standard of workmanship on these early lines was often inadequate, but that was not necessarily the responsibility of the Indians undertaking the work. In many cases, notably the larger bridges, the designs, drawn up by the British, were at fault. However, on small bridges and culverts, poor workmanship did, at times, lead to collapse and risk. A British engineer, Roger Brereton, who went out to India in 1856 to work on the Great Indian Peninsula Railway, found widespread evidence of skimping on crucial details. There were stones missing in the piers designed to support small bridges and, not surprisingly, several viaducts and bridges collapsed when trains started running over them. For his pains, Brereton, finding shoddy work on another site, was felled by a blow on the head from a stick wielded by a contractor's agent, but fortunately recovered fully and remained in India for many more years.

The extent of such 'scamping' and straightforward design failure attracted the interest of the Government of India because by the late 1860s, just fifteen years after the first line opened, 'more than 2,000 bridges and other masonry structures had failed completely or partially on the Great Indian Peninsula Railway'.[25] It was the government which had to foot the bill for these failures as the money came either from the company's capital fund, which earned the guarantee, or out of its profits, which had to be topped up to reach the 5 per cent rate of return.

This sort of malpractice was not unusual in railway construction and, given the huge cost of building new lines, was a phenomenon on similar great engineering projects across the world. On some contracts, notably in the USA, millions of dollars were purloined in corrupt arrangements created precisely for that purpose by contractors or promoters.[26] In India, there was no single figure found to be responsible for purloining vast amounts of cash, such as George Hudson, the Railway King, who created the Midland Railway in the 1840s, only to then cheat his shareholders in a kind of Victorian version of a Ponzi scheme. Despite lots of petty corruption, Kerr argues that 'India's railways had fewer major scandals, massive corruption, and speculative chicanery than railways in many other countries'.[27] This was a result of the relatively tight control exercised by the Indian government, but also because of the absence, during the early days, of a white-collar criminal class able to exploit the huge amount of money pouring into the country from UK investors.

Away from the mountains and the bridges, most of India was, in fact, relatively easy to build on, as testified by the long stretches of straight, flat line on Indian railways today. The dry soil, the even terrain and, apart from snakes, the largely benign wildlife (tigers were confined largely to the hills on the East Indian Railway and most elephants showed little interest in the process) all made ideal conditions for rapid construction, even though methods were primitive and required enormous numbers of workers. The ready availability of land, too, made the process of building railways less complicated.

Nevertheless, progress in developing the network was slow during the first few years. By the time the Great Rebellion broke out in 1857, barely 300 miles of disparate lines had been completed. The railway companies blamed the intrusive supervision to which they were subject, notably the process by which expenditure of any significant amount had to be agreed by the government before payment was made and then checked again afterwards. This meant that even very small amounts of money had to be approved and this inevitably slowed down development, especially as so many supplies were imported from the UK. A Parliamentary Commission into the start of railway construction in India was established, the first of many such enquiries, and in their report, published in 1858, the Parliamentarians rebuked the Government of India for its cautious approach and over-zealous regulation. They found several reasons for the delays, such as the animosity between engineers and contractors and the long distances on awful roads over which supplies had to be transported, especially when the nearest railhead was far away. All these inherent difficulties were intensified by the bureaucratic approach of the government, which, as we have seen, exercised close control over the projects. Because the companies had their 5 per cent guarantee, the government was anxious to ensure that they were not being profligate. Sometimes even minor matters were referred back to London, a time-consuming task given that it was not until 1870 that there was an electric telegraph connecting the UK with the subcontinent. While the railway companies were quick to blame the government, much of the responsibility lay with them for failing to ensure that they commissioned the right contractors, as we shall see in the next chapter.

In order to speed up the construction of the network, the Commission recommended that work and payments would only be overseen after the event, greatly reducing the bureaucracy. The Commission had been set up in the aftermath of the Indian Mutiny of 1857, known in India as the First War of Independence but probably best described (neutrally) as the Great Rebellion, because it had exposed the difficulties of moving troops quickly around the country. The Rebellion started in Meerut, Uttar Pradesh, forty miles from Delhi, on 10 May 1857 when a group of sepoys (Indian soldiers) mutinied over the imprisonment of eighty-five of their fellow men. Lengthy jail sentences had been imposed on them for their refusal to use cartridges which were thought to be greased with fat from pig (taboo for Muslims) or cows (taboo for Hindus). That was the trigger for a wide variety of grievances. Trouble, both in the military and in the country at large, had, in fact, been brewing for some time over a range of issues such as low pay, land expropriation by the British and fears that missionaries were preparing mass conversions to Christianity, and consequently unrest spread rapidly, first to Delhi and then elsewhere.

The railways themselves became a target. Their arrival was not always welcomed by local people, who could be downright hostile, as they feared, with some justification, that the massive embankments required to support the railway would disturb the local water management system and affect the local agriculture. Indeed, at times the hostility was so great that embankments were wrecked by gangs of local farmers at night worried that they would no longer be able to irrigate their fields properly. However, it was not just farmers who felt this way. There was a more fundamental countrywide resentment of the Western incursion that was so neatly and forcibly expressed by tracks being laid across India.

The railways were a disruptive influence on a traditional society. To devout Hindus, 'the very nature of the railway, demanding punctuality and exactitude, and breaking down caste, was alien'.[28] They were concerned, too, about Western influence generally. In the wake of the large number of engineers who had arrived in India to help build the railways, there were evangelists intent on saving souls, rather than improving transport, whose thinking amounted to the notion that if the Indians wanted railways, they would have to live with a Christian god as well. Edward Davidson concluded his book on Indian railways, published in 1868, with the sentiment that 'there is a hope that, combined with the prosperity, wealth and civilisation which have been created and fostered by the railways of India, the blessings also of a spiritual Christianity, based on the truth of God's Word, may ere [before] long spread extensively over the length and breadth of that land'.[29] No wonder some of the local population felt that their way of life was threatened by the railways, especially as Davidson's views were by no means unique, with many other writers on India expressing similar ideas.

The Rebellion was partly inspired by such fears and therefore the railways were an obvious target. Worksites on the East Indian Railway were attacked and trashed, partly built bridges pulled down, and half-completed lines destroyed. European engineers working on these projects, particularly in remote areas, had to flee or be killed. Work on the Soane Bridge on the East Indian Railway was halted in the spring of 1857 and much of the preparatory work was destroyed. The delay was costly, as wages for the European engineers still had to be paid and much material had to be replaced. It was not until December 1858 that work could restart and the bridge was not completed until the end of 1862, allowing the 430-mile railway from Calcutta to Benares to be officially opened by the Governor-General, Lord Elgin, in March 1863.

There were appalling atrocities, including numerous massacres, on both sides during the Rebellion, but within a year the British were able to overcome the rebels, who, motivated by a variety of grievances, had neither a central base, nor any united demand. The British were greatly helped by the Sikhs of the Punjab – a group that remained loyal, partly out of their dislike of the Muslims who were involved in the rebellion – and by the lack of involvement of large swathes of the population of the subcontinent, particularly in the large Deccan plateau. The unrest effectively ended with the reclaiming of Gwalior in Madhya Pradesh in June 1858 but its effects were to last far longer.

The Rebellion marked the end of the East India Company, which was seen as ineffective, with control of India being transferred to a system of direct rule from London, overseen by a Cabinet minister who quickly instituted a programme of financial and administrative reform. Officially, Indian opinion was supposed to be taken into greater account when making decisions. In fact, the Rebellion led to a greater isolation of the growing British community as there was the ever-present fear that the locals might turn against them. As J. N. Westwood explains, this nurtured 'a mildly racialist attitude on the part of many British' and resulted in 'a more patronising, often contemptuous attitude towards Indians'.[30]

However, while the British realized that changes were needed, nothing shifted the opinion of the rulers that they were in India to civilize the nation, whether its people wanted that or not. Therefore, military rule had to be strengthened and the protection of British rule became a key driver in speeding up construction of the network. The Rebellion had exposed the difficulties of moving troops around quickly and consequently the vulnerability of the British hold on a nation of 280 million people. The railways were clearly the means by which rule could be established and protected. However, the railways, as we shall see, were also a cause of conflict because the races were forced to mix when using trains. Therefore, it was often on the railway network where interactions between Indians and British became, at times, troublesome. Moreover, the railways' insatiable demand for labour meant more British people, often carrying out relatively menial jobs, came to India because the railway companies did not want to entrust various tasks to local people.

As a result, India became a much more uneasy place for the British, whose fear of the native population and concern with security had a huge impact on the design of the railways. The vulnerability of stations was recognized and new ones were designed as potential fortresses. As Burton puts it, 'the face these stations presented to the outside world was grim: high walls, rounded corners that would deflect shot, battlemented towers and firing slits'.[31] The 'fortified main station at Lahore'[32] (now in Pakistan) looked more like a medieval castle than a welcoming entrance to a key transport network. It was not just stations: the Rebellion led to 'the concern, at times an obsession, that was to last for decades among the authorities, namely ensuring the military security of the railway lines, bridges, tunnels and stations'.[33]

However, railways are very much dependent on the acquiescence, if not support, of the local population. They are often the first casualties of war since blowing up a line or causing a train to crash are relatively easy acts of sabotage with widespread consequences, as demonstrated by the activities of modern terrorists who routinely attack trains and stations. The fears of the British, therefore, may have been somewhat exaggerated as most Indians either supported or were indifferent to the advent of the railways, but they were well-founded. As we shall see in Chapter 7, Mahatma Gandhi, the leader of the Indian independence movement, made great play of the role of the railways as an instrument of imperial repression and was, at times, openly hostile to them.

THREE

CONTROLLING
THE RAILWAYS

W HILE THE GENEROUS arrangements that guaranteed the companies a rate of return may have been necessary to kick-start construction in the early days, they were neither sustainable nor practical in the long term. However, given the imperative to build railways rapidly in response to the Rebellion, the system remained in place for a further decade, by which time the rudiments of the subcontinent's railway network had been well established.

The fundamental flaw of the system was that there was no incentive for the railways to keep costs down other than through the oversight procedure. After the 1858 Commission into delays in the construction of the railways, procedures became more lax and consequently costs soared. This proved that the guarantee arrangement was inherently problematic. Before 1858, the oversight was too tight and caused delays. After the Commission's recommendations for a more relaxed system of supervision were accepted, the companies were able to exploit their position to spend without having to worry about the consequences. In effect, they were getting generous rewards without taking any risk.

It was not only the military necessity of creating a national rail network which encouraged the British government and the railway companies to speed up construction. As ever in the history of British colonialism, money was at stake, too. The development of the railways in India was big business for the British – very big business. The sharp rise in the mileage under construction meant the 1860s became boom years for British contractors, builders, engineers, and suppliers of materials and railway equipment. The 200 miles of track laid by 1856 increased twenty-fold by 1870, which made many British railway promoters and contractors both happy and rich.

The early railways were nearly all extensions of lines inland from the three major ports, Bombay, Calcutta and Madras. This was partly the result of Dalhousie's strategy but was also the most practical way of proceeding since the bulk of supplies came by ship from the UK. The economic imperative matched the military one and the railways were to play a vital part in both the Indian and the British economies for the rest of the century. In the 1860s, as a rule of thumb, each mile of railway required one ship arriving from Britain carrying some 600 tons of material. Some of this long-distance transport could have been avoided had there been more focus on local sourcing, which would have been the case had the intention in building railways been to boost the Indian, rather than the British, economy. It was not only, as mentioned in the previous chapter, that there were local supplies of suitable timber for sleepers, but there were also factories in India producing good wrought iron whose output could have been expanded. However, the iron- and steelwork required for bridges, rails and stations represented a major new market for British manufacturers and helped stimulate the economy of the colonial power. The British were not interested in encouraging and developing local industry, which, given the cheapness of rail transport and local labour, would have represented serious competition to their own industries. The few small iron-producing factories were, therefore, not encouraged to increase their output. Free trade had its limits and British interests came first.

The rapid expansion in railway construction provided substantial benefits to the City of London, too, since every journey by ship required insurance, given that losses through sinking were an ever-present risk. The overall effect on Britain's economy was significant enough to reverse its balance-of-payments deficit, initially through the supply of railway equipment and then through the enhanced opportunities for carrying imports from Britain further into the Indian hinterland that the railways afforded. According to one analysis, 'Britain kept its overall balance of payments in surplus thanks to its ability to sell large quantities of manufactured goods to India.'[1] The theory even goes that the whole economic framework of world trade in the nineteenth century, with the gradual reduction of protectionism and the growth of the free market, may not have been possible had Britain not been able to export so much to India: 'It appears likely, therefore, that the industrialisation and eventual prosperity of the Western world rested, in part, on Indian Railways.'[2] That may be somewhat hyperbolic, but it nevertheless shows the importance accorded to the railways.

The majority of the contractors during this period were British and the people carrying out the most skilled tasks, such as engineers, surveyors and supervisors, were all brought over from Britain. There were big names involved, such as Isambard Kingdom Brunel, Britain's most famous (but not always successful) engineer, and John Hawkshaw, the chief engineer of a series of railways in northern England. Both were working with the boards of the British-based railway companies as consultants while remaining in the UK. Others, such as John Brunton, who had worked on the Liverpool & Manchester Railway with the Stephensons, and Joseph Harrison, fresh from building the first railway in Egypt, came to India as the chief engineers on site. The actual work was given to contractors who were in the main British or based in one of the three port cities from where the railways were spreading. The word 'contractor' was used rather loosely. Some of the Europeans arriving to seek contracts were little more than financial speculators who would take on work and then pass it on, thereby acting purely as middlemen without investing much, if anything, in equipment or carrying out any work.

There were few local contractors, though one was notably successful: Jamsetji Dorabji, a Parsee (a follower of Zoroastrianism, an ancient religion with its roots in Iran), won at least five contracts on the Great Indian Peninsula Railway and the Sind, Punjab & Delhi Railway, which he managed to carry out 'satisfactorily, expeditiously and at less cost than his European competitors'.[3] Dorabji had an advantage as the Parsee community was partly Westernized and its members were used to trading with Europeans. Dorabji was an interesting character who had worked in his teenage years as a carpenter in the government dockyard in Bombay, where he started to cultivate friendships with Europeans. Discovering that he had the ability to recruit and use labour, he began to take on small contracts and eventually bid successfully for one on the Great Indian Peninsula Railway. Despite some difficulties with a bridge whose foundations were particularly awkward to lay, he soon earned the accolade of 'foremost Native Railway Contractor in India' from James Berkley. While his European rivals complained frequently about the difficulties of recruiting labour, Dorabji was able to earn his workers' trust and both obtain and retain them, which seems to have been down to his charm and what in modern management speak are called 'interpersonal skills'. It was the basis of his success. According to his biographer, 'he was an excellent master to his workmen, not only liberal in wages, but pleasant of speech, and constantly throwing himself into contact with them'.[4] Dorabji was also blessed with innate skills, including a prodigious memory – despite, or perhaps because of, being illiterate – and an ability to work out accurate estimates on which to base his tenders, a quality essential for a contractor. He hired competent managers, some European, to work under him and had the benefit of being able to borrow money from the Parsee community, overcoming the problem of most local and European contractors, who were perennially undercapitalized.

The handful of other early Indian contractors proved to be less successful. They had a champion in Sir John Lawrence, the Viceroy for five years from 1864, who, while favouring European contractors with sufficient capital if they were available, recognized that such people were rare and therefore he felt native contractors, who often had experience as sub-contractors, should be granted contracts. Consequently, the Sind, Punjab & Delhi Railway took on several local contractors for the line running from Lahore southwards to Multan (now all in Pakistan). These contractors largely went broke, for many of the same reasons as their European counterparts: shortage of capital, rising wage rates and lack of organizational skills (something, by contrast, which Jamsetji had in spades). Most contracts, however, continued to be offered to Europeans despite the fact that they had a similarly patchy record and, as we have seen, were generally more expensive.

Dorabji's success demonstrated that the British rail companies' insistence on handing out contracts to Europeans contributed to the high cost of the work. Many did not know what they were doing and were at the mercy of local sub-contractors. Work generally was broken down into stretches of perhaps twenty to forty miles, but occasionally much bigger sections of a hundred miles were allocated. The boom in railway construction in the decade after the Rebellion led to a rapid increase in the number of these contractors and, according to Edward Davidson, about two fifths of the work before 1868 was carried out by small contractors and 13 per cent by major international concerns, like the one run by Thomas Brassey, possibly one of the world's first truly multinational businesses.

The rest of the contracts, interestingly, were undertaken by the companies themselves as they found it was often the most efficient way to ensure the work was completed, and was ultimately cheaper as there was less need for oversight and double-checking. Note, however, that at this time, until the basis of the contracts was changed in 1869, the guarantee system ensured a good rate of return for the shareholders, while placing few constraints on the contractors carrying out the work.

Costs, therefore, were not as low as might be expected given the cheapness of labour. The average construction expenditure per mile in the period up to the end of 1868, by which time 4,000 miles of track had been completed, was £18,000, more than double the estimate of £8,000 on which Dalhousie had based his calculations. In Britain, the comparable price at the time was around £32,000 per mile, but that included the very expensive compensation claims of landowners, and the cost of fencing along the tracks, as well as the extensive legal costs required in pushing the bill to build the line through Parliament, none of which had to be paid by the railway companies in India. The situation in India was elegantly summed up by William Massey, who was finance minister under two viceroys during this period and was convinced that the cost of construction of the East Indian Railway was double what it should have been: 'All the money came from the English capitalist, and so long as he was guaranteed five per cent from the revenues of India, it was immaterial to him whether the funds that he lent were thrown into the Hooghly or converted into brick and mortar.'[5]

Apart from the flaws in the guarantee system, the other factor behind the high costs was that labour often proved to be more expensive than expected since it was not always possible to find sufficient people willing to work for the wage on the offer. The process of finding workers was complex as the contractors had to deal with dozens of sub-contractors and *muccadum*s – overseers – who were the ones with access to peasant and tribal societies that supplied the labour. On some projects, there was a shortage of local people willing to work on the railways, while on others wages were pushed up locally by the massive and urgent requirements of the construction. The difficulties of recruiting labour worsened as more lines were created, but over time a pan-Indian pool of experienced labour emerged, which made it easier for new companies to find suitable workers.

Even though many native people had no desire to work for money – India was a pre-capitalist society at the time – the railway companies found it relatively easy to train locals to carry out the skilled and semi-skilled tasks required in building the railways, such as turners, fitters and smiths, but once recruitment began, wages were inevitably driven up. This was, according to Davidson, 'very trying to engineers who have based their estimates upon current prices; and to shareholders who have accepted their calculations'.[6]

The wages were commensurately low by world standards, around 4–6 old pence (1.67–2.5p) per day, less than railway workers in any other country. The level of wages in India partly reflected the fact that on average 40 per cent of the workforce were women and an estimated 10–15 per cent boys, all of whom were paid far less than the men. Figures from the Madras Railway, for example, show that the proportion of women was, at times, even higher. In 1855, of nearly 6,000 workers, almost half (2,900) were women and 840 were boys, leaving just 2,100 (35 per cent) men.[7] This remarkably widespread involvement of women in the building of the railways is barely mentioned in many accounts of their construction – with the exception of Ian Kerr's work – and remains little recognized today.

Moreover, while the wages were much lower than in the UK, the output of individual workers was far less than that of their British counterparts – usually skilled 'navvies', who travelled from site to site for work, gaining considerable experience. The Indian labourers, by contrast, were mostly recruited locally from villages where they eked out a living on subsistence agriculture and were new to the railway and, indeed, to any kind of paid work.

Indian railways were technologically behind the times, too. While railways built contemporaneously in the UK or the US were routinely using labour-saving devices such as steam excavators and 'horse runs' – harnessing a horse to a pulley which hauled up barrows full of earth on wooden planks laid on the embankment – in India every load of earth had to be taken away in baskets carried on the heads of the labourers. Consequently, while in the UK around fifty people were employed for each mile of railway under construction, around three times that number were required in India.

Specialist workers did eventually emerge. One notable group was the *wodders* or *wudders* – they were known by various names that were corruptions of the same word in different Indian languages, such as *oddar, odde* or *vadda* – who specialized in earthworks or, more specifically, excavating. A sub-group worked solely with stone. They were the nearest equivalent of British navvies because, like them, they were both particularly skilled at their job and itinerant, moving from railway to railway to work. They even, like the British navvies, had a reputation for hard drinking.

Their simple method of breaking up stone was efficient and well suited to the needs of the railway. The *wodders* would build a fire on the surface of a rock face, generally at night, and the heat would cause expansion that would eventually result in a segment bursting off. The scattered pieces would then be broken up into fragments with a heavy boulder to create square blocks of stone. The first recorded mention of the *wodders* is on the Madras Railway in 1853 by the chief engineer, who reported how they worked in small groups under an overseer who had gathered a little capital, and thereafter 'the Wudders remained a ubiquitous and numerous presence among the railway construction workers in South India and beyond'.[8]

While the recruitment of labourers was patchy, and at times difficult, it was, according to Davidson, easier to recruit 'clerks, book-keepers and accountants ... in any number, as the Indian mind shows an aptitude for figures' and 'the young men of the upper class'[9] picked up English rapidly. The railway, therefore, was responsible for the genesis of the Indian middle class, one that would expand along with the railways and would help to spread the English language across the subcontinent.

As the construction rate became faster, the core of the network, the series of lines emanating from the ports, began to take shape and work started on several lines linking the main inland towns and cities. While the size of the network merely doubled to 840 miles in the two years following the Rebellion, a decade later the network envisaged by Dalhousie had 4,000 miles in operation.

The two pioneers, the East Indian Railway and the Great Indian Peninsula Railway, both had more than 1,200 miles. The most important line was the East Indian route between Calcutta and Delhi via Allahabad, which was completed in 1864. The Allahabad–Jabalpur branch line of the East Indian Railway opened three years later and was connected with the Great Indian Peninsula Railway in 1870, making it possible to travel from Bombay to Calcutta via Allahabad, thus connecting three of India's four most important cities. This route was officially opened in March of that year and it was later part of the inspiration for the French writer Jules Verne's book *Around the World in Eighty Days*.

At the time, Madras, the fourth key city, was also developing a network befitting its importance and just under 500 miles had been completed by the Madras Railway, which had been rather late out of the starting blocks because it had not been one of the two 'experimental' lines. It was not until 1871 that the Madras Railway became part of the wider network, with the completion of a connection to the Great Indian Peninsula Railway at Raichur providing a route between Bombay and Madras, while avoiding the city of Bangalore, which was something of an obstacle because it is 900 metres above sea level.

The next most important railway in terms of route mileage was the Sind, Punjab & Delhi, which had emerged from four separate but related companies that had initially tried to create a combined railway and steamship route from the newly established port of Karachi (now in Pakistan); however, they found that the currents of the River Indus were too strong and decided on a railway line instead. The route crossed the Sind desert and ran alongside the massive Indus, then up to Amritsar and Lahore. The company was also entrusted with building a 300-mile line from Amritsar to a junction with the East Indian near Delhi, making possible, when it opened in 1870, the rapid and efficient movement of troops to the strategically important but troubled North-West Frontier.

While the railways were becoming a crucial part of India's economy, the impact back in the UK was equally significant. In the decade following the Rebellion, some £70m was invested in Indian railways. Such a major demand for capital had the obvious result of pushing up interest rates in the UK, thereby weakening the economy at a time when capitalism was beginning to take off. This caused some consternation among 'British farmers and domestic business [who] at times complained that money for their own needs was obtainable only at unusually high rates of interest'.[10]

In India, there were concerns, too. The effect of this extensive and expensive investment in railways, backed by the government guarantee, proved to be a massive burden on the Government of India which had to make up the shortfall when railways did not earn the guaranteed 5 per cent rate of return. In fact, there were only a couple of routes which generated more than the 5 per cent. The East Indian Railway line between the two major cities of Calcutta and Delhi, favoured by low gradients, a supply of cheap coal from its own mines and well-patronized trains thanks to the high population density in the corridor it served, paid its way right from the beginning. It was a busy railway with fifteen trains daily in each direction and it struggled to cope with demand from passengers. The doubts about whether the 'natives' would use the iron road had been well and truly assuaged. Overall, freight was boosting profitability and accounted for two thirds of the East Indian Railway's income in 1869, compared with an almost insignificant 4 per cent in its first couple of years of operation. The other profitable company was the Great Indian Peninsula, which also soon reached the 5 per cent threshold thanks to the fact that, like the East Indian, it was carrying large quantities of freight.

As a result of the growth in freight and healthy passenger numbers across the railway network, by 1866 all the other railway companies, apart from the thirty-mile-long Calcutta & South-Eastern, were profitable but none, apart from the original two, had reached the 5 per cent threshold, requiring the Government of India subsidy to make up the shortfall to investors.

The soaring cost of building and maintaining the lines was the big barrier to long-term profitability. If the railways had been built more efficiently, both at a lower cost and to allow for faster operations, there would have been little need for the guarantee payments. It was the Government of India which was always the long-stop both in terms of excessive costs and lack of revenue. The bridge collapses, mentioned in the previous chapter, were a typical example of the way that the risk of the railway enterprise was placed fully on the shoulders of the Government of India – in other words, Indian taxpayers – while the companies' investors were still guaranteed their generous return. When sections of the railway needed to be rebuilt, the additional railway investment still had to earn the agreed rate of return. With the low level of profitability of most lines, by the summer of 1868 the Government of India, by no means flush with cash, had been required to fork out £23m to meet the costs of the guarantee. This might have been more acceptable had that money largely remained in the subcontinent. However, it did not. It was, in effect, a subsidy to the colonial power since, of 50,000 shareholders in the railway companies, fewer than 1 per cent – a mere 400 – were Indians. They were hampered by the fact that the shares could be traded only in London and not in India, which still had no stock exchange. Given that the vast majority of contracts were going to British-based contractors, as we have seen, just under half the total amount invested in the entire Indian railway by 1870 had been spent in Britain, not India.

The high level of subsidy could not be tolerated in the long run, either economically or indeed politically, given the tensions between Indians and their colonial masters in the aftermath of the Rebellion. Already in 1862, the Governor-General, Lord Canning, aware of the railway problem, had attempted to call a halt to the guarantee process, announcing, 'I will not guarantee a single rupee for a single day'. Like many politicians, he was unable to keep to his word. He started by taking a firm stance when he ended negotiations with the projected Oudh Railway Company on the basis that no more guarantees would be forthcoming. Instead, the promoters of the line were told to try to attract private investors, but, given that most of the early railways were not earning a decent rate of return without the guarantee, there were few takers.

Canning partly relented when James Wilson, a former engineer with the East Indian, suggested the formation of a new company, the Indian Branch Railway, to build a network of lines in Oudh, which had been one of the key centres of the Great Rebellion. Canning agreed to provide a subsidy of £100 per mile for twenty years and that attracted sufficient investors for work to start. However, the Government of India insisted that the lines be built to its normal 5ft 6in gauge to ensure a through connection with the

East Indian Railway, whereas Wilson had envisaged a smaller 4ft gauge to reduce costs. Consequently, the venture soon foundered and, in a story that is familiar in railway development across the world, the state bailed out the company with a £60,000 loan and the same 5 per cent guarantee, though with a more tightly worded contract than its predecessors had. The company was reformed into the Oudh & Rohilkhand Railway and they eventually built an extensive network linking east and north India based around Lucknow. Similarly, the Indian Tramway Company, which planned to build a branch line near Madras, was also required to search for its own private capital, but it failed to do so and was granted a 3 per cent guarantee. That was not enough to prevent the company going into liquidation and later re-emerging as the Carnatic Railway, before being absorbed into the South Indian.

These were, however, the last throes of the compensation system in its original and most generous guise. To the Government of India, the system was perceived as a recipe for corruption and inefficiency, and had to be reformed as otherwise there was the prospect of an endless and limitless series of demands for state support from the rapidly expanding railways: 'The companies were relying more and more upon state aid rather than upon energetic and efficient conduct of the railways.'[11] The Government of India decided, belatedly, to build railways itself and persuaded Whitehall to agree, even though such direct state enterprise was anathema to most politicians of the age, who were uncomfortable about government interfering in the commercial sphere. The engineers working for the Government of India were confident that they could build and operate more cheaply than the state-guaranteed private companies and pressed hard for this change. Lawrence, the Governor-General, stressed, in his dealings with UK ministers, that the Government of India was getting a bad deal: 'The whole profits go to the companies, and the whole loss to the Government [This was not strictly true since, as mentioned above, there was some profit-sharing arrangement] ... It is an abuse of language to describe as an interference with private enterprise what is only a refusal to support private speculators and to guarantee them from all possible loss by the credit of the state.'[12]

However, to the disappointment of the authorities in India, the British government agreed to soften the blow for the private railway owners by revising the contracts for the existing lines on terms even more favourable than before. In future, though, it was agreed that any additional railways would be built and operated by the Government of India. Since the entire cost of the railways was now directly the responsibility of the state, there was far more pressure to build lines cheaply and the most obvious way to do this was by reducing the size of the gauge. This was hugely controversial. The width of the gauge is one of those issues that may sound boringly technical but it pops up everywhere in the history of the railways, almost invariably the cause of much disagreement. It was to cause much angst and consternation in India and would result in no fewer than three parliamentary inquiries.

It was a matter of balance. Building a narrow railway is far cheaper in every respect, requiring fewer materials, less groundwork, and consequently less labour, and is cheaper to operate (though more expensive if costs per passenger or ton-mile of freight are used as the measure). On the negative side, narrow-gauge railways have less capacity and have the big disadvantage that both goods and people have to move from one train to another at the point where there is a change of gauge. The optimal structure for a railway network is for narrow gauge to be built for less well-used branch lines that connect with the broad-gauge main lines. In India, it did not work out like that with, eventually, nearly 20,000 miles of narrow-gauge railway being constructed, including some lengthy main lines that connected major cities, sometimes running in parallel with existing broad-gauge routes.

Dalhousie had set out very clearly to create a system of inter-connected lines using a unique gauge because he was aware that in Britain the Great Western's decision to have a much broader gauge was, at the time he was setting out the network, causing considerable trouble at interchange points. However, now that the core of the strategic Indian network had been built, and routes that were likely to be less intensively used were being considered, logic dictated that they should be built to a narrower gauge, especially as the Government of India was footing the whole bill for their construction. The issue was first raised by Lawrence, who, complaining about the high cost of the railways, argued that cheaper railway construction and operation could be achieved through railways being built, owned and operated by the state, and that in a poor country such as India narrow-gauge lines might be the only feasible option. The debate raged on for decades. As G. S. Khosla, the official historian of the Indian railways, writing in 1988, put it: 'The gauge question agitated the minds of the builders of railways, the boards of the railway companies, government authorities in India and England and the British Parliament for well over a quarter of a century.'[13] Indeed, worries about the gauge issue even reached the British Prime Minister, William Gladstone, who, in Parliament, soothed the concerns of MPs by reassuring them that all decisions regarding gauges of Indian railways would be considered carefully – a typical politician's promise.

In order to convince opponents that the concept of narrow-gauge railways was viable, their supporters in the Government of India pointed to examples of successful railways across the world. The Ffestiniog railway, a slate line in north Wales built in the 1830s to a gauge that was a fraction under 2ft, was referred to as an example of a successful narrow-gauge operation. This was, in fact, a rare example in the UK, which actually had very few narrow-gauge lines compared with most other equivalent countries, but there were already numerous other examples in British colonial territories where such railways had been built in order to keep costs down and had proved to be lucrative and useful.

The British government, which, remember, did not pay for the railways, was initially sceptical, arguing, as Dalhousie had done, that a single unified network was essential to create a smooth-running system. In particular, there were fears that having to transfer from one gauge to another would hamper the military if troops needed to be moved quickly around the country. Eventually, however, the authorities in Britain accepted Lawrence's argument that in order to open up regions without railways, the choice for India was clear. Unless these lines were built using narrow gauge, it would be uneconomic to build them at all.

The issue was finally resolved by the Viceroy of India, Lord Mayo, who was in office between 1869 and 1872 and had no hesitation in creating a second, cheaper, gauge, with the statement: 'When we have an elephant's load, we may use an elephant, but when we have only a donkey's load, we have to use a donkey.'[4] But which gauge would be the donkey? Across the world railways had appeared in a variety of sizes, ranging from 2ft to Brunel's favoured 7ft (and that extra ¼ inch). In 1862, a twenty-mile line had already been built in Baroda, one of the princely states still not directly under British rule, using a 2ft 6in gauge, and while initially it had used oxen for haulage, it later became a conventional railway. Then there was the initial nineteen-mile line of the Indian Tramway Company built near Madras using a 3ft 6in gauge.

It is difficult to exaggerate the amount of debate – much of it conducted in newspapers, which seemed obsessed by the issue – that led to the final decision. Mayo rejected 2ft 9in as that did not have a track record elsewhere and, oddly, because he reckoned that cavalry horses could not travel two abreast on such vehicles. On the other hand, he thought the 3ft 6in used elsewhere in British territories was still too large and expensive. Therefore, he plumped for the metre (3ft 3⅜in) gauge, a strange decision in a country which used the Imperial system of measurement for everything from money to liquids. The controversy continued to rage even after the decision had been made. In some cases, local people organized protests when the plans for a new railway envisaged a metre-gauge, rather than a broad-gauge, line because they felt, with some justification, that they were being offered a second-rate railway. Ultimately, it came down to money rather than practicality. Broadly, in 1880, it was estimated that a narrow-gauge railway would cost half the price of the broad gauge, about 70,000 rupees (around £4,700) per mile compared with 166,000 rupees (around £11,000) per mile.

Therefore, the last years of the 1860s marked a double shift in direction: the end, or, more accurately, the curtailment of the guarantee system, and the beginnings of the construction of what was to become a key part of India's railways, the metre-gauge network. Mayo, who was to meet an untimely end in 1872 at the hands of a murderous inmate on an official visit to the prisoner community on the Andaman and Nicobar Islands, actually wanted a bigger role for the state than merely the construction of new lines because of the failure of the guarantee arrangements to bear down on costs. Most of the early guarantee contracts did, in fact, have a clause specifying that the Government of India could take over ownership after a period, which was normally twenty-five years, after they opened. Mayo argued that 'direct action of the state was most likely to bring generally satisfactory results'[15] and consequently he favoured state ownership. This was radical stuff from a Victorian politician and contrasted remarkably with the structure of the UK railways, where such state interference would be considered anathema.

Despite the opposition of the private companies to these arrangements, for a decade the Government of India prevailed and built a series of lines, as well as taking over several others. The first to fall into government hands was the worst financial basket case, the Calcutta & South-Eastern, which had opened in 1862 and struggled for traffic. The thirty-mile line linked Calcutta with a new harbour called Port Canning, which was expected to become a rival to its well-established neighbour, but the anticipated growth in shipping never materialized. Consequently, its owners decided to surrender the railway to the government in 1868 when it became clear that it would struggle ever to pay its running expenses, let alone make any return on capital.

Soon work was started by the Government of India on various schemes which had been held up by failure to attract investment or by bureaucratic procedures. The first construction to be undertaken by the state was for a line north of Lahore (in what is now Pakistan) to Peshawar, which eventually became the Punjab Northern State. Although it was initially envisaged that the line would be metre gauge, the British government was concerned about the military implications of a break in gauge and consequently it was built as a broad-gauge line. So was another railway in what is now Pakistan, the Indus valley line, which was also seen as key to military deployment.

While the majority of the new metre-gauge lines were short branches delivering goods and passengers to the main line, others were major routes in themselves. The most significant of the early ones was the Rajpatuna (an area that encompasses today's state of Rajasthan and parts of neighbouring states) and Central India system of lines that became a vital and heavily used railway. It started life as a modest plan to provide an export route for salt from the Sambar Lake in Rajasthan, a former inland sea with huge quantities of the mineral, via the nearest main town of Jaipur. However, the railway gradually grew into a scheme to link Bombay with Delhi and Agra, which eventually had connecting stations with the East Indian, the Great Indian Peninsula and the Bombay, Baroda & Central India Railways.

For the most part, the other new metre-gauge lines followed the original intention of supplementing the broad-gauge network because, as Khosla puts it, 'the requirements of many of the districts into which it was proposed to extend railway communications would be amply served by lines of less capacity than hitherto adopted'.[16] The smaller gauge and the simple structure afforded by the government's direct involvement meant that railways could be built more quickly as well as cheaply. For example, a ninety-mile line between Hisar and Rewari in Haryana state west of Delhi was completed in June 1883, just two years after being first surveyed. Metre-gauge lines were never allowed into the key ports of Madras, Calcutta and Bombay from which the railways had originally emanated, but, nevertheless, by the turn of the century there were more than

10,000 miles of these lines. Indeed, many had substantial traffic and this caused major headaches for railway managers because they necessitated the creation of transfer stations between the gauges, which became a source of inefficiency that would blight the Indian railways to such an extent that a programme of conversion from metre to broad gauge, Project Unigauge, was initiated in 1991 (see Chapter 10).

Eventually a system of fifty-three transfer stations built up, and the administrative and practical difficulties of operating them were clear from the outset. Thanks to the delightful writings of Jim Corbett,[17] a railway manager charged towards the end of the century with running a busy transfer station, we have some fascinating details of the sheer scale of the task. Corbett, who had undertaken a variety of duties on the railway, including driving trains, was offered, at the tender age of twenty, the job of running the transshipment facilities at Mokameh Ghat (near Patna, the capital of Bihar), between the metre-gauge Bengal & North Western Railway and the broad-gauge East Indian. Corbett was sent by the Bengal & North Western at the busiest time, the summer harvest period, to find that there were around 400 wagons of each gauge waiting to be unloaded and transferred to one another. Apparently, this chaotic scene was an annual event and caused much loss to the railway. The task was made more difficult by the fact that the two railways were separated by the mighty Ganges, requiring all goods to be transshipped between them by ferry. He found the warehouse bulging with goods and the lines blocked with loaded wagons, but managed to sort it out through the clever organization of his personnel.

Previously everything had been done by a labour company, but now Corbett was to be entirely responsible and he quickly took on a workforce of 172 (his description is very precise). He reported that he was paid 1 rupee 7 annas (the equivalent of 1s 11d, or just under 10p) to move 1,000 *maunds*, equivalent to thirty-five tons. He accepts in his book, *My India*, that this 'appears incredible' as it was so little, but stressed that its accuracy can be 'verified by reference to the records of the railway'. Even then, for a three-month period he was unable to pay the workers, who were on piecework, as money was not forthcoming from the railway company. He retained their loyalty only because one of his headmen, who was about to announce that the unpaid workers would walk off the job, found that Corbett ate the same spartan meals – a couple of chapattis and a bit of dhal – as his labourers because he, too, was not being paid. The headman persuaded his team to continue working and Corbett finally managed to convince his company to send through the required funds.

There is possibly some artistic licence here since Corbett was something of a chancer, but his account broadly tallies with other stories of life on the Indian railways in the late nineteenth century. He was to keep the contract for twenty-one years, even during his absence on service in France and Waziristan during the First World War, and his later career as a hunter and conservationist led to the naming after him of a tiger sanctuary at Garhwal in the state of Uttarakhand two years after his death in 1955.

The Government of India was not the only state agency involved in railway construction. The rulers of several princely states, which were semi-autonomous monarchies more or less controlled by the British, were keen on joining the railway age and were willing to contribute towards their cost. The Gaekwad of Baroda (now part of Gujarat) built a line in the 1860s, but a more ambitious project was undertaken at the instigation of the Nizam (king) of Hyderabad (now in Telangana state) to connect the city with the Great Indian Peninsula Railway. It was a joint arrangement between the Nizam, who provided the capital, and the Government of India, which built the 121-mile broad-gauge line through reasonably easy territory, including a short branch. It was completed in 1874, three years after the start of work, and was later extended into a much bigger network, again with capital from the Nizam's government.

The longest metre-gauge line of the early princely state railways was the railway network built by the coalition of states in Kathiawar, a peninsula in north-west India that is now mostly part of Gujarat, where 455 miles of metre-gauge lines were built by the end of the century. It was a joint enterprise part funded by the local states and run by the Bombay, Baroda & Central India Railway.

The Government of India may have been successful in building and operating railways, but it failed in one important respect. While, as we shall see, workshops for maintaining the permanent way and the rolling stock sprung up all around India, there was no attempt to create a genuine rail supply industry in the subcontinent. This is well illustrated by the source of locomotives throughout the pre-Independence era. By the end of 1869, just over 1,000 British steam locomotives were in main-line operation, with none having been built in India, and that domination would continue throughout the colonial period. Supplies of materials and equipment, therefore, largely still came by ship from the UK. Despite this, the private Indian railway companies based in the UK were unhappy with the involvement in the railways by the Government of India and, in the mid-1870s, launched a concerted lobbying campaign to reclaim the main role in the development of the network. This was hardly surprising given the generosity of the past arrangements and they argued that it was only the private sector which had sufficient capital to fund further investment, a familiar position taken by their counterparts in today's debates around the sale of government assets. The companies' case was given a boost thanks to an unlikely source, a famine that swept across parts of India in the mid-1870s, which they were able to exploit for their own ends.

FOUR

STARVING OFF THE LINE AND FIGHTING ON IT

I NDIA HAS HAD many famines in its history, triggered generally by weather or war, or a combination of both, but invariably made worse by hoarding and profiteering. These occurred at regular intervals, roughly every forty years, but their number and intensity increased in the late eighteenth century and the nineteenth, with much of the blame being attributed to policies of the British rulers.

One of the worst in Indian history, the Great Bengal Famine, occurred soon after the East India Company established control over much of India following the gradual disintegration of the Mughal Empire. The famine began with a poor harvest in 1768 and was exacerbated the following year because of the absence of the monsoon rains. In 1770, there was widespread starvation, with the ultimate death toll being estimated at 10 million, a third of the population of the area.[1] The impact would last for decades, with swathes of formerly cultivated land returning to jungle and many areas coming under the control of bandits and 'thuggees'. However, much of the blame for the extent of the famine lay with the East

India Company as it had recently increased land taxes significantly, charging as much as 50 per cent of the value of the land's produce, which had the dual effect of deterring production and preventing peasants from stocking up for the lean times. The company had also made the situation worse by encouraging the replacement of food crops in favour of poppy and indigo cultivation, and forbidding the storing of rice. Worse still, even when it became clear that there was a widespread shortage of food, East India officials did nothing to alleviate the situation and were only interested in the continued profitability of the company.

There were several other major famines during British rule, notably in Madras (1791–2) and Agra (1837–8), but the first of the railway age did not occur until 1860–61. It was known as the Upper Doab famine and affected parts of the North-Western Provinces, the Punjab and Rajpatuna. There followed a series of food shortages in the subsequent decades in various parts of the subcontinent that prompted the creation of a Famine Commission, with the improvement of transport as a key part of its remit. In the age before railways, the difficulties and inefficiencies of transport meant that famine relief was either slow or non-existent. The simple logistics of bullock-cart transport militated against solving a famine crisis. The maximum range of a bullock cart was around fifty miles for the basic reason that beyond this distance the animals would have to eat more than they could haul. Moreover, during famines, there are likely to be few healthy bullocks precisely because there is insufficient food for them.

The potential for railways to relieve famines soon attracted the attention of the authorities. In an 1874 famine, Tirhut (now part of Bihar) was able to receive supplies thanks to a railway connection with Patna, 100 miles away. It was not only main-line railways that were needed but also lesser lines able to reach deep into the countryside. In the particularly deadly Madras famine of 1877–8, when around 2 million died, grain had rotted at stations near the famine areas because there were no bullocks to carry it and no silos to protect it against rats and rain. If there had been more railways to transport the grain, then many lives might have been saved.

The idea that railways could be part of the solution to famine gained currency and cleverly the private railway companies, which were hostile to the system of state building of lines, exploited the situation by arguing that they would be able to build new routes far more quickly than a state-run enterprise thanks to their commercial acumen and access to private capital. The Famine Commission established in 1880 suggested that India would not be safe from episodes of widespread starvation until its railway system connected all major regions, requiring a network of 20,000 miles, more than double the 9,300 mileage at the time. The Commission showed a touching faith in the ability of the private companies to deliver these new lines: 'There would be manifest advantage in giving free scope to the extension of railways by private enterprise, if it were possible.'[2] That might have had something to do with the fact that the Commission was chaired by Sir Richard Strachey, who became chairman of the East Indian Railway a decade later.

The Famine Commission, which heard from many railway witnesses, accepted the criticism of the previous guarantee system, but hoped that a new system of privately built lines could be created that was not so dependent on government backing. This was typical of the constant tension within government that saw private enterprise as the acme of the political system and yet, at times, recognized that the development of the railways on a purely profitable basis would never deliver the large comprehensive

network which the country needed. Railways are natural monop-
olies since, as the Commission recognized, building parallel lines is
expensive and wasteful and therefore, once a line is completed, it is
unlikely that investors would ever pay for building a second one in
competition with the original one. There is always a risk, therefore,
once railways become better used, which may be some years after
completion, that the owning company can make excessive profits
by exploiting this monopoly. The advantage of state railways is that
those profits can then be reinvested in the transport network to fund
further development. In order to distinguish between profitable
and unprofitable railways, the Commission developed the concept
of 'protective railways', which were unlikely to be remunerative but
might have a future key role in preventing famine. Obviously, these
'famine railways' were to be funded by the state as the private sector
would not want to invest in them. However, they were to be built
and operated by private companies since the British government,
imbued with the Victorian obsession with laissez-faire economics
(so familiar, of course, today), wanted to give the impression that
the private sector was the provider.

In fact, the state system had been successful during the brief
period it had been given a free rein: the Government of India had
built 3,000 miles of railway in just over a decade, a faster rate than
achieved previously under the old guarantee system. Indeed, it
was just at the point where the state system was reaching a peak
of activity that it was reined back. In the fifteen months to the
end of March 1881, 1,142 miles of new lines were opened (all but
twenty-two miles state sponsored); the quickest period of growth
since the inauguration of railways in India. Many of the railways
built by the state would never have seen the light of day had it not
been for state involvement. However, the private companies were

able to argue that the government lines were less profitable than those built under the original guarantee system. While this was true, it was not necessarily a reflection of the way in which they were funded and built.

Overall, in 1880 the railway network as a whole was proving reasonably profitable, earning around 4.7 per cent on the capital invested, providing a perfectly respectable return for investors that was better than in the UK, where the average at the time was just under 4 per cent. The state railways in India were far less profitable than the average in India, delivering around 1.5 per cent, but their profitability was constrained for several reasons. The companies which had operated under the guarantee system until 1868 had been able to cherry-pick the routes that were most likely to deliver significant profits. The state lines, in contrast, were being funded precisely because the private companies had shown no interest in building them. Moreover, the state lines were newly completed and, as the 'guaranteed' companies had learnt, it took time to build up traffic and operational efficiency. Many of the state lines were branches where traffic flows tended to be in one direction, again in contrast to the most profitable private lines, which benefited from being heavily loaded in both directions at all times. Moreover, the state lines had found it difficult to find a suitable workforce and through necessity had spent much on training up its staff. Several, too, were in areas where coal was expensive, which also pushed up costs. As Khosla sums it up, 'state railways had not been long enough [in existence] for their financial results to give a tangible guide as to what their future prospects would be'.[3]

None of these subtleties were the concern of the private companies. They argued that the state had no business in the field of railway construction and should get out of it – and they won their argument. Famines in India and war in Afghanistan and elsewhere had drained the Government of India's coffers and the companies claimed they had the resources to build lines. Consequently, in 1879, the Secretary of State for India instructed the Government of India to stop building lines apart from under exceptional circumstances such as famine or conflict: 'Thus the valuable experiment of having state-owned and state-operated lines, functioning contemporaneously with privately owned and operated lines, was brought to a close.'[4] However, at least these new arrangements were not quite as generous as the old guarantees, as the rate of return was lower.

At the same time, rather oddly, since it seemed to contradict its overall policy of reining back the private sector, the government took over the East Indian Railway at the expiry of its original twenty-five-year initial contract. However, as Khosla explains, 'it was never the intention of the state to work the line itself'.[5] Most of the shareholders were bought off with bonds paying out 4 per cent per year. That, too, was to be the new level of guarantee for the shareholders of railway companies, which was still high enough to attract investors now that railways were a more mature industry that appeared to be a largely risk-free option – especially given the guarantee. As the other '5 per cent' railways reached twenty-five years, most were taken over in the same way, with the management being handed back to the company. Thus, neither the personnel nor the operations were much affected by the transfer, although the government did require running rights for state-owned trains on the privately operated lines.

Oddly, the government did not exercise its option to take over the other inaugural railway, the Great Indian Peninsula Railway, despite having a similar arrangement. Instead, shareholders were able to continue benefiting from the guarantee, through which, as a result, 'observers estimated the Government of India lost tens of millions of pounds and left fortunate shareholders with another twenty-five years of annuity-like dividends'.[6]

The new guaranteed lines were a further burden on the Government of India, which protested against their imposition by the colonial power in London to no avail. The cost was leavened somewhat as the Government of India still shared any profits above 4 per cent – they were entitled to 80 per cent of the excess profits, after various expenses were deducted, for the East Indian and 60 per cent for most of the other railways which obtained contracts in this period, and over time, as railway use went up towards the end of the century, most of the companies' income exceeded the guaranteed level. The hope of the British government was that eventually private companies would come forward to build lines without seeking a guarantee, but this proved to be over-optimistic.

The private companies realized that after the report of the Famine Commission there was a renewed sense of urgency in government circles to expand the railway network and consequently they were able to drive hard bargains for the funding of new lines. The difficulty for the government was that the railway companies had become subsidy junkies and had come to expect the customary generous guarantees in return for investing in the Indian rail network. No wonder they had baulked at the state building railways itself because of the lost opportunity for profits. Khosla notes wryly, 'capitalists in England had become so accustomed to consider a Government guarantee as a sine qua non, that it was difficult to float an undertaking without State aid [being] given in that form'.[7] Instead, subsidies took other forms, mostly through free use of land and support from local district boards.

Other than 'famine' railways, there was another important group of lines, largely built in the last quarter of the nineteenth century, which benefited from generous government largesse and were to prove to be mostly redundant, despite the massive expense and the enormous engineering challenges required to build them. These were strategic military lines built at the instigation of hawkish politicians mostly because of the perceived threat from Russia. There were always two aspects to the military's interest in the railways. The first, as we have seen, was to ensure that troops were able to make use of the railway in order to move around the country quickly to quell unrest. The other was the construction of lines specifically for military purposes, given that the roads were so inadequate in remote areas.

Most of these railways were built on the North-West Frontier, the border of what is now Pakistan with Afghanistan, and their construction was stimulated by a recurring fear that Russia was constructing railways in central Asia with designs on invading Afghanistan, seen as a buffer state, and perhaps India itself. The railways in what is now Pakistan were built on the plains relatively early, but the huge rivers, flowing out of the Himalayas to the north, were natural barriers that took years and considerable funds to breach. The construction of the bridges over these rivers was a particularly challenging project because of the unpredictable nature of the water flow. Floods can occur at any time of the year because of potential breaching of natural dams formed by ice or debris. Therefore, several stretches of line ended at a river crossing and in many cases there was a gap of several years before the bridge linking them was built. Transport in the plains before the arrival of the railways was by steamship on the Indus, a perilous and, upstream, a very slow journey. Gradually, the Sind, Punjab &

Delhi Railway, whose investors benefited from the guarantee system, completed sections of line parallel to the river, but it was not until 1878 that a chain of railways across northern India united Calcutta with Karachi, and even then the Indus had to be crossed by ferry until the opening of the Lansdowne Bridge in 1889, which was the longest cantilever span in the world at the time. By this point the Scinde, Punjab & Delhi had amalgamated with three state-owned railways north of Delhi to form North Western Railway, which had 1,800 route miles, and would become the beneficiary of a little-used series of railways stretching deep into the deserts and mountains of the north-west.

The advocates of building these strategic lines had their eyes firmly on the Russians, who were rapidly building railways in central Asia. The most significant was the Trans-Caspian, which was started in 1879 and reached Merv (now in Turkmenistan) in 1886. To the consternation of the British, that line was extended further south to Panjdeh and the western Afghanistan border, which was reached in 1889. The big question was whether the construction of these lines by the Russians was born of commercial interests or were part of an expansionist military strategy. The issue of how to respond became a major subject for debate in the UK parliament, with strong protagonists on both sides. Those who supported responding to the perceived threat by constructing lines that went through barren territory and would inevitably attract minimal civilian traffic argued Russia was intent on using its railways for invasion. The evidence for this was not strong. Russia had struggled in its recent wars, losing in Crimea and only just managing to overcome the Turks in 1877–8. Moreover, Afghanistan has always been hostile territory, as Britain had discovered in the first two Afghan wars, which started in 1839 and 1878 respectively

– both ended inconclusively with much British bloodshed. Crossing on foot through the country, with its potentially hostile tribespeople and its extreme climate, to reach India would have been a daunting, if not impossible, task for a large Russian army. Afghanistan, as the subsequent century and a half has shown, is a place where wars are lost, even if they are seemingly won. The opponents of these military lines saw them as a waste of money and a distraction given the need for more useful railways in many other parts of the subcontinent. Nevertheless, with the support of some of India's Viceroys – they numbered both hawks and doves over the years – and much pressure from the UK government, various military lines were built in the last third of the nineteenth century into territory approaching Afghanistan, but none of these railways would ever cross the border.

The Second Afghan War (1878–80) provided the impetus for the construction of these railways, both in the short term, with a rush to lay down lines to help the war effort, and in the longer term, as it gave the military the justification it needed to build further lines into the deserts and mountains of the North-West Frontier, particularly as the Trans-Caspian was being extended. During the war, the most remarkable project was the construction of the Kandahar State Railway, ironically named after a town in Afghanistan which it never came close to reaching. Once fighting broke out, in September 1878, the Government of India decided to build an all-weather line into Afghanistan. Surveys had been carried out earlier but otherwise the scheme had languished until, suddenly, resources – both men and money – were thrown at its construction.

The route involved a stretch of 133 miles before reaching the mountains and, remarkably, this was completed by January 1880, with the railway reaching Sibi a mere 101 days after work had started. However, further construction was held up as the difficulties of the terrain became apparent and it was obvious that the line could not be completed before the conflict was over. The extension by the Russians of the Trans-Caspian railway to Merv gave renewed impetus in 1883 for construction to resume and the line reached Chaman, on the border, a decade later. The construction was a heroic task, equal in difficulty to the first assault on the ghats east of Bombay forty years previously. In fact, two routes were built, one through Quetta, which had only been occupied by the British in 1876, and another to the north, which became known as the Sind Pershin State Railway. Remarkably, the British Prime Minister, William Gladstone, had given orders that these works should be carried out in secret, as he was fearful that the military intent of building a railway was all too obvious. Therefore, for several years the project, which went through a town called Harnai, was known as the 'Harnai Road Improvement Scheme', a ridiculous name which rather implied it was some kind of suburban bypass project.

Despite doubts about building through to Afghanistan, a huge depot was established at Chaman and stocked with rails, sleepers and even bridge girders, with the intention of completing the further sixty-seven-mile line through to Kandahar, but the British never dared to risk the wrath of the Afghan ruler and the equipment was left to gather dust and rust. The line through the difficult Bolan Pass was started in 1880 but was interrupted by the Battle of Maiwand, which took place nearby and was another bloody defeat for the British. Work resumed in 1885 and reached Quetta, the capital of what is now Balochistan in Pakistan, the following year. However, the track was washed away three years later and an alternative route had to be devised and constructed.

Not only did those working on the lines have to cope with the desolate, rocky terrain, but they also faced attacks from nearby tribes. Dealings with local people required careful negotiation and diplomacy, but occasionally a dispute would arise that led to an attack and the inevitable bloodshed.

Several difficult bridges were built, too, some of which did have the secondary effect of allowing remote areas to be better connected. The most impressive was the fording of the Indus at Attock. The railway had reached the river in 1881 but the bridge would take another two years to complete. The passage of the Indus there had long been one of the greatest hazards of the Silk Road because the size of the river varies from a gentle flow to a raging torrent, fed both by monsoon rains and sudden releases of water from breaches in natural dams. The Government of India had long sought to erect a bridge but the cost and difficulty had stymied the project until the military imperative led to its construction. Sudden rushes of water have been known to raise the level of the river by seventy feet, and the design of the bridge had to ensure it was robust enough to withstand such a flood. The five-span bridge was eventually completed in 1883, but had to be reconstructed in the 1920s because of damage from the river flow.

The question of who paid for these railways was a subject of much controversy. They aroused much anger among Indian nationalists, who saw them as unnecessary and serving merely to entrench British rule. Their location meant that for the most part they were utterly useless as methods of transport, but several were in fact paid for out of the Government of India's transport budget, reducing available resources for far more useful lines. Back in Britain, too, there was much opposition, and the debate in UK government circles over the necessity of building these lines raged for more than half a century between Russophiles and Russophobes and their respective camp followers. The British, incidentally, were miffed that the Russians were able to lay their lines for around £5,000 per mile, about a quarter of the amount that the railways through what is now Pakistan were costing. That was partly because the Russians did not use contractors but instead the state itself commissioned and built the lines, whereas the British used private companies.

If the famine railways failed in their basic task, at least they proved in the most part to be useful for local people. These military lines, running through sparsely populated territory, barely provided any kind of service. The usual provision was for a train per week in each direction, principally with the sole purpose of providing supplies to the railways themselves. Amazingly, there would be another burst of construction in these lines during the boom time of the Indian railways in the 1920s, including the conquest of the Khyber Pass (see Chapter 8).

Meanwhile, more useful railways were still being built. One successful line was the Bengal & North Western, created in 1881, which was the only significant railway that never received any government aid throughout its existence. When it was taken over by the state during the Second World War, it boasted 1,270 miles of metre-gauge track serving the area north of the River Ganges to the south of Nepal. Its management structure was typical of the time and demonstrates the extent to which the railway companies were run from Britain. The Bengal & North Western's board sat in London, controlling the company through a general manager (who, oddly, throughout India was known as the 'agent') and his staff in Gorakhpur in Uttar Pradesh. Interestingly, too, despite the fact that the railway received no financial support from government, except free land and buildings at the outset, the state still took a share of the profits above a 6 per cent rate of return on capital. Moreover, 'the system was subject to government inspection and sanction for all but the most petty expenditure, and government approval of fares and freight rates, routes and working practices'.[8] The contract with the government even gave the state an option to buy the railway after thirty, fifty or ninety-nine years, though, in fact, it did so after sixty-one years.

The Bengal & North Western was one of three railways without guarantees that sprang up in the 1880s as a result of the new system. The other two were not as successful, demonstrating that the ideal of self-supporting railways built without state aid was illusory. The Rohilkhand & Kumaon received a subsidy for ten years and was subsequently taken over, while the Bengal Central was a classic case in demonstrating the limitations of privately sponsored railways. The Bengal Central had backing from two major banks with worldwide interests, Rothschilds and Barings, which gave encouragement to the government in its hope that substantial investors would be prepared to support railway construction. However, the company sought government support when it undertook to build the seventy-five-mile line between Calcutta and Jessore, and obtained a guaranteed rate of return of 4 per cent on its investment for the first five years. This was to be repaid from profits in excess of 5 per cent made in subsequent years and the government had the right to purchase the line on favourable terms after thirty years. Nevertheless, this example shows just how difficult it was for the government to persuade private investors to take all the risk of investing in the railways.

The new system also resulted in the creation during the 1880s of three railways that did benefit from the new guarantee system, but the government managed to negotiate down the guarantee in most cases to 3.5 or 3 per cent. These were presented as famine relief railways that reduced the risk of food shortages, but, in fact, their role in relation to the market for agricultural produce was actually far more complex and less obviously beneficial.

Two of these new railways had connections with the Great Indian Peninsula Railway, whose system was becoming the dominant one on the subcontinent: the Indian Midland had a series of routes connected with older lines at three places, including Delhi and Agra, and was soon subsumed into the Great Indian Peninsula; and the Bengal Nagpur, which ran from Calcutta (in fact, Howrah on the other side of the river) to Nagpur (now in Maharashtra), where it connected with the Great Indian Peninsula. The Nagpur line, in fact, had originally been a government project halted by the change in policy and lack of funds, and by joining the East Indian at Asansol (West Bengal) provided a shorter route between Bombay and Calcutta. It eventually became a significant railway by acquiring part of the state-built East Coast Railway that ran south from Calcutta to Madras and by running branches into the coalfields of Orissa and Bihar.

These two railways were the biggest beneficiaries of the funds available for famine relief. Business plans for these lines were presented to the government by the promoters emphasizing their value in ensuring regular food supplies, but there was little evidence that this was the case and the information about potential traffic was wildly optimistic. There was a rather remarkable aspect of the way that the owners of these railways were remunerated, because, perversely, they were partly funded by those they were supposed to help feed. When, in 1878, the Governor-General, Lord Lytton, had set up the Indian Famine Relief Fund, he decided that rather than raising the money from government funds or from taxing the better-off sections of society, it was the poor peasants who should be forced to contribute to the fund through extra taxes paid when their harvests were plentiful. Lytton's view of the government's role during famines was strictly in line with the Victorian zeitgeist: 'There will be no interference of any kind on the part of Government with the object of reducing the price of food.' Famine relief, too, was seen as interfering with the market and consequently discouraged: 'Mere distress is not a sufficient reason for opening up a relief work.'⁹ Therefore railways were seen as a way of making the existing economic and transport framework more efficient, rather than as a form of government intervention, which would elicit the criticism of the fervent free marketeers.

The famine funds were in fact not to be used to relieve shortages but rather to build railways that would facilitate the transport of food. Consequently, in 1885, Randolph Churchill (Winston's father), the Secretary of State for India in the Whitehall government, decreed that these funds should be used to pay interest to the owners of these two railways. Since the Bengal Nagpur railway was funded by the Rothschild family, this led to the irony of the richest family in the world benefiting from taxes extracted from poor peasants in order, supposedly, to prevent them starving. Other investors who benefited from this absurd scheme included several politicians and former Indian civil servants. It was too much even for some of Churchill's fellow Tories to stomach: 'This misapplication of famine monies to add multiple guarantees, for "gentlemanly capitalist" investors, was condemned by Churchill's fellow Conservative party representatives, Viceroy Curzon and Secretary of State for India Lord George Hamilton.'¹⁰

Even worse, it is doubtful that these famine relief railways even managed to relieve famine. There was another famine in the

Central Provinces, through which the Nagpur line ran, just after the railway was completed in the mid-1890s, and the railway seems, according to a subsequent assessment by the Famine Commission, if anything, to have exacerbated matters. Quite simply, railways operate in both directions and consequently food prices went up in some parts of the region as grain was exported on the supposedly beneficial railway. In some parts of the region the shortage caused by exports led to grain prices rising by up to 100 per cent. Even Nagpur, the terminus of the line, suffered from grain riots because of shortages.

The other beneficiary of the famine railway investment funds, the Midland, didn't do much to relieve famine either. In fact, it was effectively a vehicle for the expansion of the Great Indian Peninsula Railway, as the composition of the boards of the two companies was identical and the two railways merged in 1900. Those directors, therefore, benefited from the 5 per cent guarantee enjoyed by the main company, as well as from the famine funds on their affiliate. Yet, the Indian Peninsula did little for famine relief as it was criticized by subsequent Famine Commissions for its high freight charges and inefficiencies. Overall, the famine relief railways did not succeed in their fundamental purpose: 'While these railway companies were recipients of substantial government support, they failed to provide the level of service and fare structure required to deliver cheap wheat to famine regions.'[11]

Support for funding these railways from public funds relied on the assumption that famines were caused by regional shortages of food, rather than an overall nationwide deficit. This argument was rather undermined by a widespread famine in 1899–1900, which was precipitated by the failure of the monsoon rains over vast swathes of western and central India. The area around Bombay was the worst hit, but neighbouring regions were also affected and, as often happened, the heaviest death rate was in the second year, when malaria and cholera epidemics rampaged through the weakened population.

This was, however, to be the last major famine until a particularly severe but local episode in Bengal in 1943 caused by the war. While the railways may have played a small part in allowing for more efficient distribution, it was their role in providing better access to markets for farmers, and consequently greater profits, which in turn led to the ability to store savings for hard times, that was more important than their direct role in providing transport for food supplies at times of shortage.

Changes in the pattern of agriculture were the main reason for the absence of major famines in peacetime during the twentieth century. Thanks to better farming practices, the predominantly subsistence agriculture of the nineteenth century was being replaced by a more diversified economy, with more produce being grown for cash and consequently export, principally by rail. The demand for labour from the wider growing economy meant that surplus labour could be absorbed in the cities, thus reducing the number of mouths to feed in the impoverished rural areas. The risk of famine was also reduced by the adoption of a more humanitarian approach from government, a departure from the cruel *laissez-faire* policy of relying solely on market forces favoured in the Victorian era. By the early years of the twentieth century there was a much greater readiness to intervene early, born both of humanitarian concerns and of the recognition, in the context of the growing nationalist movement, that Indian public opinion could no longer be simply ignored. Ultimately, therefore, the railways had only a minor role in reducing the risk of famine and certainly did little that could justify the generous subsidies they had obtained from the Famine Relief Fund. The money would undoubtedly have saved more lives if it had been spent in more direct forms of intervention.

There was one exception to the lower guarantees given to the new railways. In the province of Assam, which until the early 1880s had no railways, pressure from tea plantation and mine owners led to the construction of a series of railway lines. In the early 1870s, the Government of India had been reluctant to sanction construction as Assam was a remote area which was effectively a dead end. However, a decade later, the government changed its mind under pressure from British investors, who argued that a railway would be an economic boost for the local tea and mining industries. The government also, belatedly, recognized that there was the strategic advantage of connecting Burma with the Indian railway network. Oddly, so strong was the government's desire to bring the iron road to Assam that the initial line – the seventy-eight-mile metre-gauge Dibru–Sadiya railway – benefited from a generous 5 per cent guarantee, rather than the lower rate which had then become the norm. This was partly because of the unstable political situation in Assam, but also because of the difficulties of constructing lines in the mountainous region. Not only did the London-based railway company receive the guarantee on its investment – paid, incidentally, by the Province of Assam by taxing local people – but it was also granted valuable rights to exploit coal, timber and oil in the region. The railway soon proved to be highly profitable, playing a key role in the economy of Assam, and its chairman claimed that by the turn of the century it was carrying more goods per mile than any other metre-gauge line in India. However, as Sarah Hilaly, the author of a history of the railways of Assam, notes, the motive behind the signing of the contract was purely to support the interests of the British company: 'The colonial policy of upholding commercial interests above all factors was largely responsible for the initiation of such a project.'[12]

Several other lines and branches were built in Assam during the run-up to the First World War and a 575-mile connection with the Bengal port of Chittagong was completed in 1904. Sir Richard Strachey, the former head of the Famine Commission, who, as mentioned previously, became chairman of the East Indian Railway in 1898, managed to persuade the government to fund the Assam–Bengal line, arguing it was important for both famine relief and military purposes, as well as being commercially profitable. However, it became something of a white elephant. The line included a mountainous middle section between Badarpur and Lumding which proved so difficult that expert tunnellers from Cornwall were brought over at great expense, and inevitably the line cost far more than the original estimates. Earthquakes and landslips added to the construction challenges and, according to Hilaly, 'the financial allocations for the Assam–Bengal Railway were marked by expenditure in excess of projected estimates, which had no parallel in the history of railway construction in India'.[13] This might be a slight exaggeration, given the cost of building through the ghats in the early days of the railways in India, but the line was for a long time a major financial burden on the Province of Assam, which was responsible for paying the guaranteed rate of return – set at 3.5 per cent – on the line. The Assam–Bengal Railway suffered, too, from competition on the network from navigable waterways in the region which limited its commercial potential: 'The system of subsidy was an immense drain on the internal resources of the province and the country at large ... The masses were not benefited by the large-scale expenditure on infrastructure development.'[14] Later, Lord Curzon criticized the construction of the line, ridiculing 'the half-digested combination of famine, military, and commercial arguments, which had absorbed over £9m of taxpayers' money [against a construction budget of £4m]'.[15] It was only much later, especially during the Second World War, that the Assam–Bengal Railway proved to be a very useful route, opening up Assam and becoming a vital military supply artery.

The biggest of the new railways in India, stimulated by the shift back to private-sector construction, would eventually be the metre-gauge Southern Mahratta Railway on the western side of the Deccan plateau, which stretched to 1,600 miles by the turn of the century. Its principal route connected Poona (now in Maharashtra), seventy miles east of Bombay, to Bangalore and Mysore (both now in Karnataka), while another line stretched across southern India from Bezawada on the east coast to Goa, still a Portuguese colony, on the west.

The basic pattern under the new system was that as the old companies' contracts ran out, generally twenty-five years after their creation, the government would take over ownership, buying out most of the shareholders while allowing the existing management to continue running the railway. Most of the major companies followed this pattern, but there were exceptions. With the Sind, Punjab & Delhi in the north-west, for example, the government insisted it would operate the railway directly because of its strategic importance. It became part of the state-run North Western Railway, which had an extensive network connecting Delhi with Amritsar, as well as Lahore and Karachi (which are both now in Pakistan), and later, in the 1920s, with the Khyber Pass.

Towards the end of the nineteenth century, a new category of railways emerged: lines up to hill towns used by the British to escape the extremes of temperature during the sweltering Indian summers in the valleys below. The concept of connecting the hill stations with the rail network was not new. It had first been suggested by Hyde Clarke, the editor of the *Railway Times* in a pamphlet, published during the Rebellion of 1857, whose very title, *Colonisation, Defence and Railways in Our Indian Empire*, is revealing. His idea was that the hill stations offered a much better environment from which the British could govern India all year round thanks to the climate that made them much more like 'English towns'. They would not only accommodate the leaders of the Government of India, but also attract immigrants, at the rate of 50,000 per year from the UK, encouraged by land grants like those which were, at the time, being granted in Australia. It would not only be the elite who would benefit: 'The Eurasian and European clerks and mechanics who worked on the plains could settle their families in the hills and visit them frequently with the aid of cheap second and third class return tickets.'[16] (Eurasian referred to people of mixed descent, usually an English father and an Indian mother, but over time came to mean any person with some European blood.) By moving away from the plains, where the debilitating climate thwarted British attempts to impose their way of life on the subcontinent, Clarke argued that 'in the hill stations everything from joint-stock companies, appropriate domestic influences and Christianity to a militia to defend India from internal and external attack, would flourish'.[17] From these hilltop enclaves, whose likeness to a medieval castle towering above the lands of the local peasantry was not coincidental, Britain would rule India.

In fact, once work started on the hill-station railways, these grand ambitions had been somewhat tempered by the realities of colonial India. Three of these railways were built in a twenty-five-year period spanning the end of the nineteenth century and the first few years of the twentieth. Bizarrely, just to add to the range of railways in India, they were all of different gauge. The first to be started was the line up to Darjeeling, where the hill road, completed in 1861, involved a tortuous and at times perilous journey that took two to three days to cover the sixty miles from Siliguri in the valley below. Even the 400-mile journey north to Siliguri from Calcutta was no easy matter as it involved a railway trip for half the route, followed by a steam ferry journey on the Ganges, before the long trip up the hill in the inevitable bullock cart, and it was not until 1878 that the line from Calcutta to Siliguri was completed. Oddly, a metre-gauge railway was built almost simultaneously to Siliguri from the north, but it was felt that the steep incline made it too difficult to continue the line up to Darjeeling.

However, the two new rail connections to Siliguri encouraged the authorities to consider a rail route up to Darjeeling. With the number of Europeans living in India increasing, the demand to reach the hill stations more easily once the summer heat became unbearable put pressure on the government to support a railway scheme. After years of debate and delay, construction was finally started on the Darjeeling Himalayan Railway in 1879. That was a result of pressure from Franklin Prestage, an official of the East Bengal Railway, whose original plans to build a line up to Darjeeling had been abandoned following the decision by the Government of India in 1868 to shift railway construction to the state sector. Prestage, who deserves his accolade as the 'father' of the railway, nevertheless kept on pursuing the idea, seeing it as an opportunity to reduce the cost of transport to Darjeeling, which was limiting the economic potential of the tea plantations and causing great hardship since, for example, the price of rice more than doubled between Siliguri and the hill station. By reducing the cost of transport and speeding up journeys, the railway could, Prestage felt, quickly become a profitable enterprise. Prestage's attempt to build it under the auspices of the East Bengal was rejected by the government, but, instead, he put together a plan for a new company to build the line funded entirely by Indian investors.

Work started in March 1879 and it was no easy task. From the terminus of the line at the joint station of Siliguri, the 2ft-gauge railway zigzags over deep ravines and precipices and rises up steep inclines, climbing 7,000 feet to reach Ghum four miles from Darjeeling, after which it descends slightly. The fifty-mile-long line incorporated two innovative ways of running the tracks up the hill that obviated the need for any tunnels. First, a series of loops, where the railway circles around and passes over itself on a bridge to attain a higher elevation, were created to ease the gradient up the hill, though the average still remained 1 in 25, very steep for a railway. Then, using a similar technique to the Bhor Ghat, a series of Z-shaped reverses were used, with the train entering a siding (or head shunt) carved into the mountainside. Just as with the Bhor Ghat, the points are then changed to allow it to reverse and continue the climb. It was cumbersome and slow, perhaps, but cheap and effective.

Despite the difficulties, the line was built remarkably quickly, helped by the fact that such a narrow-gauge line required far fewer earth movements than conventional broader-gauge lines, and could cope with bends that were far tighter than would be possible even on a metre-gauge line. For much of the route, the railway followed the path of the cart hill road, which also speeded up progress. The first section of eighteen miles was opened in March 1880 by the Viceroy of India, Lord Lytton, a rail enthusiast who took advantage of his position to ride the train up to its temporary terminus. The following August, the line was opened as far as Kurseong, nearly 5,000 feet above sea level, thirty-two miles from Siliguri (which is only 400 feet above sea level), and the line all the way to Darjeeling was completed a year later. The steep gradients severely restricted the maximum weight of the trains, as they needed sufficient adhesion, even when the rails were wet, to climb up the hill and descend safely.

Although the small gauge and consequent tiny engines have led them to be called the 'Toy Trains', attracting rail fans from around the world, they were nothing of the sort. They were the main link, the veritable lifeline, for both passengers and freight between Darjeeling and the valley, and the line was kept open despite frequent landslides and other mishaps. Their description in the official history of the railways nevertheless concedes that the trains were an odd sight: 'Ornamentally painted in green, the locomotive looks almost like a giant war horse straining to draw a heavy chariot as it pants and throbs, struggling to pull its loads up sharp inclines.'[18] The Darjeeling railway (I travelled on it in 2000) offers a unique experience as it takes passengers up through remarkably contrasting landscapes, from thick forest and tea plantations to rather stark mountain scenes, with, if you are lucky (which I was not, despite spending three days there), views of 20,000-feet-high snowcapped peaks.

The town expanded rapidly as a result of the advent of the railway, and many buildings were copies of English bungalows and town houses. Lady Iris Wedgwood, an accomplished author and travel writer, who journeyed across India by train in the mid-1930s with her husband, Ralph, as he was compiling a report on the railways, was not impressed with the result: 'Darjeeling is, to my mind, a mere bungaloid growth upon the hill side, architecturally trivial and vulgar; the Swiss would have made a better job of it. For the most part, the buildings are a most unsatisfactory aspect and seem simply to have come for the weekend, which gives a makeshift caravan-like appearance to the little town.'[19]

Despite such criticisms, with such stunning scenery (when the fog recedes), and the mountain air, the railway, not surprisingly, boosted the use of Darjeeling as a summer resort for Europeans. However, the line was also a busy freight railway. It helped the tea industry, which had only been started in 1841, to expand rapidly and send its produce more easily to Calcutta and beyond. An interesting side issue, one of great excitement to railway enthusiasts, was that when the line to Darjeeling was completed, Siliguri became the only station in India – and quite possibly the world – to be served by railways of three different gauges.

The second hill railway to be built was the metre-gauge Nilgiri, from Mettupalayam, the terminus of a branch line of the Southern Railway between Madras and Kerala, up to Ootacamund, dubbed the 'Queen of Hill Stations' because of its beautiful setting on a plateau in the heavily forested Nilgiri mountains. It was a more difficult railway to build than the Darjeeling line, requiring a series of tunnels and viaducts to be carved out of the side of a valley. The incline was so steep that a twelve-mile section was fitted with a rack and pinion system since mere adhesion would not have been sufficient to counter the 1 in 12.5 gradient. Rack railways had been developed in the early nineteenth century but little used until they were adapted to enable mountain railways to climb much steeper gradients than would otherwise have been possible. They had been introduced in the USA with the Mount Washington cog railway and in Switzerland with the Vitznau–Rigi line near Lucerne about thirty years previously, but the Nilgiri was the first such line in Asia.

Ootacamund had become the summer resort for government employees and other Europeans based in Madras during the first half of the nineteenth century, and though it soon boasted boarding schools, churches, clubs and all the other amenities favoured by Europeans, the only access, as with Darjeeling, had hitherto been a narrow hill-cart road. As with many such challenging projects, there was a long period of gestation with a variety of proposals suggesting different ways of reaching Ooty (the name generally used by both the British and locals) being considered. The most outlandish scheme came from the Duke of Buckingham, the Governor-General of Madras, in 1877, who suggested two sections of rail line linked by a two-mile-long inclined ropeway up to Lady Canning's Seat, a popular picnic spot. There was only one problem with this plan – the ropeway had to be up a gradient of 1 to 1.5, which made it highly unlikely that the sahibs of Madras, let alone the memsahibs, would agree to be hauled up on such a precarious contraption.

Eventually, after much negotiation over the level of guarantee and the cost of the project, and further delays while the Nilgiri Railway Company raised the necessary capital, work started in 1891 with the involvement of Niklaus Riggenbach, the inventor of the method used on the Vitznau–Rigi line. The company, however, soon went bust and, with the government reluctant to step in, progress was held up for several years. It was not, therefore, until 1899 that the line was completed to Coonoor, seventeen miles from Mettupalayam, which included the rack section that took the trains up the steep climb. The route up from Coonoor is on a gentler gradient through the tea plantations and consequently does not require the aid of the rack and pinion system, but due to lack of money and the relative ease of travelling by road up to Ooty from Coonoor, work on this section did not start until 1907 and was completed the following year. The twenty-eight-mile railway, which has a series of wonderfully English-named stations such as Runnymede, Hillgrove and Glendale, was a great triumph given the severity of the incline and the need for sixteen tunnels covering a total of three quarters of a mile, as well as countless viaducts, many of which are elegant structures blended into the contours of the mountains.

The other notable hill railway was the line to Simla, which had become the summer capital of India in 1863. This meant a twice-annual transfer of the whole apparatus of government, involving a difficult 1,000-mile journey between Simla and Calcutta, which remained the capital of India until superseded by New Delhi in 1931. Simla enjoyed the most British-like climate of these hill stations and was the headquarters of the British army, whose officers' behaviour meant it developed a rather louche reputation for adultery as many women coming to India to seek marriage visited the hill station only to be tempted into illicit relationships.

Although the idea of a railway to Simla had been mooted as early as 1847, the difficulties of building the line meant it was the last of the three main hill stations to become accessible by rail. Indeed, the engineering challenge was far greater than for either of the other two railways. The line was, at sixty miles, not only the longest of these hill railways, but had to run through even harder terrain than the Nilgiri, requiring more than 100 tunnels, totalling three miles in length, as well as nearly two miles of viaducts.

Kalka, at the base of the hill, was reached by a broad-gauge railway in 1891, which made the idea of building the line up to Simla feasible. The contract for the line – originally, like Darjeeling, just 2ft gauge – was obtained by the privately funded Delhi–Ambala–Kalka Railway Company. However, the estimate of the cost of construction was soon exceeded and eventually twice as much was spent on building the line than had been envisaged. It was opened after five years of construction by Lord Curzon, then the Viceroy, and the railway company was allowed to charge higher fares per mile as a result of the increased building and maintenance costs, but nevertheless it soon fell into financial difficulties. Consequently, the line was sold to the government in 1906 and widened to 2ft 6in, strangely almost the median of the other two early hill railways. The basis for this decision was that the tiny and cheap 2ft of the Darjeeling was insufficient for the needs of what was effectively a capital city, as well as being inadequate for military purposes, while metre gauge was too expensive.

All three of these lines survive today and have been combined as a Unesco World Heritage Site, ensuring their preservation. Remarkably, some of the engines still in use on the Darjeeling line date back to its opening in 1880, though nowadays it is little more than a tourist attraction. Somehow, though, it manages to employ some 750 people, but is, nevertheless, in a very poor state of repair, with frequent minor derailments that require the numerous workers to physically manhandle the stock back onto the tracks.

A fourth, much shorter, hill railway, and a recent addition to the Unesco World Heritage Site, was built to Matheran, a favourite hot-weather resort for residents of Bombay, sixty miles away. Less well-known because Matheran was not used as a hill town by the British, the railway also used a 2ft gauge and runs thirteen miles from Neral, on the line between Bombay and Poona, to Matheran. The construction of the line, started in 1907, was funded by Sir Adamjee

Peerbhoy, a cotton magnate and philanthropist who started life in abject poverty selling matches on the streets of Bombay and later became the first president of the Muslim League. His son, Abdul Hussein, was in charge of the construction and completed the line in 1907. It remains open today, though it has been closed several times due to floods and landslides.

The final hill railway, and what became the longest at just over 100 miles, was built in the late 1920s. The 2ft 6in Kangra Valley Railway, constructed by the Northern Railway in the sub-Himalayan region of Himachal Pradesh, is also the least known of these railways, as it is in a remote region and was originally conceived principally for freight. Its most remarkable feature is that, unlike on the Simla line, there are just two short tunnels in the whole length, but instead there are countless bridges (nearly 1,000), which makes for a particularly scenic journey. The line soon became a busy passenger railway, despite the fact that the road trip is actually shorter, as it carried pilgrims to various holy Hindu sites as well as tourists.

In several ways, therefore, 1880 was a turning point in Indian railway history as the new arrangements based on private-sector companies became the predominant way of building new lines until 1924. The ownership and operation of Indian railways was by then a complicated hotchpotch of private and public, both national and local, interests. To make matters more complex, the princely states had continued to build lines under various arrangements with the Government of India, and some minor lines were built at the behest of local district boards, which either owned them directly or provided a guaranteed rate of return. These district boards were encouraged to build branches by the government, which offered them up to 10 per cent of the earnings gained by main-line companies from the traffic they provided; a complex but satisfactory arrangement that enabled them to make a profit and pay dividends. Some lines were built by private companies at the behest of local district boards and financed through their tax revenue.

There were, therefore, private lines owned by companies guaranteed under the old contracts as well as under the new ones; state-owned lines worked either by private companies or by the state; lines built and supported by local district boards; railways supported by the famine fund; and princely state lines run either by the government or by the princely states themselves. There were even lines run in foreign territories, since both France and Portugal had built lines in the areas they controlled. Overall, 'in 1902 the Indian railways were worked by 33 separate administrations including 24 private companies, four government agencies and five princely states'.[20] It was a fluid situation, as Westwood suggests: 'railways were continually being formed, built, amalgamated, bought up and sold'.[21] And, as noted above, many of these companies were still run from boards sitting some 4,500 miles away in London.

In order to provide some coherence to this complex situation, the government convened a Railway Conference, which first met in 1879, bringing together senior officials from all the various railway administrations across the country to help the system function as a genuine network. One bugbear had been the use of rolling stock owned by one company operating over another's track, and an early decision of the Conference was to ensure unrestricted interchange of rolling stock between different broad-gauge lines. Another early decision, influenced by the chaotic situation in the UK over braking systems, where the use of a variety of designs had resulted in inconvenience and greater safety risk, was to ensure that the mechanism for continuous braking, a key safety feature of the railways, was standardized. This would ensure that coaches from different companies could be attached to operate as a single train. India, thus, benefited from the mistakes made on the railways of its colonial power, and from its late adoption of this technology. That may have marginally increased safety on the railways, but there was still a long way to go to making travel on them pleasant or comfortable for the majority of passengers.

LIFE ON THE LINES

A s we have seen, by the turn of the century, the Indian railways were a fiercely complicated and rather incoherent set of lines with a variety of gauges, and a wide range of ownership and operating structures. Dalhousie's vision of a unified system with a single gauge had been disrupted by subsequent political differences and changes in policy that resulted in the creation of a plethora of companies, ranging from fully state-owned to completely free-standing – though all were obliged to run services in line with government requirements. The system was not the result of a clear strategy on what kind of railway system was best for India. Rather, it was, in modern management speak, sub-optimal, as Dalhousie's vision had been subverted by circumstances and capitalism.

The system's deficiencies were all too apparent for the growing number of passengers. Their needs were rarely at the forefront of the thinking of the various companies' directors based in far-distant London, who were solely concerned with the financial bottom line rather than the comfort or needs of their passengers. This was the Victorian era, when parsimony was saintly and profligacy a sin. Right from the outset, Indian train travellers, particularly those travelling in the cheaper classes, felt the impact of that philosophy.

By the end of the century, the Indians had got the railway habit. It had taken a bit of time, however. After almost two decades of existence, the railways carried only 19 million passengers in 1871, but this figure grew more than tenfold by the end of the century. The vast majority of these journeys were in third class, since barely 10 per cent of Indians could afford second or first. While conditions varied somewhat between different companies and routes, by and large in third class 'their discomforts and indignities exposed them collectively to the intertwined structures of capitalist profit'.[1]

As in the UK, the promoters of the early lines had expected the railways to be principally freight carriers, hauling raw materials to ports and distributing imported manufactured goods inland. The East India Company had been sceptical of the desire or ability of the impoverished Indian population to travel on the railways and had expressed those doubts publicly, suggesting there would be little business from a population 'rendered immobile by poverty, a landscape of isolated habitations and religious restrictions'.[2] The company was to be proved utterly wrong and even the expectation that religious and cultural issues would deter people from travelling proved misplaced.

At the beginning, curiosity attracted half a million people to travel on the inaugural line between Bombay and Thana in the first year, and some 4 million used the railways in 1860 on what was still a tiny network. There were other promising examples, such as the fact that 300,000 people travelled on trains between Lahore and Amritsar in the year following its opening in early 1862.

However, the early lines were not constructed with the idea of maximizing the number of passengers, but were, as we have seen, built principally to carry freight to and from the ports and to ensure that troops could be mobilized quickly and despatched rapidly to trouble spots. The railways quickly proved their worth in that respect. Kerr mentions that 'when disturbances led by the Kukas occurred in Punjab in January 1872 ... four days were needed to move a mountain battery of artillery, 100 cavalrymen, a regiment of British infantry and a regiment of Gurkhas 161 miles from Delhi to Ambala'.[3] While noting that this was rather slow, since there had been a delay caused by a collapsed bridge, by historic standards it was something of a triumph. A much more unequivocally successful and longer use of the railways to deploy troops was in the albeit disastrous Second Afghan War: 'At the height of deployment, eight troop trains per day carried men with all their guns, supplies, horses, baggage and stores through Punjab.'[4]

As more lines were completed, the companies realized that they were missing a trick in not providing for India's growing population. The success on the inaugural lines established the fact that there was a strong demand for rail travel but accommodating it was a task fraught with numerous intractable issues for the railway companies. The first problem was the heterogeneous nature of the Indian population. Not only was there the troubled issue of religion, with the deep divisions between the Muslim and Hindu populations, but there was the even more complex question of caste. Add to this the desire of some sections of the population for women-only carriages and the specific demands of more affluent Indians, and the dilemmas facing the railway operators were all too apparent. The extent to which they needed to accommodate these cultural, social and religious considerations was an issue that would tax many directors' meetings over the coming decades.

The railways all provided first-, second- and third-class accommodation, and some even had a fourth, 'coolie', class intended to attract 'people seen walking between towns and villages on the public roads and railway tracks'[5] (this was clearly not successful, since even today the railway tracks are full of people using them as the shortest route for their journey). Several of the early railways, notably the East Indian and the Great Indian Peninsula, experimented with the provision of open wagons, without seating, for fourth-class travellers, some of whom travelled with their livestock, but it was third class that was used by the vast majority of travellers. Indeed, for the whole colonial period, more than nine out of ten passengers travelled in third class. Later on, an intermediate class emerged between second and third, often as a result of upgrading fourth to third but sometimes as an additional distinction.

The companies were extremely reluctant to break down the provision of accommodation on their trains to meet the demands for separate accommodation for every specific religious group or caste. Not only would providing these facilities be expensive, but they were, rightly, concerned that such separation would make filling up their trains far more difficult. They feared the prospect of Hindus clamouring to get on trains that had lots of empty carriages earmarked for Mahommedans (as they were called at the time) or vice versa.

One early suggestion had been that Europeans would all travel in first class, and then separate sets of accommodation in both first and second class would be offered to Hindus and Muslims, with yet more separate compartments for women. In fact, the first decision which the railways had to make was whether to go for separate compartments, as in the UK, or open carriages like those in the US, where a central passageway allowed passengers to walk along its whole length. In the end, the latter seemed more appropriate for a democratic society of pioneers like the US than for

India, given its cultural, social and religious divides, and the Indian railway companies universally chose the compartment structure.

Having compartments did not, however, solve the difficulties over allocation of space. The railway companies initially provided compartments allocated on the basis of class, gender and race but not caste. There were first- and second-class carriages which were often, but by no means always, divided into carriages for Europeans and Indians, and European women. Third class was assumed to be entirely for Indians, though in fact some poorer Europeans used it, with some companies providing separate compartments for women.

The disparity in standards was enormous, far more marked even than in the class-ridden UK, and reflected the different worlds in which Indians and Europeans lived. According to Laura Bear, the author of a book on the social implications of early Indian railway development, 'First-class carriages were lavishly upholstered like Victorian drawing rooms with beds that pulled down, their own bathing facilities and a small room for servants.'[6] In fact, 'so grandiose were the furnishings of second class carriages with their wicker and cane seating panels' that she reckons even second class was better than anything provided in the UK. Samuel L. Clemens (better known by his nom de plume, Mark Twain), an experienced traveller who toured extensively round India in 1896, was delighted with his accommodation: 'On each side of the car, and running fore and aft, was a broad leather-covered sofa – to sit on in the day and sleep on at night. Over each sofa hung, by straps, a wide, flat, leather-covered shelf – to sleep on. In the daytime you can hitch it up against the wall, out of the way – and then you have a big unencumbered and most comfortable room to spread out in.' He concluded that first-class Indian accommodation was the best of any luxury trains in the world: 'No car in any country is quite its equal for comfort (and privacy).'[7]

No such joy for his fellow travellers. The contrast with third class, used, as mentioned before, by 90 per cent – or more on many railways – of travellers, who, according to Mark Twain, 'were packed and crammed into cars that held each about fifty',[8] could not have been greater. While a few poor whites were forced to venture into third class, they were a rarity; the vast majority of its occupants were Indian and the conditions they endured were a reflection of the hierarchies of the colonial system. By the turn of the century, the average Indian train carried just one first-class passenger (suburban trains had no first class, which rather reduces that average), five in second class, eleven in intermediate and 187 in third. Those proportions would, by and large, remain the same up to Independence in 1947.

Third class, thanks to sheer numbers, was the money spinner for the railway companies but that was not reflected in the provision they made for the different classes. An assessment in 1894 by Horace Bell, the consulting engineer for railways, quoted a manager who believed 'it would pay him to give every first-class passenger twenty rupees to stay away'.[9] It was not like today's airlines which make their money out of their premium-class passengers. On the contrary, the luxurious facilities offered in the top two classes were expensive to provide but used by a tiny minority. One could argue that it was precisely because the conditions in third class were so cramped and the facilities so basic (or non-existent) that it was so profitable, but, in fact, there would still have been ample money to be made had the railway companies spent substantially more on making life just a bit more tolerable for its poorer passengers. In a report for the Government of India published in 1903, Thomas

Lord Dalhousie (1812–1860), Governor-General, who planned and pushed through the construction of India's first railway lines.

Alice Tredwell took over the contract for the construction of the railway across the Bhor Ghat when her husband Solomon died a month after arriving in India, and saw it through to a successful conclusion.

The inauguration of the East Indian Railway to Burdwan in 1855. The East Indian opened up the region's coalfields, which became key to the railway's profitability.

The construction of the railway through the ghats to the east of Bombay were one of the great engineering achievements of the age, engendering terrible losses, through accident and disease, to the workforce, which reached 42,000 at its peak.

Creating a railway through the ghats involved innovative techniques, such as this reversing station which obviated the need for tunnels, and which was used until the line was electrified and tunnels built in the late 1920s.

Rudyard Kipling visited the site of the Empress Bridge over the Sutlej River during its construction, inspiring his short story *The Bridge Builders*.

In the early days of India's railways, bridge collapses, such as this one on the East Indian Railway in 1863, were a cause of several disasters as the strong river currents in the monsoon period required new techniques to protect supports.

Following the rebellion in 1857, the British built stations as fortresses, like this one in Lahore (now in Pakistan), so they could be easily defended against protestors and rioters.

However, by the time Victoria Station (now Chhatrapati Shivaji Maharaj Terminus) was built over a ten-year period starting in 1878, the style was more relaxed and designed with similarities to London's St Pancras, which had opened a decade previously.

Worksites on India's railways were often perilous, such as this one on the
Bengal–Nagpur Railway in 1890.

Several remarkable mountain railways were built to ease the journeys of British
expatriates who travelled up to hill stations in order to escape the summer heat
of the plains. These included the Darjeeling Himalayan Railway, completed in
1881 and a vital link despite being nicknamed the 'Toy Train'.

An obsession with protecting the North-West Frontier (now in Pakistan) with Afghanistan from invasion led to the construction of several 'strategic' railways, including the Khyber Pass Railway which opened in 1925. They proved to be hopeless commercially and were little used since no invasion attempt was ever made, except by the Japanese from the east in World War Two.

Typical railway station scene at Rawalpindi (now in Pakistan) in the North-West Province in 1910.

Freight, such as these cotton bales being loaded at Akola station in Maharastra, *c.* 1930, has been the most profitable part of the operation of the railways in India.

The railway helped to create an Indian middle class, such as the workers in this booking hall at Victoria Station in Bombay, *c.* 1930.

The poor conditions of travel for Indians using the railway helped to stimulate the rising independence movement and was highlighted by Gandhi, who was himself a frequent passenger, pictured here receiving a donation from a wellwisher.

As a key part of India's infrastructure, the railways were targeted by nationalist protesters, such as this group of demonstrators blockading the railway in 1945.

In the troubled summer of 1947, the Partition of India and Pakistan led to millions of people moving from one country to the other on the railways, which were the scene of terrible massacres.

Robertson, a special commissioner who had been sent to India to assess the functioning of the railway system, 'emphasized how unappreciative railway administrations were of their third-class traffic, which he described as "the backbone of the passenger business of every railway in India"'.[10]

And so it was. There was one mitigating factor in the companies' attitude: the fact that fares were kept low for third-class passengers. Initially, in the 1850s the railway companies had pitched their fares relatively high because, protected by the government guarantee of a 5 per cent return on their investors' money, they were unconcerned with the number of travellers. However, under pressure from the Government of India, the ultimate paymaster, they reduced fares and consequently, rather unexpectedly, attracted considerable custom. (As an example, the East Indian Railway charged ¼ of an anna per mile in third, ¾ of an anna in second and two annas in first, giving an eightfold ratio between the highest and lowest, far greater than the ratio in the UK or on railways elsewhere.) These fares might have seemed low but, in his report, Robertson argued they could have been reduced further while still enabling the companies to be profitable. He argued that fares and freight rates should have been set at around one sixth of those in the UK, given the disparity in incomes and wages, but they were, in fact, considerably higher than that.

The quid pro quo of these relatively low fares was basic provision in overcrowded carriages that allowed for no human dignity. Ritika Prasad, author of a book on the impact of the railways on India, quotes an official from the North-Western Provinces whose description typifies the railway experience for Indians in the nineteenth century: 'The natives [were] penned up in carriages, 10 or 12 in a compartment, with seats 14 inches wide and 15 inches between them, with their legs dangling down in a way the most uncomfortable to them, and with no space to lie down to get any real rest.'[11]

The overcrowding was the result of the fact that the railway companies sold tickets for their trains with little regard to how much accommodation was available. Despite this, the companies blamed the Indians themselves, implying that they preferred overcrowded conditions in exchange for cheap fares. Some officials even suggested that Indians would prefer to travel in carriages with no seats if they were cheaper. A manager of the Calcutta & South-Eastern Railway, Captain F. Firebrace, told a railway conference in 1871 that Indian passengers would 'put up with every inconvenience in order to save themselves the extra pie [there were 192 pies to a rupee] per mile'. He therefore suggested that the key to economic success for the railways was to provide the barest accommodation for Indians. In fact, the evidence was to the contrary, as Firebrace himself reported. He quoted the fact that on his own railway when third- or fourth-class accommodation was provided at the same fare, passengers would make great efforts to rush to fill the better-appointed compartments.

It was not only a matter of discomfort. Death as a result of this overcrowding was not uncommon, particularly in desert crossings during the fierce heat of the summer. The companies steadfastly refused to accept that the higher rate of mortality on trains travelling in the hot conditions was the result of overcrowding. While the local population died in considerable numbers, the dangers were not confined to them. During a rapid troop transfer in the summer of 1915, thirty-two British men perished from heat exhaustion on a train crossing the Sind desert when temperatures reached 125°F and no ice to cool the train had been provided. That tragedy, incidentally, caused a scandal back in the UK resulting in the sacking of the Quartermaster-General in India, a Brigadier-General Roe, who had foolishly allowed the ship on which the troops arrived to dock at Karachi rather than Bombay. That meant the poor troops, unaccustomed to Indian conditions, had to cross the Sind desert, a journey that was usually not allowed in the summer heat. Indians, however, were expected to routinely put up with such conditions, despite travelling in far more cramped carriages than the military.

The discomfort and danger were heightened by the fact that railway companies were in the habit of locking their third-class passengers into the carriages, a practice that was still, at the time the first railways were built in India, the norm in parts of Europe and had been partly responsible for the high death toll in several accidents, notably one near Paris on one of France's first lines. In India, the custom was institutionalized, becoming the norm despite the obvious safety risks it entailed and the string of previous disasters around the world.

The awful conditions in third class led to repeated complaints but change was resisted strongly by the companies, even though the Government of India itself was critical of the levels of overcrowding and pressed for improvements. Companies were supposedly required to display the number of passengers allowed in each carriage and were banned from exceeding these limits, but there was little enforcement of these rules. This inaction was very much the result of the contemporary norms whereby interference by the state in the affairs of private companies was perceived as inappropriate and an unnecessary restraint on entrepreneurs. This attitude affected rules governing many other aspects of railway operations and partly explains the ability of the railway companies to simply ignore regulations from government. Self-regulation was the order of the day, despite considerable evidence that it did little to restrain the worst excesses of the railway companies. Rather than make improvements, the companies were inclined to blame the behaviour and customs of their own passengers for the poor conditions on trains. As Prasad puts it, even when the companies were presented with clear examples of the issuing of an excessive number of tickets for a particular train, this was 'attributed to a peculiar habit that they argued was endemic to native passengers: of "following one another like sheep into a crowded carriage"'.[12] There were even suggestions from railway managers that Indians, apparently unlike the rest of the human race, disliked empty compartments where they could sit in comfort. As for the high death rate in hot conditions, the companies again blamed it on the passengers themselves for boarding the train when they were too 'old, ill or unfit to travel'.[13]

Overcrowding was the railway companies' dirty secret, a pretty open one to anyone using the railways, but one which they repeatedly refused to recognize. Even modest suggestions, such as the requirement issued in the early 1900s to reduce the number of passengers in each compartment to six for long journeys, were ignored by the railways. There was, though, an even dirtier secret: toilets, or rather the lack of them. Somehow, no thought had been given to their provision by the railway companies. Or at least not in third class. Moreover, rather than simply acquiescing to complaints about the absence of sanitary facilities, the companies remained reluctant to provide for this very basic need, and it was not until toilets became a political issue in the early twentieth century that the matter was resolved, and even then it took several years.

The amount of debate and discussion expended on the matter of toilets was remarkable and quite bizarre given that the case for their provision seemed irrefutable. Admittedly, the style of carriages made installation more difficult. In the US, open-plan coaches had quickly become the norm, partly because of the long distances travelled. No such considerations had been taken into account by the Indian railway companies when they chose the compartment-style layout. The lack of a corridor meant providing toilets was impossible, since having one in each compartment was clearly impractical. Some trains had a connecting running board outside that allowed transfer between compartments, but this was clearly too perilous for most passengers and was used principally by railway staff.

There was something almost sadistic in the companies' obdurate and continuing refusal to consider this issue, particularly in relation to women and the elderly, who found it far harder to improvise either on the train or at stops. In the first couple of decades, not only were there no toilets in any class but, remarkably, many railway officials were reluctant to unlock the doors of the third-class compartments to let their occupants out to use station facilities. Moreover, sometimes trains did not stop long enough for passengers to risk going to the toilet through fear of not being able to return in time to their carriage. A North-Western Provinces official, Colonel Fraser, reported: 'When I arrive at a station, I am at once let out on the platform while the Natives are detained, penned up in a crowded state till the ticket-collector has taken their tickets – a very slow process when there are many passengers.'[4]

Again, the railway companies took up their usual defensive 'not our fault, guv' stance in response to complaints. They claimed that safety regulations required them to lock the passengers in between stations but the railway officials were often slow to open the doors once the train stopped. In fact, the regulations clearly stated that they were supposed to allow passengers out if they wanted to step onto the platform, but 'even as reports of third-class passengers remaining locked up in carriages trickled in, railway companies argued that they were complying with all requirements'.[15]

While toilet facilities for first- and second-class passengers quickly became the norm, often with en suite facilities in every compartment in first, the railway companies resisted providing them for third class. On the station platforms, privies and urinals were provided for the European passengers in buildings while Indians had to make do with *tatti*s, in effect holes in the ground protected by flimsy bamboo or grass shelters.

The companies fought a long campaign against being forced to provide onboard toilets in third class. At a Railway Conference in 1882, their representatives spoke strongly against demands for universal provision, even though the idea was supported by senior military commanders anxious for their native troops to be accommodated. The companies argued that the use of station facilities was sufficient but some went further, offering spurious excuses. One contributor to the Conference made the point that allowing excrement to be dropped on the line – retention tanks were for the future – would harm the permanent way and require a large labour force to clean it up. Another submission, rather revealingly, mentioned that the main consideration was perhaps not sanitation but profitability. Its author, a railway official, argued that providing toilets on trains would be costly and result in a reduction of 6 or 7 per cent in available revenue-earning accommodation. In 1884, the consulting engineer for Bombay, in response to demands for facilities, argued that it was difficult enough 'to keep a closet in a 1st class compartment occupied by two or three European travellers sweet and clean during a long journey', let alone one used by '30 or 40 native passengers'.[16] That perhaps said rather more about contemporary Western toilet habits than possibly he intended.

The Indian Railways Act passed in 1890 required railways 'to provide latrine accommodation to one compartment reserved for females when the train ... runs for a distance exceeding fifty miles'. The Public Works Department of the government, which was at the time responsible for the railways, twice sent out circulars reminding companies of their obligations, but its policy of maintaining only the lightest regulatory touch meant those injunctions went unheeded. It was not until 1902, when a prominent Indian, Ramachandra Gungadhar Karwe, wrote a note to the Viceroy, Lord Curzon, after a lengthy tour around the railway system, that concerted action was at last taken. Karwe pointed out that while the companies provided onboard toilet facilities to first- and second-class passengers, it was those in third who provided the bulk of their revenue and yet suffered from lack of facilities. Karwe begged Curzon to show 'mercy to the poor' and, while there are doubts whether Curzon ever read the note, it certainly led to a change in attitude.

Curzon was highly critical of the railway companies' reluctance to respond to the requirements of the 1890 Act. His official memoirs[17] later revealed that he found their attitude 'old-fashioned, prejudiced and mistaken' and that he rejected the idea that excreta would be dropped on the line in such quantities that it would 'frighten the gang men'. As an aside, he highlighted an issue that might well have been of concern to the London-based railway companies, steeped, as they were, in Victorian morals, by dismissing the notion that the toilets might be used for an 'immoral purpose' when stopped at stations – the contemporary equivalent of the 'mile high' club beloved of today's oversexed air passengers. He went into remarkable detail on the sanitary issue, even suggesting that to ensure faeces were not dumped at stations, there should be a mechanical arrangement 'by which the bottom of every pan was closed as soon as a train entered a station, and released as soon as it leaves'. It seems a brilliant idea but clearly the scheme was not implemented given the plethora of 'do not flush this toilet at stations' signs found not only in India but across the world. Merely locking the toilet doors at stations, as happens in some countries, might have been a simpler solution to both the sanitary and moral issues.

Curzon immediately issued orders to local government to ensure that railways began providing facilities 'as soon as possible' in all intermediate and third-class carriages on fast trains, and later on slower services. Sensibly, suburban services running for less than fifty miles were exempt and consequently, by 1908, more than 5,000 third-class carriages had been fitted out with toilets, which showed that where there was a will, there was a way. Nevertheless, although relief was at hand for many passengers, not all railways complied, and even by the outbreak of the Second World War fewer than half of the Bengal & North Western Railway third-class carriages were fitted with toilets.

One of the reasons for treating third-class passengers so badly was the notion that they included numerous criminal elements, who necessitated a disciplined approach. While the vast majority of rail passengers were law-abiding, there is no doubt that the railways afforded unprecedented potential for thieves and 'ne'er-do-wells' to steal and rob. The railway thief was as old as the railways themselves, but in India there was a particular problem as organized gangs from outlaw tribes, with generations of criminal experience behind them, adapted their traditional practices to take advantage of the new opportunities afforded by crowded stations and trains. There were, of course, the normal casual thieves prominent on many systems, such as pickpockets who specialized in working the areas around ticket offices and the opportunists who would make away with unattended baggage at stations. The hot weather, which meant windows on trains were permanently open, offered the opportunity for thieves to walk along the running boards on coaches without corridors and remove valuables from clothing or bags left lying around by insufficiently alert passengers.

It was the activity of certain gangs and tribes using the identical modus operandi which frightened the law-abiding traveller and the railway companies alike. The long-distance trains, which included overnight travel en route, offered a particularly enticing prospect for groups who specialized in targeting and robbing rail passengers. The level of sophistication was such that it seemed a shame that their ingenuity could not be put to more honest endeavour. These gangs were often based in tribal villages and highly trained in the skills required for their particular speciality, having been apprenticed – Oliver Twist-like – to their life of crime at an early age. One method was for two men to operate as a pair in a compartment. The first would wrap himself in a large blanket to cover the activity of the second, who would crawl underneath the seats with a sharp knife in his mouth – a technique that involved not inconsiderable skill – and slit open bags, handing the stolen valuables to his partner. In order to delay any discovery, he would sew up the tear, allowing him and his colleague to make their escape before suspicion was aroused. Westwood reckoned the most sophisticated of these gangs were members of an outlaw tribe from near Aligarh, in what is now Uttar Pradesh, who used long-nosed secateurs in the course of their agricultural work. In the hot season, when activity on the farms stopped, 'they took these secateurs on railway expeditions, and would imperceptibly snip off the necklaces and bangles of sleeping passengers. The more experienced, faced with victims asleep in an inconvenient position, would tickle the soles of their feet with a feather until they turned.'[18] Another tribe specialized in the old dummy bag trick. They would carry a bag stuffed with old newspapers and rags, sidle up to a hapless passenger carrying a similar one, and swop them when the opportunity arose.

Various measures were taken over the years to reduce the ability of thieves to operate on the railway. Bars on windows – a feature of trains today – and doors that were lockable from the inside helped, as did removing the running boards from outside trains without corridors. The gangs largely faded away in the interwar years as a result of targeted policing, more sophisticated investigation methods, such as fingerprinting, and centralized reporting of incidents, which helped to pinpoint the activities of organized groups.

The authorities found policing third-class passengers easier than making their lives better. While being so reluctant to improve the lot of these passengers, the railway companies in contrast expended much energy on the matter of the travelling arrangements for 'respectable' women, the small minority of relatively affluent ladies able to afford higher-class accommodation. The provision of three or four separate classes was deemed not to take into account the requirement of the well-heeled and, consequently, mostly very conservative elements of Indian society. The *zamindars* – landed gentry – and the Indian aristocracy were consulted by the companies in 1869, through the agency of the British Indian

Association, to which many belonged, on the issue of women travelling on the railway. Across the country, local members of the Association were asked for their views, following numerous representations to the companies from the upper echelons of Indian society who had complained that respectable women were unable to travel in conditions that befitted their rank. There were even reports in the local press that female missionaries were travelling in third class in order to proselytize and convert their fellow travellers to Christianity.

The *zamindars* made a clear distinction between lower-class and, by implication, less respectable women, who were, in any case, seen in public all the time, and their own family members, who were shielded, thanks to their wealth, from the view of strangers. These two distinct types of women, they suggested, should be kept apart as mixing with these lower-caste women would in effect contaminate their superior sisters. In any case, the lifestyles of these poorer women, they argued, meant that they did not need separate accommodation on trains. The *zamindars* suggested that rather than women-only carriages, where the classes and castes mixed, there should be 'family compartments', where male escorts would be able to look after their women folk, who 'become quite helpless in the absence of their male relatives and protectors'. Bizarrely, they suggested that these compartments would not even need seats, since their women were used to sitting on the floor cross-legged, and that benches were 'a form of seat Indian women are never accustomed to and make use of with great reluctance'. So, the carriages should be emptied of seats and be 'plain and unadorned so that the inmates may freely use it in their own way'.[19] Effectively, they were suggesting that the majority of women could be bunched together in conditions that befitted them, while the minority of 'respectable' ladies travelled with their families in secluded compartments, which some even wanted screened off so that strangers could not see the women. The Association's views were picked up in the press, which 'stressed the "serious inconvenience" that "Hindu ladies faced" when travelling "in the same carriage with women of the lower classes such as sweepers, *chamars* [an untouchable caste] and the like"'.[20] In their view, class was a more important consideration than gender.

The *zamindars* were particularly concerned about interaction with railway personnel and sought to ensure they would have no interaction with middle- and upper-class women. They grumbled that the staff, particularly the Europeans and Eurasians, 'give themselves airs at every step and generally look down upon the passengers as if they were creatures of an inferior order or goods soon to be packed off' – a familiar complaint made by many of today's travellers on subcontinental railways. Simply talking to a man not in the family was deemed intolerable and therefore female railway guards and waiting-room attendants should be employed. The fact that these women would have to deal with male passengers, too, was an irrelevance, of course, since they would be of a lower – and therefore by implication less respectable – class.

These dilemmas were the result of the fact that the railways were breaking new ground in Indian society. The public spaces of the railways, whether waiting rooms or train compartments, were often the first place where Indians of every caste and class had ever mingled and, unlike in the bazaars and streets, were enclosed together for long periods. This unprecedented mixing was bound to raise fundamental cultural issues and later resulted in conflict and litigation. Interestingly, the railways were both a levelling experience, since all but the poorest could use them, but simultaneously also reaffirmed, and at times heightened, class, religious and caste hierarchies and differences. One can almost hear the groans of the railway company managers who had to deal with these sensibilities in the knowledge that causing offence to such an important element of society could be disastrous for their companies. Equally, so could accommodating these demands, since they were financially burdensome, resulting in unfilled seats on trains where potential passengers might well be turned away because they were of the wrong sex, religion or caste. Moreover, acquiescing to these demands from conservative elements damaged the railways' reputation as a liberalizing force in Indian society, opening it up to European – and by implication progressive – mores. One of the justifications for government support for the railways was that they would transform India into a modern state, and therefore pandering to what were seen as these primitive customs went against the grain. As Laura Bear puts it, the measures introduced by the railway companies 'helped to mark Indian women with signs of respectability or immorality depending on which ticket they could afford to buy for their passage'.[21] That was not supposed to be their role.

The contortions required to meet these demands could be viewed as an early example of businesses facing the complexities of what today is known as 'political correctness' and led to the railway companies seeking solutions that satisfied as many interests as possible. The issue of female ticket collectors was, however, generally seen as a step too far for the companies, mainly because the task was entirely carried out by Europeans and Eurasians and they feared that employing Indian women would open up the way for fraud, while the notion that respectable European women would want to work on the railways was unthinkable.

The *zamindars'* views proved to be influential in persuading some of the railway companies to change their policies. In July 1869, the lieutenant-governor of the North-Western Provinces, William Muir, produced a minute that set the tone. Muir was one of those British administrators who saw the role of the colonial power as one of spreading civilization and enlightenment to the Indian masses, but he accepted that existing practices had to be taken into account. He recognized that the separation of the sexes was 'not only practised among the rich, but also among the vast majority of respectable classes, whatever their means'[22] and therefore needed to be accommodated, simply to ensure that women were able to travel, as that would help bring about 'general enlightenment' of the population. He suggested, therefore, that reserved first-class compartments for the upper classes should be provided, as well as a compartment to which women would have access in their *palkis* (screened carriages carried to the station by servants). There was also to be a third or intermediate class (slightly better than third but not as good as second), with compartments at each end shielded by venetian blinds, in which families would be able to travel together while ensuring the women could not be seen by other passengers. For other women passengers in third class, there would be separate carriages, but somehow 'prostitutes' and other disreputable women would be barred; Muir said they would be easy to identify but did not explain how.

The East Indian Railway was the most assiduous in following these rules. Second-class accommodation was provided for Indian families in a US-style open-plan coach with a passageway down the middle. On one side, there was private space for ladies, including toilet facilities, while on the other male relatives could intermingle. Women-only accommodation was also provided in third class by separating two compartments in each carriage, one of which was designated for full purdah, with no access from the platform, while the male relatives could sit in the adjoining compartment. For women travelling without their families, there were all-female open carriages. Even waiting rooms with separate accommodation for Hindus and Muslims were provided by the East Indian in its efforts to follow Muir's injunction to the letter.

The East Indian, though, was something of an exception. Other companies were reluctant to follow, not least because of the cost and the lost revenue. Some, in fact, actually scrapped female-only carriages because they accepted the argument that respectable women would invariably travel with their families, while others merely provided screens to shield women from view, more or less successfully. Others refused to provide separate accommodation for women, except in third class, arguing that very few passengers would benefit since not many Indian travellers could afford even intermediate, let alone second or first class. The most serious case, which, in fact, was the one which prompted the railway companies to make changes, occurred in 1867, when a woman on the East Indian Railway was assaulted by a fellow traveller, a European called Samuel Horn. In an attempt to escape, she jumped out of a window and was killed. The complaint from the Indian population was not only about the extent of assaults, but also the comparative leniency with which those accused or even convicted of the assaults were treated.

Every solution, however, was fraught with difficulties and pitfalls. The biggest sufferers from these changes, more often than not, were precisely those that these convolutions were supposed to help – women travelling on their own – since the very separation from the safety of the crowd made them vulnerable to attack. The contemporary newspapers were full of incidents of women being assaulted, or raped, sometimes by railway personnel, often after they had been unable to pay their fare or had unwittingly overridden the station for which they had a ticket. Ticket collectors, too, were not averse to taking advantage of their position for a bit of inappropriate touching. There were also reports of women becoming separated from their husbands with whom they were travelling, due to some ticketing discrepancy or simply in the crowded conditions in large stations, and as a result being assaulted or even raped. These incidents were, of course, the exception rather than the rule, and for the most part relations between passengers and railway officials passed off without trouble.

None of this was new or unexpected in a society where even touching a member of a different caste was abhorrent to many. Arguments sometimes arose because women travelling without men refused to hand over their tickets directly to an official as it involved touching a man, preferring to ensure there was no contact by leaving them on a table or chair, and the ticket collector, finding this unacceptable, would refuse to pick them up. As we will see in Chapter 7, the issue of assaults on women became a cause célèbre during the fight for nationalism, and some of the stories appearing in newspapers were embellished to suit the political aims of those reporting them, in particular by exaggerating the proportion of attacks carried out by European and Eurasian railway employees rather than fellow travellers. However, there is no doubt that women were put at risk on the railways precisely because of attempts to protect those perceived to be 'respectable'. The implication of the separation of the more affluent women from their peers was that anyone travelling in all-female accommodation was therefore assumed not to be respectable and perhaps a prostitute or loose woman.

By 1871, as a result of trying to accommodate these various requirements, there were various individual carriages running on the system marked 'first-class European, first-class Indian, second-class European and Eurasian, intermediate-class Indian, third-class Indian, third-class female, European female, family and fourth-class coolie'.[23] The following year, Lord Northbrooke, the new Governor-General, told the railway companies that they needed to simplify their class structures and types of rolling stock. His efforts were largely in vain since, as we have seen, the companies were in the habit of ignoring such requests from government. However, no company, not even the East Indian, provided all these different types of accommodation simultaneously, but, nevertheless, the increasing breakdown of types of passengers into discrete groups was a constant headache for railway managers. The tradition of seclusion varied, in fact, from region to region and in large parts of India there was little demand for these complicated arrangements. The railway companies, though, run from central headquarters in India and ultimately governed from London, found it difficult to accommodate the precise and often disparate requirements of their passengers. Eventually, the Indian Railways Act 1890 mandated female-only carriages for the lowest class on every passenger train but, as with toilets, suburban trains were excluded. Even then, it took years for all the companies to comply.

As well as issues around women and sanitary facilities, there were complicated questions over the provision of food and drink. Similarly to the complications over seating arrangements, the issues of caste and religion had to be addressed. The railway officials were more receptive to the need to provide different eating facilities for Muslim and Hindu passengers than they were over the question of sanitary arrangements. There was, however, still a contrasting attitude towards the provision of facilities for Europeans and those for 'natives'. Station refreshment rooms for Europeans rapidly became the norm, but these were deemed unnecessary for Indians because, it was argued, 'natives' did not generally take their meals at regular hours and therefore were best served by vendors on platforms. The system, while appearing haphazard in the hubbub of the platform environment, was actually tightly regulated by the railway companies. The vendors – who are still commonplace today – had to buy a licence from the railway and wear clothing that identified them, and were expected to sell food that was fresh and hygienic. Those who occupied stalls had to pay rent to the railway, and, yet again, there appeared to be a measure of discrimination favouring Europeans. Ritika Prasad notes that 'On the Great Indian Peninsula Railway, the annual fee for a European refreshment room was fixed at 360 Rupees, while those for native stalls went as high as 3,500 Rupees per annum.'[24] This is in spite of the fact that a stall with no seating covered an area far less than the refreshment room, which was in essence a small restaurant.

After the turn of the century, the railway authorities did begin to recommend to the companies that refreshment rooms for Indians, as well as Europeans, should be provided on stations served by long-distance trains. Consequently, by the middle of the second decade of the twentieth century, they had become commonplace. Hindu establishments, which were more widely available, were usually split into veg and non-veg sections and some even offered meals for Muslims. At other stations, there were entirely separate facilities for the two religions. The company which made the most effort in catering to the needs of its wide variety of passengers was the Madras & Southern Mahratta Railway, which 'provided not only a "general stall for the sale of sweets for all castes" and "a kitchen with a Brahmin cook who cooks for all castes" but also a separate dining room each for Brahmins and non-Brahmins, as well as "a Muhammadan cook" and separate dining rooms for Muslim passengers'.[25] The East Indian Railway, in its efforts to ensure that taboos were not broken, encumbered itself with four types of food inspector – 'Junior Mahomedan' and 'Junior Hindu', and 'Senior' equivalents for both religions. Caste, class and religion were both serious and expensive matters for the railway authorities.

There was also some pressure to provide dining cars on trains, but, unlike in Europe and the US, they were very slow to catch on in India. That failure can be explained both by the reluctance of the companies to introduce them and by cultural expectations. Several companies objected to the idea in principle, saying that it would be impossible to cater for the range of religious and caste requirements of their passengers. Moreover, such cars would reduce the amount of accommodation available to third-class passengers. Experiments by a few more entrepreneurial companies to provide dining cars proved to be short-lived, often because they fell foul of religious prejudices. In 1912, the East Indian Railway introduced dining cars on the line between Calcutta (Howrah) and Mughal Serai, a junction in the United Provinces, but soon withdrew them after finding that 'high caste Hindus were averse to eating "in the same compartment as a Mohammedan or a low-caste Hindu"'.[26] Providing separate facilities did not seem to work either. On the Bombay, Baroda & Central Indian Railway, which did offer segregated cars for Hindus and Muslims, the failure was put down to the reluctance of third-class passengers to leave their seats – presumably on the grounds that they were wary of losing them – and the competition from platform sellers, whose wares were cheaper.

The provision of water was a surprisingly contentious issue. The reluctance of the railways to allow third-class passengers off the trains meant they found it difficult to access the hydrants and taps provided on platforms. Instead, passengers were reliant on the watermen who carried buckets and ladles to supply them for the journey ahead. There were often not enough vendors, especially in hot weather, and in this regard the companies were relatively responsive both to the overall shortage of watermen and in ensuring that the right ones were available. Upper-caste Hindus would only accept water from Brahmin watermen and Hindus and Muslims required separate provision. One compromise was to have a Brahmin for the upper-caste Hindus and a lower-caste Hindu *bhistee* for everyone else. The railways were keen to show they recognized these sensibilities, with the Great Indian Peninsula Railway emphasizing it provided watermen 'of different castes' for 'various classes of passenger'.

It was not only as passengers that Indians suffered discrimination. The railways were becoming massive employers and yet again the contrast between the treatment of European and local people was all too obvious.

SIX

WORKING ON
THE LINE

B Y THE TURN of the century, with a network of 23,600 route
miles, the railways had not only established themselves but
become a key part, indeed the mainstay, of the subcontinent's
transport system. In a country with little industrial development,
the railways were by far the biggest employer, and, through a vast
array of functions needed to train, keep and pay for that huge
labour force, they were developing a series of institutions that were
instrumental in modernizing the nation.

The raw figures of the level of employment on the railways
were quite astonishing (and actually remain so to this day, as we
will see in the final chapter). For the construction of the railways,
the best estimate is that an average of around 200,000 people
were directly employed during the whole forty-year period
running up to the end of the nineteenth century. This estimate
excludes all the workers in the supply chain, whether simply
transporting material to the worksites or providing plant and
equipment for the railways, which might have amounted to a
similar number.

However, the number of workers constructing the railway would soon be exceeded by those directly employed in the wide variety of tasks to operate and maintain the iron road. By 1870, there were already around 70,000 permanent railway workers, and in 1905, after a strong growth spurt in the early years of the twentieth century, 437,500 were employed directly by the railways, of which 6,300 were European and 8,600 Eurasian. (Therefore, while Eurasians, who were also known as Anglo-Indians, or by the somewhat derogatory term 'chi-chis', formed less than a half of 1 per cent of the population, they accounted for 2 per cent of railway workers.) This disproportionate pattern was partly the result of a deliberate policy of apprenticeship and recruitment by the railway companies and their targeting of orphanages where Eurasian children, who were the result of brief liaisons between soldiers and local women, often ended up. As well as simply recruiting from these orphanages, the 1850 Apprentices Act gave the railways, as employers, the right to take on the role of parent for these children in return for indenturing them as apprentices, thereby providing a ready source of workers who were seen as more reliable and loyal than their pure native counterparts – and were, of course, far cheaper than men brought over from the UK.

Right from the outset, the arrival of the railways in a country that was still essentially feudal and agricultural had an impact that far exceeded their direct reach. Naturally, the prejudices and institutionalized racism which pervaded the provision of services, outlined in the previous chapter, were a constant influence on the employment practices of the railway companies and inevitably resulted in strife and conflict. While the companies were aware that the expansion of the railways would require a huge permanent workforce to run and maintain them, there was great apprehension about employing Indians for safety-critical tasks. In 1844, well before the opening of the first line, Rowland Stephenson, the founder of the East Indian Railway Company, warned that European staff would have to be responsible for all aspects of train operation in order to protect the interests of British investors. This notion was further elaborated by the Parliamentary Commission on the Colonisation of India, which set out the qualities required by British personnel working in India, as it was worried that those without sufficient resilience would fall foul of the 'degeneracy' prevalent in the subcontinent. The British would take on all the supervisory roles, but only the right sort of chap would be up to the task and be able to resist the Eastern temptations. Therefore, when the East Indian Railway started recruiting, the pattern for office work naturally followed the traditions of the Indian Civil Service, with British managers and Indian subordinates. However, as Laura Bear notes, in the railways this model was extended to all aspects of its functioning: 'More surprisingly, any work that dealt with the running or repair of trains also had to be in the hands of British agency.' There was an added justification for this – the fear of disaster: 'The threat of technological accident that hung over all railway enterprises took on a particular tenor in India.'[1] The concern that Indians were simply not up to the task of ensuring the safety of the railways underpinned the justification for excluding them from vast swathes of managerial and supervisory roles.

There was some tension in this respect between the companies and the Government of India, which oversaw their work and was the ultimate paymaster. Local labour was, after all, considerably cheaper and consequently there were repeated calls for many of the manual tasks, such as engine driver or train guards, to be 'Indianized' in order to enable the railways to make sufficient profits and thereby no longer require continued government support. In response, the companies, unfussed about whether their 5 per cent rate of return came from the fare box or government subsidies, placed a series of overt and covert barriers in the way of Indians progressing up the career ladder. For example, Indians were widely employed as firemen, stoking the fires of locomotives, often in pairs, while Europeans or Eurasians would drive the train. In the UK there was an established process by which after a period of several years, firemen would be promoted to replace drivers who had retired, but this did not happen in India as even highly experienced local firemen were simply barred from taking on the role. While accepting the separation of office tasks between Europeans and locals, Lord Canning, the Governor-General from 1856 to 1862, made repeated calls for Indians to be allowed to drive trains or take up posts as stationmasters, but the railway companies resisted. Instead, the East Indian Railway, for example, sought to try out particular ethnic groups, such as Sikhs, Parsees and even Chinese, in various roles but ultimately considered that they were only suited to lesser tasks in each area of work. Therefore Indians were allowed to shunt locomotives around yards or drive goods trains on branch lines, but were barred from operating services that carried passengers. They became stationmasters but only in minor locations with little traffic rather than at major stations. Backed by their government guarantees, the railway companies could afford the luxury of using expensive European labour which fitted well with their prejudices.

Their reluctance prompted the Government of India to adopt an official policy of Indianization in 1870, when it announced that all posts should be open to locals. Even that radical shift failed to make much difference. There were always good reasons to stop

Indians being promoted, with the ever-present implication that accidents would result if they rose above their station. Laura Bear uncovered countless examples in old railway company files of explanations from railway managers, such as Indians did not have 'the judgement and presence of mind' to deal with emergencies, or that they 'seldom have the character to enforce strict obedience'. Indians could not become engine drivers because they lacked sufficient 'talent, energy, general knowledge and reliability' and would be unable to cope with the hard work as a result of 'privations which caste rules subject them to'. Essentially, the qualities required were, strangely enough, those in which Englishmen apparently excelled and which they uniquely possessed. The locomotive superintendent, for example, needed to be 'a sharp, ready hardworking man with sound judgment, great nerve when suddenly brought into danger. He must have in himself a sharp turn for mechanics which makes him fond of his profession. He must be sober and of good constitution.'[2]

There was, in fact, another largely unstated but crucial reason why Indians could not be allowed to take over too many key positions within the railways, which was revealed by a senior British official. A certain proportion of trustworthy Europeans and Eurasians had to be retained, he argued, in order to maintain 'the security of the country, both from a military point of view and from the point of internal security, and that had to be taken into account in dealing with the recruitment of staff'.[3] If Indians ran the railways, the trains might not be available to deal with a repeat of the events of 1857.

Europeans were not only paid far more than their Indian colleagues, but, as an inducement for them to come to India, their wages were greater than they would have received for carrying out the same job in the UK – an average, in 1870, of £270 per annum for a driver compared with £115 back home. In addition, there were numerous other expenses associated with employing them that further dented the rail companies' profits. Most were on four-year contracts, which included a P&O trip back to the UK at its termination, and all received allowances for housing and moving home. Not only were salaries better than in the UK but there were plenty of opportunities for overtime. Moreover, the sickness rate among Europeans was high because of the heat and the prevalence of fevers, resulting in long absences or, sometimes, death. They were also 'notorious for their licentious lifestyle, drunkenness and verbal abuse of Indians'.[4] These absences, together with difficulties of recruitment, meant that on occassion there was an overall shortage of drivers, notably when extra trains were needed to deliver grain at times of famine or to bring people to the numerous large festivals held regularly around the country.

Despite the extra costs and the difficulties of recruiting Europeans, there was a great reluctance to allow Indians to carry out what were seen as supervisory or safety-related tasks. Moreover, the European and Eurasian staff were ever ready to thwart attempts to be replaced by Indians and this led them to create a local branch of the UK-based Amalgamated Society of Railway Servants, India's first trade union, in order to protect their interests. The pressure to reduce wage bills did, over time, lead to some 'Indianization'. By 1881, although a third of the East Indian's 375 drivers were Indian, they were still confined to minor duties and only allowed to drive on plain line track with no curves or gradients, and handle slow-moving goods trains. By contrast, all but 61 of the 790 firemen were Indians.

Bear notes that Indian guards, deemed to have a key safety role, 'were only permitted on goods and coal trains when their responsibilities were shared with a brakeman'.[5] Given the limitations placed on Indians, it hardly seemed worthwhile training them and, indeed, the East Indian Railway reined back on its experiment within a few years, arguing that 'men of the Babu [a respectable Hindu male] class have not the physique for the work or the spirit of loyalty which goes so far with the bulk of the European staff of Guards in ensuring hearty and willing cooperation in times of real pressure'.[6]

The policy of reserving many tasks for Europeans, including several that were the preserve of working-class men, engendered its own complications. As well as requiring more pay than Indians, Europeans were difficult in another respect. While it was relatively easy to lure young men without families to the subcontinent with offers of wages higher than they would receive in the UK, retaining them, especially when they married and had children, was not easy. The railway companies had to strive to create conditions which made living in India not just bearable but actually attractive to these men. There was, too, the constant worry about both their moral and physical health, as highlighted in the 1858 report of the Committee on the Colonisation of India. The solution came in the form of railway communities, backed by a clear set of rules governing the behaviour of railway workers, both Europeans and Indians, and which addressed the ever-growing concerns about the moral risks created by the spread of the railways.

As early as 1859, less than a decade into the railway age, the companies and the government began to establish railway colonies. These, ideally, would be quite separate from the existing Indian towns, where the bazaars and brothels were a constant temptation, and would provide all the facilities needed to create a home from home. Their ostensible purpose was twofold, to guard against degeneracy but also to offer a space where European values could survive and thrive. However, the thinking behind the establishment of these colonies went much deeper. The railway system and, indeed, the whole colonial project would be put at risk if thousands of men arrived from the UK and behaved in a way that was counter to the prevailing Victorian ethos. They would set a terrible example and arouse hostility from the locals. Previously, administering India had been carried out by a small group of civil servants, essentially from the officer class. The only members of the working classes who were needed to maintain control by the colonial power were the lower ranks of the army and they were subject to military discipline and rules. Now, with the arrival of large numbers of men to carry out a wide variety of tasks on the railway, similar rules as those in the military were required to police and discipline them.

The effect of this was to turn the railway system into a kind of state within a state. The powers given to Indian railway companies to control both passengers and staff were far more extensive than those accorded to their counterparts back in the UK. The first Indian Railway Act passed in 1854, in the immediate aftermath of the opening of the first line, reflected British practice but went beyond it in terms of the regulation of employees. The rail companies in Britain had aspects of a military regime, as expressed through uniforms and the rigidity of the hierarchy (British Rail used to have separate canteens for officers, NCOs or middle management, and the rest), but it was nothing like as rigid as the system created by law and regulation in India.

The duties of all staff, from stationmasters and platform porters to signallers and drivers, were prescribed by a lengthy series of regulations set out in a rule book which they were required to carry at all times. Each set of workers had a clearly defined hierarchy, akin to the way that the military operates, which meant, for example, the stationmaster was responsible for all personnel at his station and permanent way staff were answerable to an inspector. Employees could face immediate dismissal or have fines imposed for transgression of the rules but they did have the right to appeal to the 'agent', invariably the European who was in charge of the railway and reported to the directors in London. Each company added its own by-laws to the standard regulations, in line with its particular circumstances. The rigidity of the hierarchy was a response to the specific conditions of the subcontinent and, in particular, the fundamental mistrust by the company directors of both local and European workers: 'A strict hierarchy founded on both military models and a notion of moral obligation for self-governance emerged as the solution for the inadequacies of the Indian and potentially wayward European/Eurasian railway worker.'[7]

It was not only the workers who were subject to the strict rule of law on the railways. The railway companies assumed extensive powers over passengers as soon as they set foot on railway land. The laws went well beyond British practice in numerous ways, such as giving the companies jurisdiction over the station and adjoining premises, unlike in the UK, where that was confined to the track itself. Additionally, whereas in the UK passengers who were apprehended by railway staff had the right, if innocent, of suing for false arrest, there was no such equivalent legislation in India. The railways were judge and jury, and the difference with UK legislation was neither trivial nor accidental. It effectively meant that staff saw themselves as having the right to police passengers and, inevitably, such unfettered authority led to abuses and, worse, a general attitude of contempt towards users of the railway. There are still signs today on the railway which remind passengers that 'Ticketless Travel is a Social Evil'. This tight control over passengers at stations exhibited itself most strongly in relation to the fear and threat of disease, as examined in the next chapter.

There were no fewer than twenty-three offences that could be committed by passengers, many of which were not even against the law in the UK. Misbehaving Europeans were also of particular concern, which led to the passing of the European Vagrancy Act in 1869; this law gave magistrates the power to send Europeans found begging or destitute at railway stations (and elsewhere) to workhouses and, for repeat offenders, to be transported to Australia. Oddly, as Laura Bear notes, 'the result of the Vagrancy Act was that any European spotted on the railway platform by station staff or the police was immediately under suspicion simply for travelling'.[8] Not, of course, if they were able to buy a first-class ticket. However, poor whites in third class were at risk of being wrongfully arrested and there were numerous reports of the railway authorities mistreating them, which are all the more poignant because many were former rail workers who had fallen on hard times, often as a result of alcoholism. White people who fell foul of the law, or were the victims of crime, were not, however, expected to have to deal with Indian police officers. Instead, the railway police force had a much higher proportion of Europeans than its counterpart in the towns and cities. That was to ensure that the fundamental police functions for the British community were carried out by Europeans, not Indians. A special rank of 'reserve inspectors', aided by a few sergeants – both relatively lowly positions that would normally be expected to be filled by Indians – was created for Europeans to ensure that there was always a white officer available to deal with their compatriots, whether as miscreants or victims. This was not based on any operational needs, but, rather, 'the existence of a special class of European inspectors and sergeants, while owing nothing to any legitimate administrative or public safety concern, speaks volumes about the race-oriented peculiarities of British colonial society'.[9] Partly, this was out of a desire to provide the sort of service that British people might expect from police officers back home: 'They were white policemen for a white people whose natural expectations of police accountability and courteous manner were far greater than anything the villagers and townsfolk of colonial India could ever expect from their police.'[10]

The railway companies' intense concern over wayward whites and idle Indians underpinned the policy of establishing railway communities or colonies separate from the towns and cities in which they were located. These communities were also crucial in the companies' efforts to attract European workers to India to work on the railway. By definition, railway jobs are located at many different places and it was unthinkable that new arrivals from Europe would be expected to live cheek by jowl with Indians. It was fortuitous, therefore, that the creation of these communities, motivated by concerns over degeneracy, also helped make life more palatable to the incomers and consequently reduce the high turnover of staff, which was both inconvenient and expensive for the companies.

The housing in these communities was deliberately designed not to be like barracks for soldiers, who lived in large communal dormitories, but rather to create the sense of a real home. The cottages were built to house two men sharing or a married couple as, later on, women were encouraged to travel to India to join their husbands due to the fact that having a family was seen as likely to help them keep on the straight and narrow. In order to facilitate the arrival of women and children, companies paid for half the passage and at times even advanced the rest.

The deliberate way that these railway communities were created as enclaves meant they had to be set well apart physically from the towns and villages adjoining them. In particular, they were to be sited as far away as possible from bazaars and native housing. If locals started to encroach, or a bazaar sprung up in the vicinity, the native huts would be torn down and relocated. Bazaars, in particular, were perceived as a great threat as they were considered to be places where morals were lax and prostitutes rife. The East Indian Railway even introduced Sanitary Police 'for the proper enforcement of sanitary regulations and for the security of the settlement'.[11] Even the vegetation was subject to a kind of biological apartheid. Any trace of local plants was to be removed and the areas around the houses were laid out with the sort of flowers and bushes that could be found in the garden of a British country cottage. The seeds were specially imported from a British company and provided free to the residents, who were expected to do the gardening in order to preserve their health and morals. There was an obsession with fresh air and ventilation, too, as according to a lecture given at the Railway Mechanics Institute in Howrah in 1863 'it is to a great extent the air we breathe which moulds the form, temper and genius of a people'.[12] Good ventilation and other sanitary measures, the lecturer went on to say, were the only way of fostering British genius.

The communities in large towns became pastiches of English villages or small towns. The settlements would be laid out like American towns with a grid system and there would be a clear-cut *classification* – in its literal sense. The European managers would occupy houses at one end, often closest to the Anglican church (complete with spire), and would frequent a railway club, open only to senior staff, while a railway 'institute' would cater for the other ranks, who were housed on the opposite side of the enclave. There were numerous sports clubs, too, with separate ones for Europeans and Indians.

This policy of encouraging married staff in order to make the labour force more stable caused further complexity as it led to the need to provide schools. Initially, little thought had been given to the lack of educational facilities for the children of lower-paid European and Eurasian staff. A series of hill schools had been built in the 1860s, due to an initiative by Lord Canning, the Governor-General, but the fees were so high that only the children of well-paid administrators could afford them. After pressure from Archbishop Bayly of Calcutta, who was appalled to find that only a third of poorer European and Eurasian children attended school, the government pressed the railway companies into taking action. Following the churchman's intervention, in 1879 the Viceroy, Lord Lytton, wrote a minute supporting the extension of schools to poorer European and Eurasian children, suggesting that funds would be made available from both government and private sources. As a result, a series of eleven schools in the hill stations were founded by the railway companies and churches, and several boarding schools were also opened in the plains, notably at Jamalpur in Delhi on the line between Delhi and Calcutta. The poorer European railway workers were encouraged to send their children to these schools, which had an emphasis on vocational rather than academic education, teaching the pupils basic skills of woodwork and needlework, but, more importantly, encouraging them to learn and develop European mores.

Throughout this schooling, which normally ended at fourteen, the boys were required to carry out frequent military drills, and the older ones were attached to railway battalions of the Auxiliary Force, known as the Railway Volunteer Force, or simply the 'volunteers'. This was somewhat of a misnomer. These units were an important part of uniting the Europeans in the workforce and of acting as a permanent deterrent to repeats of the 1857 Rebellion, given that the authorities realized there were never enough fulltime soldiers to crush a nationwide insurrection, and consequently involvement in the 'volunteers' was effectively mandatory. This was noted by Rudyard Kipling, writing in 1888, on a visit to the headquarters of the East Indian Railway in Jamalpur, who revealed:

> On Tuesdays and Fridays the volunteers parade. A and B Companies, 150 strong in all, of the E.I.R. [East Indian Railway]. Volunteers are stationed here with the band. Their uniform, grey with red facings, is not lovely, but they know how to shoot and drill. They have to. The 'Company' makes it a condition of service that a man must be a volunteer; and volunteer in something more than name he must be, or someone will ask the reason why.[13]

Kipling pointed out that it was these men who would need to defend local Europeans in the event of a mutiny, since there were no army barracks in the 350 miles between Calcutta and Danapur, and even the latter was more than 100 miles away from Jamalpur. The real intent of the force, rather than the endless drilling and ceremonial activity, was exposed by the fact that Indians were barred from joining. The 'volunteers' were issued with rifles and a uniform but not much else, as Kipling complained: 'They are as mobile a corps as can be desired, and ... hence the Government may possibly be led to take a real interest in them and spend a few thousand rupees in providing them with real soldiers' kits – not uniform and rifle merely.' They did have access to a firing range which, Kipling noted from the condition of the grass, was well-used, especially by army veterans who, he observed, were much sought-after recruits to the railway.

On some railways, training was even more serious. The Oudh & Rohilkand Railway gave 12-pounder quick-firing guns and old machine guns to the railway corps. They were mounted, according to the *Railway Gazette*, 'in an armoured train, with which there is extensive annual practice in combination with other arms, regular and volunteer'. The *Gazette* reporter was impressed at the extensive training that was given: 'The attendance at the annual camps runs to a figure not far short of one third of the total strength and at these the men bivouac, build block houses, dig trenches and exercise with the trains, doing as much as is possible to fit them for the efficient defence of the long lines of railway communications in time of war. Another 200 men had training in ambulance trains.'[14]

There were plans to make military use of the railway in a more direct way. On a visit to Lahore, just prior to his trip to Jamalpur, Kipling had noted the workshops there had built an armoured train fitted with heavy artillery and machine guns, which he assumed was a precursor to many others. However, in the event, armoured trains proved to be an unwieldy weapon and were little used, apart from, according to a Colonel Phillips writing in 1968, the deployment of the Lahore train on field days, 'when its main function appeared to be to supply tiffin [afternoon tea] to the officers, a dining car being added to its composition for the purpose'.[15]

Kipling found Jamalpur, which, like most of the communities, had deliberately been sited far away from any existing large city or Indian settlement, pleasant but somewhat overbearing, a re-creation of an Arcadia that never was:

> Its designers allowed room for growth, and made the houses of one general design – some of brick, some of stone, some three, four, and six roomed, some single men's barracks and some two-storied – all for the use of the *employés*. King's Road, Prince's Road, Queen's Road, and Victoria Road – Jamalpur is loyal – cut the breadth of the station; and Albert Road, Church Street, and Steam Road the length of it. Neither on these roads nor on any of the cool-shaded smaller ones is anything unclean or unsightly to be found.

There was a thriving Masonic lodge, whose members proudly boasted that all the fittings had been made by them, half a dozen well-used tennis courts in the grounds of the Institute, a library with thousands of books, and swimming baths. It was, Kipling reckoned, all too quiet, as there was none of the hustle-bustle that characterized towns and cities back in the UK. There was little necessity for 'wheeled vehicles' since most people could walk easily to work.

For the white men, wages were good and the career ladder as high as their ambitions wanted it to be. Even those starting as ticket collectors at 65 rupees per month could soon be earning ten times that and be in charge of several hundred Indian workers. Other Europeans had been recruited from the United Kingdom – Scotland was a particularly fertile source of engineers - to fill key posts, such as head of department, locomotive superintendent or stationmaster. Kipling toured the workshops and engine sheds at Jamalpur, which was heaving with hundreds of local men working in a hierarchy under a few heads of department who were:

> silent, heavy-handed men, captains of five hundred or more … They are men worth hearing deferentially. They hail from Manchester and the Clyde, and the great ironworks of the North: pleasant as cold water in a thirsty land is it to hear again the full Northumbrian burr or the long-drawn Yorkshire 'aye'. Under their great gravity of demeanour – a man who is in charge of a few lakhs' worth of plant cannot afford to be riotously mirthful – lurks melody and humour.

For the Indian workers, life was of course very different. Just as with the workers building the railway mentioned in Chapter 3, the recruitment of large numbers of local people to operate and maintain the system was a task without precedent. While there were a smattering of industry and a few factories by the mid-nineteenth century, there was nothing on the scale of the railways. The very concept of paid labour was novel for most Indians, apart from agricultural workers employed seasonally, but the railway companies realized that for reasons of both economy and practicality most of their employees would have to be hired locally.

There was a plethora of tasks, and while many were relatively menial, they still required training, basic competence and the discipline of the work ethic. Almost half the workforce was engaged in activity which was called 'engineering', though most were solely concerned with keeping the track in good repair, a massive and continuous task that was safety-critical. Clerical staff, looking after accounts and stores, policing the network and providing medical services accounted for about one in twenty workers, while most of the rest were in 'telegraph and traffic', which included the more skilled tasks, such as driving trains and providing the workforce for the workshops and engine sheds that sprang up around the country to maintain the locomotives and other railway equipment.

While many staff were scattered throughout the network to work at stations or on permanent way gangs, the biggest centres of employment by far were the workshops like the one visited by Kipling at Jamalpur, which at the time employed more than 4,000 people and would eventually, by the mid-twentieth century, have almost three times that number of workers. There were numerous similar sites across India, including a handful of similar large complexes to Jamalpur, and a far greater number of smaller engine sheds scattered throughout the nation which housed locomotives overnight and carried out basic maintenance. The large workshops undertook every task required to keep railways operating and the workforce was divided into a huge range of 'shops', which Ian Kerr, citing the huge Moghulpura works in Lahore built just before the First World War to replace an older, smaller site, sets out in a list: 'The tender shop, the erecting shop, the fitting shop, the light machine shop, the heavy machine shop, the tool room, the brass finishing shop, the millwright shop, the boiler shop, the coppersmith shop, the blacksmith and spring shop, the brass and iron foundries, the pattern shop and the case hardening and tool hardening shop.'[16]

The existence of such a wide variety of functions reveals the range of skills that the largely Indian workforce had to acquire. But, just as with the workers who built the railways, there were complaints that they were not as efficient as their UK counterparts. An official commission into the efficiency of Indian labour at the time of the First World War found 'there was general agreement between the European officers at Jamalpur that the outturn work per man was not more than one-third that of corresponding workmen in British shops'.[17] Of course, wages were concomitantly far lower and it is unclear the extent to which this assessment was accurate. Certainly, the range of jobs that they carried out helped develop a key skills base that stood the railways in good stead. They included fitters, turners, blacksmiths, carpenters, tinsmiths, machine men and many more.

It was not only blue-collar workers. Kipling was full of admiration for the *babu*s, the Indian clerks who filled every office in huge numbers: 'The Babus in the traffic department, in the stores' issue department, in all the departments where men sit through the long, long Indian day among ledgers, and check and pencil and deal in figures and items and rupees, may be counted by hundreds.'[18] He pointed out that it was thanks to them that the railway companies were financially viable since not only did they do an excellent job, but it would have been prohibitively expensive for the railways to depend on imported European clerical staff, who would have cost far more:

> The Babus make beautiful accountants, and if we could only see it, a merciful Providence has made the Babu for figures and detail. Without him, the dividends of any company would be eaten up by the expenses of English or city-bred clerks. The Babu is a great man, and, to respect him, you must see five score or so of him in a room a hundred yards long, bending over ledgers, ledgers, and yet more ledgers – silent as the Sphinx and busy as a bee. He is the lubricant of the great machinery of the Company whose ways and works cannot be dealt with in a single scrawl.[19]

Of course, for all these men, there was no equivalent of the railway communities built for the European and Eurasian staff. Consequently, large settlements arose around the major workshops, often tacitly sanctioned but always at risk of being pulled down.

A study by two economists suggests that the railways, both in construction and in operation, employed 50 per cent of those working in the 'modern' sector, the businesses and small companies involved in capital enterprise, throughout the whole period between 1850 and 1940. There is both a positive and negative side to that figure. On the one hand, it demonstrates the importance of the railways in stimulating the beginning of industrialization in India, but on the other shows the extent to which the railways failed to be the catalyst for wider economic development as they had been during the nineteenth century in so many other countries around the world. If the railways had stimulated greater development across a range of industries, then they would have represented a far lower percentage of this type of employment. While the railways undoubtedly represented a great new asset for India, enabling people to travel in a way that would have been impossible otherwise and facilitating the transport of goods to open up markets, they were also a missed opportunity because they were part of a colonial project whose motives did not include the rapid development of the Indian economy (or take-off, as economists call it).

As we saw in Chapter 3, the methods of construction of railways imported from the UK were, over time, subject to some adaptation necessary for the hugely different environment on the subcontinent. There was a gradual recognition that in some respects local methods, the result of traditions handed down through the generations, could provide the basis for different types of work processes. In basic tasks, such as earth moving and dredging,

European techniques were adapted through the medium of traditional Indian ways of working to create an amalgam that was far
more labour-intensive than contemporary practices elsewhere.
This included animal labour, with bullocks being widely employed
to carry out heavy lifting, in contrast to the methods in the UK,
where by the end of the century sophisticated machinery was
widely deployed. For example, at the site of the construction of the
Bezawada Bridge on the East Coast State Railway in the 1890s, the
dredging was undertaken by a team of sixteen dredgers, requiring
a total of sixty-four bullocks. A Railway Board report reckoned
they were 'as fast, efficient and cheap as the other more civilized
methods', a reference to steam-worked dredgers. The steam dredger
was 'only so much better than the primitive bullock system as to
justify its retention as a reserve to overawe the bullock-drivers, who
were a troublesome and bad-tempered lot, always ready to strike'.[20]
While the greatest adaptations to Indian conditions were in the
simpler more labour-intensive tasks, other more complex aspects
of railway building, such as tunnelling, track laying and especially
bridge building, 'were never transferred undiluted'.[21]

In contrast, as far as the operation and maintenance of the rail
network were concerned, by and large, British machinery was
simply imposed with little consideration of local circumstances.
This was particularly true of locomotive and carriage technology.
The occasional adaptation was made to standard equipment, such
as the addition of US-style cowcatchers – which are effectively cow
killers – to the front of locomotives because, unlike in the UK, the
railway was not fenced, but usually 'only minor cosmetic adaptations were made'.[22]

The same attitude which resulted in Indian people being
considered incapable of carrying out many tasks also underlay the

attitude towards the ability to manufacture railway equipment locally to the required high standard. According to Mark Tully, the veteran BBC India correspondent, 'as early as 1865, India demonstrated the possibility of establishing railway industries by manufacturing a locomotive which competed in price and quality with British products'.[23] However, the railway companies ignored that development, continuing to buy expensive British equipment, a situation which continued throughout the colonial period. By Independence in 1947, only 700 locally produced engines had been introduced on Indian railways, while 12,000 (94 per cent of the total) had been imported from the UK. John Hurd, the author of a chapter on railways in *The Cambridge Economic History of India*, suggests that this was a key limiting factor in India's ability to begin the industrialization process: 'India's loss from the purchase policies of the railways was not limited to her lack of progress in developing heavy industry. She also failed to reap the benefits of the spread effects of industry which would have occurred.'[24] There was nevertheless some limited technology transfer in the workshops. J. N. Sahni, the official historian of the Indian railways, notes that 'in the early stages almost all spare parts for the maintenance of rolling stock were imported from Britain but to attain self-sufficiency, their manufacture was gradually developed in the railway workshops and other indigenous factories'.[25] However, this process was slow and it was not until Independence that it was accelerated to create genuine self-sufficiency.

Because India was a captive market for British-built locomotives, the wider economic effects of the huge investment in the railways benefited the UK. Indeed, of the world's nations which built major railway networks in the nineteenth century, such as Britain, the US, France and Germany, India was the only one which by the end of the century had not become a base for major locomotive production. Japan, too, offers an interesting contrast in this respect. From a situation where it imported all its equipment when the first railway was built in 1872 – nearly two decades after India's first line – Japan was manufacturing three quarters of its railway carriages by the turn of the century. In order to boost locomotive production, which required greater engineering knowhow than carriage manufacturing, the Japanese government set up four companies to build locomotives and within a few years they came to dominate the domestic market. Consequently, the railways were a key catalyst in Japan's industrialization which took off in the late nineteenth century and early twentieth.

While India was not allowed to manufacture locomotives and other railway equipment and Indians were barred from many jobs on the operating railway, the British owners of the railway companies had no choice but to employ them for the majority of tasks in the workshops. The companies could not possibly import the huge number of staff required to keep the railway functioning and were forced to take on thousands of local people. There was no little irony in the fact that the same workforce reputed to be unable to manufacture locomotives or even to drive a train with passengers had to be skilled enough to maintain and operate the complex and varied machinery needed to keep the railways running efficiently and, crucially, safely every day.

The breakdown of the workshops into a series of different 'shops' led to the division of the workforce into a plethora of separate groups and, as a result, the formation of small unions, which often recruited solely from those employed on a particular task. These divisions were reinforced by the fact that activities in certain shops and operating divisions became the specialism of particular racial groups, thus entrenching the separation. For example, on the East Indian Railway in 1900, according to Laura Bear, 'a quarter of locomotive department employees were Muslims. In contrast Muslims were a tiny minority in the traffic department in roles as stationmasters, signallers, and the like'.[26] Also, in the Kharagpur workshop in West Bengal, 'Punjabis built the carriages, specializing in the fine carpentry necessary for this task. Biharis and West Bengal Muslims worked on the boilers. Members of North Indian hill tribes were put to work in the foundry making the components for the carriages.'[27] And so on. In that way, particular jobs became associated with particular castes and racial groups.

It was inevitable that the management style of the railways, combined with the sheer scale of the enterprise, would result in industrial unrest both in the workshops and in railway operations generally. There had, of course, been sporadic strikes and protests during the construction of the railways, but the temporary and unorganized nature of the workforce meant they were generally quickly resolved, quite often through mass dismissals.

The situation in the workshops, with vast numbers of permanent workers, was bound to be more conducive to difficult industrial relations and conflict. One of the first recorded instances of strike activity in the workshops was on the vast Lahore site, first established in the 1860s and the biggest in India at the time (of course, now in Pakistan). It was the hub of the North Western Railway, which, by 1905, through merger and expansion, encompassed a system of 4,000 route miles that required 750 locomotives and 2,400 coaches to provide for the passengers, as well as 11,600 wagons to carry freight, and employed a total of 63,000 people. In March 1895, a group of 150 workers in the iron moulders' shop went on strike in protest against the introduction of a system of piecework payments, rather than the fixed wage they had been receiving. This change infuriated a workforce already aggrieved by the harsh treatment of the management, whose response was, perhaps predictably, to dismiss most of those who had withdrawn their labour. The strike escalated as fellow workers in the carriage works came out in sympathy and within a week around 2,800 of the 4,000 workers in the workshops had joined in. The management, however, held firm, helped by the fact that the Europeans and Eurasians stayed at work and remained loyal to the company, putting in extra shifts which enabled the workshops to keep functioning. Nor did the strike spread to the operational railway, which would have damaged North Western's revenue. As a result, most of the workers soon sought to go back to work but many were barred from doing so by the company. As is common in such disputes, the management identified 'ringleaders', many of whom were *mistris* – supervisors in the shops – and those singled out were put in front of local magistrates for breaches of railway legislation to be bound over to keep the peace.

Even though on this occasion the action was largely unsuccessful, Ian Kerr suggests this was a key event in making railway workers, by far the biggest industrial group in India, aware of their ability to wield their industrial muscle: 'Regardless of its outcome, the 1895 strike represented a significant manifestation of worker consciousness among the workshop employees.'[28] Indeed, industrial disputes on the railways became commonplace with, for example, signallers on the Great Indian Peninsula Railway going on strike for higher wages in 1900, and numerous other disputes across the network in the early 1900s. It was not only Indians, and when trouble spread to white workers, the authorities became even more concerned. In 1897, the Eurasian and European guards on the Great Indian Peninsula Railway walked out in protest at the arbitrary fining system imposed by management for breaches of behaviour, and there was a further strike by Eurasian guards and drivers on the Indian Midland Railway three years later.

Worse, there were several train-wrecking incidents in the troubled North-Western Provinces, carried out by Indians aggrieved by the railway. The combination of these attacks and strikes led Lord Curzon to call for the creation of a commission to look at the issue of railway defence, which reported in 1902. The Commission noted that the role of the Volunteer Force, which Kipling had observed training, would be essential in the event of any recurring troubles but required reinforcing and professionalizing. The volunteers, it recommended, should be given clear tasks in the event of an emergency, e.g. protecting key parts of railway property, such as tunnels and bridges. Each section would be allocated a segment of the railway to protect and would ensure the safe passage of the garrisoned troops in the event of an emergency, enabling them to travel rapidly to counter rebellions. The 'volunteers', therefore, would be transformed into a quasi-military force, far better organized than hitherto. It was to focus on being prepared for action, rather than merely undertaking endless ceremonial drills, turning what had been a rather shambolic Dad's Army into something that was more akin to today's semi-professional Territorial Army. According to Laura Bear, this change in role was important in two respects: 'European and Eurasian railway workers would be made to feel their duties and loyalties more keenly . . . They would act as a line of defence against any uprising, whether this took the form of political strikes, external attack, or internal rebellion against British rule.'[29] Giving the members of the force these added responsibilities inculcated them more in the colonial ethos.

A separate simultaneous inquiry was also held into the possibility of employing more Europeans and Eurasians and to examine the roles played by the 'different creeds and castes' in the railway. The report confirmed the concentration of particular groups in specific roles and suggested that there should be a more even distribution among the various tasks. How that could be achieved was unclear. The reason for the concentrations, as mentioned above, was the tendency of groups from the same caste and religion to work together on particular aspects of the railway and there was great resistance to breaking up these affinity groups. Regional, caste and religious identity could not simply be disregarded without causing widespread disaffection.

More significantly, the authors suggested that increasing numbers of Eurasians and Indian Christians – deemed to be more reliable than members of the indigenous religions – should be employed on the railways, rather reversing the 1870 policy of Indianization. The railway companies rather baulked at this idea. They were concerned, as before, about costs, given that the Eurasians were better paid than Indians in order to maintain their European lifestyle. Moreover, they could not be sent to remote stations away from other members of their communities as they could not be expected to live solely amongst Indians. They had a separate status, even if they were not quite European.

The railway companies eventually compromised, agreeing to recruit more Eurasian guards and locomotive crews, which meant allowing Indians to drive a wider range of trains and take more responsibility for safety. The best way was to get them young by apprenticing Eurasian and local European boys, the sons of existing workers, and similarly there was a recruitment drive for young Christian Indians. One advantage was that they tended to be more rootless than native Indians, who were tied to their caste and religious groups, which meant that it was easier to move them around the railway to take up jobs in different locations.

The Eurasians became increasingly important in the government's eyes as a source of stability in the railways. They were rarely allowed into the top echelons of the hierarchy, but they filled many middle-grade posts and were paid at rates between those of European and Indian workers. For the most part, they were fiercely loyal to the Raj and 'became the key passenger and mail train operatives and strike breakers'.[30] There was no little irony here. Some of the Eurasians were nothing of the sort and were pure-bred Indians who decided to go European if they were light-skinned or could point to some distant white ancestor. Sometimes they managed to become 'Eurasian' by virtue of obtaining a supervisory job and then gradually adopting European mores and mixing with Eurasians, a kind of polar opposite of 'going native'. There were obvious advantages in doing this thanks to the Eurasians' higher earning capacity and better living conditions.

The encouragement of more Eurasians into the industry did not resolve the industrial-relations issues that had been festering for many years. In fact, quite the opposite. In 1906, for example, there were strikes against several railway companies across India. On the East Indian Railway in July, there was a strike by clerks of the traffic and locomotive departments at Asansol in West Bengal, which led to the formation of a union but was quickly defeated. The railway dismissed 206 men for failing to fulfil their duty and endangering the public by striking, while those who stayed at work were rewarded with medals. At Kharagpur, a major workshop in West Bengal, the workers in the carriage construction department struck for better pay and increased grain allowances.

The relationship of the small number of Eurasian and European staff with the Indians remained strained, not least because of the latter's dissatisfaction at the lack of opportunities for promotion. As the Acworth Committee, which reported just after the First World War, put it, 'the 7,000 [Eurasian and European workers] were like a thin film of oil on the top of a glass of water, resting upon but hardly mixing with the 700,000 [Indian workers] below'.

Inevitably, the strikes became part of a wider political movement. As the authorities feared, *swadeshi* – political agitators – helped stir up these disputes, and while most disputes were undoubtedly based on well-founded grievances, they were seen as an opportunity by nationalists to garner support for their cause. The *swadeshi* were not averse to resorting to unscrupulous tactics in attempts to force out those reluctant strikers. Laura Bear recounts that 'those who didn't strike were threatened with being made to eat cow or pig flesh, according to their Hindu or Muslim origins'.[31] There were even piles of cow bones strategically placed along the roads to the workshops to throw at potential scabs. The strikes could last for quite a long time as the workers received outside support, and while the particular battles tended to end in failure, the accumulation of industrial action in many parts of the country, together with the authorities' fear that it would lead to wider political discontent, meant they did result in gradual improvements in pay and conditions. As we shall see in the next chapter, one consequence of the unions becoming stronger and more politicized was that the outbreaks of industrial unrest inevitably became increasingly entangled with the nationalist cause.

SEVEN

NOT ALWAYS LOVED

THE RAILWAYS WERE not only the country's largest industry and biggest employer, but also a visible and physical demonstration of colonial rule. By the turn of the century, through merger and expansion, the railway companies had become extremely powerful entities and the government responded by launching an inquiry into the administration and working of the railways. The period from the beginning of the century up to Independence was characterized by numerous such government-inspired inquiries and commissions into various aspects of the operation and development of the railways, stimulated by the ever-present feeling that the railways were not functioning effectively. There was, too, constant angst in government circles, in both India and Britain, about the relationship between the state and the railways. In the event, the early decades of the twentieth century would see a gradual strengthening of government control over the railways as their importance to the Indian economy grew and as the way they were run attracted increasing criticism from those seeking independence. The process of nationalization and consolidation into a single entity was to prove inexorable, and one by one the major companies were subsumed into state ownership. The constant tinkering with administrative aspects of the railways was a reflection of a far greater concern about their operation.

The government-inspired inquiries were invariably undertaken by advisers or experts from the UK, which gave their findings more credibility and resulted in a greater expectation of their recommendations being implemented. The first was undertaken just after the turn of the century by Sir Thomas Robertson, who was later described rather unkindly by J. N. Westwood, in his short history of Indian railways, as 'one of those experts who became so familiar in the mid-twentieth century: men of no particular talent but regarded with some awe in underdeveloped countries'. Westwood went on to say that the result was a report produced after 'months of agreeable all-expenses travel' which consisted of 'an ill-written string of platitudes' resembling 'the work of a first year undergraduate'.[1]

Nevertheless, parts of the report, published in 1903, were to prove influential. Its central recommendation, which was to transfer oversight of the railways from the Indian Public Works Department to a newly created three-member Railway Board, was swiftly implemented by the government, an arrangement that would survive, in various guises, to this day. The idea was that the Board would establish some order out of the complex structure of ownership and control in the railways, with their myriad different, and at times conflicting, arrangements. The creation of the Board gave railway managers a measure of independence, though the Board still reported to the Government of India's Department of Commerce and Industry. Robertson also highlighted the fact that there was not enough investment in the railway system to ensure it was in good working order, let alone to keep up with growing demands for extra capacity, and therefore suggested the establishment of a railway capital fund, managed by the new Board, both to maintain the existing system of lines and build new ones.

Robertson's effort was quickly followed by a report by Sir James Mackay (clearly a knighthood was a key qualification for this type of work) which, oddly, given the new regime had only just bedded in, sought to free the Railway Board from the daily oversight of the Department of Commerce and Industry and give it more independence from government. This was the start of the creation of a national rail network, owned by the government and managed by a relatively independent board, that would take until four years after Independence to come fully into fruition.

The colonial power's attitude could be put, in modern parlance, as 'What is there not to like about the railways?' After all, the railways enabled millions to travel cheaply and rapidly, they created massive employment, they helped modernize India, boosted the economy and were a source of pride for its people. That, of course, only told half the story and it was inevitable that criticisms of the iron road helped stimulate the nascent nationalist movement and would play a part in its rise.

Nationalism had its roots in the second half of the nineteenth century. Following the 1857 Rebellion, a political movement for independence began to emerge among the more educated and westernized Indian middle classes. Its most significant manifestation was the establishment of the Indian National Congress in 1885. Congress was initially more a debating society than a political party, meeting annually and making gentle suggestions to the government, which mostly ignored them. By 1900, however, it had established itself across the nation as a political organization, though it was undermined by the fact it did not attract Muslim support.

Other political forces were stirring, some motivated by religious causes, others by radical, principally left-leaning, ideology. A key event which stimulated protest was the decision by Lord Curzon to partition Bengal in 1905; he felt the province was too large to administer properly but he also sought to split apart the two main religious groups. His decision resulted in the separation of the largely Hindu western part from the Muslim-dominated east and angered the more-educated sections of Hindu society, who, rightly, saw it as an attempt to curb growing nationalism and to reduce the influence of Bengal in national politics. It was part of a wider British strategy to encourage the Muslim and Hindu populations to identify with their religion rather than their country in order to weaken pressure for independence. In other words, it was another example of that great British colonial strategy of 'divide and rule'. Even though the decision was reversed six years later, partition of Bengal was to remain a cause célèbre, and, indeed, the state would be divided again in 1947 when East Pakistan, now Bangladesh, was hewn out of India.

As the most potent symbol of the rule of the Raj, the way the railways were owned and operated was an early nationalist cause. This hostility to the iron road exhibited itself at two levels – a growing feeling among the educated classes that the railways were built solely in the interests of British commerce while being paid for largely by Indian taxpayers, and an increasing awareness among the masses travelling on them that they were being systematically mistreated. The railways were an easy target for the nationalists who exploited their failings to the full, as pointed out in a paper by two Indian historians: 'The imperial rulers of course presented the introduction of railways as a great boon to India, made possible by its association with Britain ... The Indian nationalists bought none of this.

A critique of railway policy was an integral part of *economic nationalism*, the foundational phase of the Indian national movement.'[2]

As mentioned in the previous chapter, the nationalists were concerned that India had missed out on the economic development that the railways had stimulated in many other countries. Worse, there was a feeling that the advent of the railways had disrupted the economic ecology of India. Because the arrival of the railways had not been accompanied by a rapid upsurge in economic development, the destruction of indigenous handicraft industries by cheaper imports transported by rail was not matched, as had happened elsewhere, by the creation of new alternative jobs. The economist Mahadev Govind Ranade, a member of the Indian National Congress, summed up the argument by saying that the railway had not 'only made competition with Europe more hopeless over larger areas, and facilitated the conveyance of foreign goods', but had also 'killed our local indigenous industries and made people more helpless than before by increasing their dependence and pressure on agriculture as their only resource'.[3]

To add to the complaints, many of the blue-collar and manual jobs associated with the railways, such as coalmining and steelwork, went to British-based companies, which therefore meant there were none of the sort of 'multiplier' effects that stimulate rapid growth and are at the root of Keynesian economics. As a result, the railways were accused of being responsible for much of the destitution found in rural areas, where traditional industries had been wiped out by competition enabled by the railways.

The nationalists argued, too, that because much of the capital came from Britain, the overall impact of the railways on the Indian economy was to shift money out of the subcontinent. Not only did this take place in the form of dividends and debt interest, which was the case in many other countries where the railways were built by foreign investors, but the Indians were additionally penalized because payments had to be made in pounds and the rupee was in a permanent state of decline against sterling. India's balance of payments suffered further through having to pay for imported materials and for the services of European staff, who, as noted previously, took most of the top jobs, which, of course, created another source of resentment when these well-paid employees sent remittances back home. The overall effect on the Indian taxpayer, too, was largely negative since the railways required considerable subsidy and the nationalists were particularly critical of the guarantee arrangements because of the drain on India's finances. However, this argument lost much of its force at the beginning of the 1900s when the overall financial situation of the railways improved so much that, taken as a whole, they began to make a profit, which meant, for the most part, they were no longer a burden on the Indian taxpayer. Even then, however, some of the guaranteed railways still required subsidy to pay the shareholders, as did new railways being built at the instigation of British-controlled companies and the London government.

The more violent elements among the nationalists started a campaign of sabotage against the railways in 1907, mostly concentrated in Bengal because of the widespread anger over Partition. There were repeated attempts to blow up trains carrying Andrew Fraser, the Lieutenant-Governor of Bengal, and during one such attack it was only by luck that his carriage stayed on the tracks despite being bent by the force of the explosion. There was also a series of attacks on trains carrying valuable consignments which were stolen to fund the nationalist cause. As with other periods of terrorist activity, it was difficult at times to determine whether these acts of *dacoity* (banditry) were perpetrated for political or simply criminal reasons. Either way, there was a sharp rise in such attacks in the years running up to the First World War, which caused enormous concern in government circles.

As ever, overreaction from the authorities stirred up further anger. A series of bombs thrown at trains in 1908 led the Eastern Bengal State Railway to establish a special patrol on the section of line around the Dum Dum junction on the outskirts of Calcutta, where most of the attacks had taken place. While this was a fairly unremarkable response, the fact that the annual cost of 75,000 rupees had to be financed through a special levy on local residents living within two miles of the line raised widespread resentment.

In 1908, the authorities responded with legislation that provided for harsher penalties for offenders carrying explosives, but it was not until the introduction of the more draconian Defence of India Act in 1915, which was specifically aimed at curtailing nationalist activity, that the outbreak of railway sabotage ceased, albeit temporarily. Inevitably, though, the repressive new legislation, which lapsed after the war, created yet more dissent and anger among the Indian population.

While the violent attacks on the railways abated during the war, the verbal ones did not. Bit by bit, the nationalists unpicked the arguments in favour of the railways. Interestingly, however, few of the critics of the railways suggested they should not have been built at all. Quite the opposite. They generally supported the creation of the network as an important modernizing force, but were critical of the way the development of the railways had favoured British interests and exploited local people.

One important line of thinking was that too much money had been spent on railways rather than on other potential ways of stimulating economic development. The most obvious example, according to the nationalists, was the failure to invest sufficiently in irrigation. Ensuring a supply of water, rather than constructing railways, was the key to increasing agricultural production and thereby reducing the risk of starvation and providing food security. This was particularly true of the period between 1892 and 1905, when the expansion of the railway system was at its peak, with nearly 1,000 miles added to the network in each of those years. These lines were not necessarily remunerative and this spurt in growth of the network angered the nationalists. Should the money not have been better spent on other investment? The railways, after all, were not delivering the wider economic benefits for the rest of society and were not the catalyst for economic take-off as they had been elsewhere. The railways, they argued, absorbed much available capital that could have been used to improve other parts of the Indian economy, notably agriculture.

The nationalists set the railways and irrigation against each other by arguing that both were large capital projects that were potential remedies for famine. Irrigation, they suggested, went to the heart of the problem of intermittent food deficiencies, while railways were a mere palliative, as they simply were used to transfer produce from one area to the other. Yet, in the early 1900s, far more money went on improving the railways than was invested in irrigation projects. Worse, according to critics, the whole focus of government activity and the attention of politicians were centred on the railways. As R. M. Sayani, the president of the India National Congress, argued in the Viceroy's Legislative Council in 1898, 'While railways absorb so large a measure of Government attention, irrigation canals, which are far more protective against famine, are allowed only … one thirteenth of the amount spent on the railways each year.'[4]

Irrigation works could, too, be financially far more rewarding than the railways, offering annual returns of between 6 and 9 per cent, according to contemporary economists. The most common explanation for the difference in levels of investment gave easy ammunition to the supporters of the nationalist cause, as expressed by R. C. Dutt, the prominent economic historian: 'Preference was given to railways which facilitated British trade with India and not to canals which would have benefited Indian agriculture.'[5]

Simplistic, perhaps, but difficult to deny. The Viceroy, Lord Curzon, however, tried to counter these arguments in a speech introducing his 1900/1901 budget, when he argued that irrigation of desert tracts only encouraged population growth, thereby exacerbating food pressures. He insisted on pressing on with the railway expansion plans in order to ensure that remote parts of the hinterland were connected with the system. He did, nevertheless, appoint an Irrigation Commission, which recommended, in its report published in 1903, an increase in the area of irrigated land, but not on a scale sufficient to meet the complaints of the nationalists.

Rather ironically, the construction of railways through agricultural land actually created antagonism and tensions in some of the very rural areas they were designed to help because of the need to build embankments to protect the railway from flooding. As was often the case in India, what was *supposed* to happen in theory differed starkly from the reality. Embankments to raise the level of the track above the surrounding countryside were widely used in hilly terrain since railways require as level a surface as possible. Even where the topography was relatively flat, such as on the Gangetic plain, embankments were required to protect the railway from flash flooding in the monsoon period. However, it was a requirement under the legislation through which railways were built that the inevitable damage that the embankments caused to local drainage had to be alleviated by the companies through the construction of tunnels, culverts and drains. The local authorities were supposed to enforce this regulation by ensuring that sufficient infrastructure was provided by the railway company, but, as Ritika Prasad notes, 'this legal mandate notwithstanding, railway embankments continued to be built with inadequate waterways; sometimes, railway administrations closed off or blocked waterways that had been sanctioned and built'.[6]

The railway companies were supposedly responsible for damage to agricultural land resulting from their embankments or from their actions in blocking water courses, but they were frequently able to wriggle out of making any payments because of the complex issue of determining the precise cause of such incidents. The companies even argued at times that the embankments acted as dams, preventing damage to the side of the line that did not flood.

Disputes over the damage from flooding caused by railway embankments were almost as old as the railway in India itself. Ritika Prasad cites an account from Burdwan in West Bengal, where the line, built by the East Indian Railway, caused massive flooding by the Damodar River. The local paper, the *Urdu Guide*, described the damage as unprecedented and extensive: 'Thousands of dwellings have fallen, hundreds of lives been lost, countless number of cattle and a large quantity of grain been destroyed', and was unequivocal about where the blame lay as the people living in the villages 'had never dreamt of such dangers and losses, before the construction of the railway'.[7] There were numerous other similar cases stretching well into the twentieth century and at times local people did manage to obtain compensation. For example, the Oudh & Rohilkund Railway was deemed responsible for severe floods in the Ramgana valley in Uttar Pradesh caused by the embankment blocking the normal drainage and, in 1873, was required to pay more than 5,000 rupees in compensation, as well as being forced to rectify the situation.

At other times, local people took matters into their own hands, which led to serious unrest. In August 1917, a group of 500 local farmers, angered by repeated flooding, tried to destroy several sections of the railway embankment of the Bengal & North Western Railway in the Monghyr District of northern Bihar. The embankment had long been a source of grievance to local people, who had complained that there were not enough drainage courses beneath the railway to allow for the free flow of water. In 1915, there had been exceptionally heavy rainfall and a branch line built over a dried-up stream, a tributary of the Ganges, had caused a flood, which local villagers complained had swept away their cattle and would have drowned them had it not been for the intervention of the local district magistrate, who arranged boats to convey them to safety. The railway argued that the damage was merely the result of the normal vagaries of the weather, rather than the fault of the embankments. Even though a magistrate subsequently endorsed the villagers' complaints, the railway refused to act, arguing that additional culverts would undermine the whole embankment, and the local authorities refused to press the company to resolve the problem. Indeed, the railway's actions in trying to prevent erosion of its embankments exacerbated the situation.

Further floods in the subsequent two years spurred the local people into action. When floodwaters rose again in August 1917, hundreds of local villagers organized themselves in several groups aiming to breach the embankment in a number of different places.

They targeted the main line of the railway, which ran parallel with the Ganges at a height of around eight to ten feet and was clearly causing drainage problems since the water was several feet higher on the Ganges side. The authorities got wind of the attack and fired shots to disperse the protestors, but not before several breaches in the embankment had been made, partly as a result of their action but also as a result of the sheer scale of the inundation. The railway was blamed for blocking culverts, claiming it was necessary in order to prevent the line being washed away, but clearly this made things worse. The authorities were split about what to do, with some local police being sympathetic to the cause of the villagers whose crops were being wrecked, pushing them into destitution. The more senior district officials, however, tended to side with the railway company, but eventually decided that its action in blocking culverts was illegal and should not have been done without permission from the local authorities. Some prosecutions for sabotage under the Railways Act were initiated but it was difficult for the authorities to find the culprits, especially as most people had fled the floods by the time they tried to make arrests.

The dispute continued locally for several years and similar events occurred elsewhere, notably in Rajashahi in northern Bengal in 1922, where an incident came to the attention of Meghnad Saha, a noted astrophysicist who was several times nominated for a Nobel Prize. The floods that year were particularly heavy and destroyed the local paddy fields, which can withstand gradual flooding but not the onset of massive amounts of water. The subsequent investigations exonerated the railways, blaming heavy rain, but Saha, who was involved in the flood relief programme that followed, pointed out that similar heavy floods in 1871 had receded very quickly, saving the crops, whereas in 1922 the waters remained high for a long time. He argued that the railway embankment effectively acted as a dam and that the report blaming heavy rain was 'an ill-concealed attempt to blame nature instead of railways'. There was no doubt, he said, that 'ultimately the peasant was sacrificed to railway interests'.[8] His teacher, P. C. Ray, went further and blamed the British owners of the railway companies for refusing to build the required culverts and bridges: 'The fact is that railway lines are always constructed with an eye to the interest of foreign shareholder. The less the cost, greater the expectation of dividend.'[9] Consequently, proposals for new railways in Bengal, particularly in the lowlands, attracted widespread opposition, as the *Railway Gazette* found that 'any demand for further extension for railways in Bengal, especially for those railways running across the general line of the country, will meet with considerable criticism'.[10]

Clashes over flooding caused by the railways continued throughout the interwar period. In some areas, a game of cat and mouse between the police and villagers took place nightly during heavy rains as the authorities tried to stop local people opening culverts or breaching the embankments. As late as 1939, 36 local people were convicted of causing damage to the railway by breaching the embankment on two branch lines of the Eastern Bengal Railway in West Bengal, despite the fact that they said that the embankment had ruined their crops. (Interestingly, the same issue is arising in several parts of India today with the construction of new highways on embankments that are causing similar damage as those built for the railways.)

Floods caused by railway embankments were not the only type of environmental degradation laid at the feet of the railways, as Ritika Prasad notes: 'The disruption caused by railway embankments was part of the profound and long-lasting impact that a range of colonial projects of "improvement" had on India's natural environment'.[11] In particular, the railways required vast quantities of wood, especially in the early days of construction, when it was needed for sleepers and other parts of the construction process, as well as for fuel, since many early locomotives were wood-burning. Parts of the Himalayan forest as well as forests in the Upper Ganges and Indus basins were devastated; Paul Varady, an American professor of environmental policy, has written that the railways were 'agents of deforestation' which helped cause soil erosion.

If these environmental considerations at times raised hostility against the railways, anger from the railway passengers about the depredations of travelling on the railways proved to be a far more potent force in creating a general sense of dissatisfaction about the rule of the Raj. One notable source of discontent was the treatment of pilgrims. Pilgrimage had long been a feature of the subcontinent's history, conducted not only by followers of the main religions, Hinduism and Islam, but also by Sikhs, Jains and others. The numbers, even before the railway age, were large, but travelling was difficult and only a minority, mostly those relatively well-off, were able to undertake such journeys. The railways radically improved the experience of travel: rather than weeks on bullock cart and foot, the pilgrims could take a train journey for a few days at the most.

However, their experience of train travel was no picnic either. The high demand at particular times of the year meant that every available carriage had to be called into use, even those that were rotting in sidings during the rest of the time. Worse, many pilgrims suffered the indignity of travelling in covered freight wagons. These were not only dirty, since they were normally used for livestock and perishable goods, but had no sanitary facilities and ventilation in the worst type was only provided by keeping the side door open. As mentioned in Chapter 5, there had been some use of these on normal-service trains, particularly in fourth class, but the railways had phased them out for routine timetabled traffic. However, freight wagons continued to be used for pilgrims because the companies claimed that there was no other way of meeting demand of travel to holy places at peak times. This was not entirely true, since despite claims by the railway companies that these wagons were only deployed at the busiest times, Ritika Prasad found that 'the phenomenon was more widespread. Passengers continued to be transported in "pilgrim specials" and "*mela* [festival] rakes" even when visiting places of pilgrimage that attracted people all the year round'.[12]

The local pilgrim committees, which were official bodies appointed in 1912, were highly critical of the use of these wagons, particularly because they had no sanitary facilities and it was inevitable that the wagons soon became major sources of infection. Nevertheless, the railway companies insisted on retaining this primitive form of accommodation and justified their decision with the usual obfuscation: 'The NWR [North Western Railway] argued there was as much danger of infection in a passenger carriage as in a wagon, while the EIR [East Indian Railway] insisted that seats would increase the discomfort of passengers and wooden wagons were harder to disinfect and thus more likely to carry disease.'[13] Several other railways, such as the Oudh & Rohilkund, the Madras & Southern Mahratta, and the Bombay, Baroda & Central India, were still using them during the period of the First World War, while the South Indian Railway was one of the few which overtly eschewed their use, despite overcrowding during pilgrimages.

Pressure from the committees led to the companies no longer using steel wagons without ventilation, which were clearly unsuitable in the summer heat. However, for the most part, the railway companies' response was much like their earlier excuses about not providing toilets and cramming people into third-class carriages, arguing that these were the conditions in which local people were content to travel. This attitude was summed up neatly by the suggestion from the directors of the narrow-gauge Barsi Light Railway that the pilgrims on the way to Pandharpur (in Maharashtra) for the Vithoba temple were lucky to have an extra – and consequently cheap – way of travel that was denied to their European counterparts.

The pressure on the companies during the final years of the First World War not to use these wagons intensified after the end of the conflict and resulted in an agreement that they would only be deployed when there was genuinely no alternative. The Railway Board tried to discourage the operation of these wagons by requiring the companies to report every occasion they were deployed, but these records show clearly that they were used right up to Independence. Some companies resorted to charging pilgrims a premium, usually one anna, to provide better sanitary facilities, an arrangement that caused particular anger among passengers who thought they were being asked to pay for their religious beliefs.

The pilgrims and other passengers travelling in conventional third-class accommodation fared better, but conditions were by no means ideal and frequently led to complaints. As early as 1873, a doctor, M. C. Furnell, recounted the scene at Allahabad when his train stopped to pick up many pilgrims: 'The confusion, noise and apparent helplessness of the people surpassed anything I have ever seen.'[4] He went on to describe how the pilgrims, mostly elderly, were packed rather brutally by the British guard into the carriages until the train 'swallowed the crowd ... like a gorged boa constrictor'. He was rather shocked that when he pointed out to a European guard that the pilgrims were in some difficulties, the somewhat cheery response was that the 'pilgrims is worse than 'osses, Sir'.

This type of treatment seems to have been routine well into the twentieth century. The advent of the railways may have made the pilgrims' journey a lot faster, but not much more pleasant. Various petitions sent to the Viceroy from pilgrim organizations in 1914 replicated many earlier complaints about their treatment. The overcrowding and unsanitary conditions caused a range of problems. There was the ever-present fear of sexual impropriety and breaches of caste sensibilities, with one petition describing 'the promiscuous huddling together' entailed in railway journeys and stressing how such proximity left Hindu pilgrims 'unable to eat or even drink water because people of other castes were present in the same compartment'.[15] There were well-founded concerns, too, that disease would be spread by the cramped conditions and the failure by the companies to clean carriages. In response to this threat, the Government of India hired the internationally renowned rail travel company Thomas Cook and Son to improve facilities for pilgrims and to help them whilst in transit at stations. The arrangement, which began in 1886, lasted for seven years and, as Ian Kerr points out, was an 'ironic effort': 'The English firm that pioneered tourist travel (including the use of railways for excursions) in its modern form, a Christian firm (Thomas Cook was devout) headquartered in London, had been given the task of facilitating the perfor-mance of the hajj by South-Asian Moslems.'[16] Thomas Cook's involvement petered out when fewer pilgrims sought to use the company's services.

The privations of the journey did not prevent a significant increase in the numbers travelling to pay their respects to the gods once they were able to travel by train. The railways gave an opportunity for hundreds of thousands of new pilgrims, but, as we have seen, the companies made little effort to make the journeys of these pilgrims bearable. Mahatma Gandhi, in fact, was rather scathing about these new pilgrims, suggesting that, without going through the hardship of a long walk or journey on a bullock cart, the experience of worship was degraded. This seemed rather unfair. Holy places were now able to attract the old and the infirm who would not have been able to travel on the arduous roads. More women, too, became pilgrims because the trip took less time, ensuring they could return to their domestic duties more quickly, and because they could travel more safely.

The railway companies may not have treated the pilgrims well but they realized that pilgrimages were a good earner and ran publicity campaigns in conjunction with religious groups to attract greater numbers. In 1911, the Railway Board published a guide, strangely in English, a language spoken by few pilgrims, to places of pilgrimage, and there were occasional features in the *Indian State Railways Magazine*. Enterprising companies like the Bengal Nagpur Railway encouraged pilgrim travel to particular festivals by handing out leaflets in villages accompanied by the beating of drums. In the 1930s, there were even films produced by the Central Publicity Bureau of Indian Railways 'encouraging travel to pilgrim centres', to be screened in travelling cinema cars on the state-managed railways, though clearly these were aimed at the more affluent potential pilgrims. At the other end of the scale, 'handbills, pamphlets and posters in the languages of South Asia were displayed and distributed at stations, municipal and local board offices and at schools in a context where the literate few could spread the message to the illiterate many'.[17] The 1933/4 annual report by the Railway Board was enthusiastic about the fact that the attempts to foster pilgrim traffic had resulted 'in a remarkable improvement over other years'. The railways were, in a way, the victims of their own success in stimulating pilgrimages.

As with so many aspects of the advent of the railway, its influence was transformational of the nature and extent of pilgrimages. The ability to travel by train to holy sites did not just allow far greater numbers of travellers – it revolutionized the very nature of the experience of pilgrimage. Numbers increased exponentially: 'Railways were the mechanism, the necessary if not sufficient cause of mass pilgrimage.'[18] This was the case right from the outset. In 1846, a surveyor for the Great Indian Peninsula Railway had, three years before the line was approved, undertaken a study into the fares that potential pilgrims would be prepared to pay in order to replace a ninety-two-mile journey by bullock cart with a railway journey taking a matter of hours. The holy sites also changed radically, expanding rapidly to cater for greater numbers. Moreover, the pilgrimage season grew as people no longer travelled in groups to arrive for specific holy days, but, instead, came at different times throughout the year. The holy days remained the busiest period, but the huge increase in numbers meant that many places attracted visitors all year round rather than solely at peak times. Pilgrimages became even more of a business than previously – although in truth there had always been a commercial side to the phenomenon.

Pilgrimages became bound up with another aspect of train travel that was to prove oppressive and attract much criticism from the Indian masses: the attempts to stop the railways becoming the means by which infectious diseases were transmitted across the subcontinent. The prevalence of disease had been largely dismissed in the days of the East India Company as merely one of the penalties of life in the tropics. However, during the Rebellion of 1857, many garrisons were undermanned because soldiers were struck down with disease, and the soldiers' propensity to be ill increased when they travelled. Restricting the spread of disease, therefore, became an important part of military strategy, as Mark Harrison, the author of a book on the colonial public-health programme, explains: 'Public health provisions in British India grew out of, and continued to be shaped by, anxieties aroused by the Indian mutiny of 1857; particularly the unhealthy state of British troops.'[19] The greater good of the native population did not seem to have been a factor in these concerns.

The railways were perceived by the authorities as responsible for the spread of disease, and, therefore, during epidemics stringent control measures were imposed, to the great disquiet of passengers. This response to fears about the spread of disease resulted in travellers being treated as potential carriers who were submitted to a range of indignities. The railways acted as a kind of medical police force, imposing inhumane rules on those seeking to travel in areas affected by disease.

The authorities had become convinced that it was not a coincidence that the increase in the extent and severity of epidemics of cholera and plague in the second half of the nineteenth century happened simultaneously with the growth of the railways. There were lengthy debates about the precise mechanism by which the railways increased contagion of diseases. The numerous cholera epidemics across the subcontinent in the second half of the nineteenth century had led to epidemiologists analysing the source of these outbreaks. There were strong advocates on both sides – 'contagionists', who believed the railways were responsible, and 'non-contagionists', who pointed out that many areas reached easily by the railways did not have outbreaks of the disease and, commensurately, epidemics occurred in places with a sparse or little-used rail network. One of those most vehemently opposed to the idea that the railways spread cholera was the government's sanitary commissioner, J. M. Cunningham, who concluded in his 1875 report that 'over great parts of the country in which cholera was most severe, there are no railways and the roads are often indifferent'.[20]

There was naked politics at play here. Cunningham's assertion was rather at odds with contemporary medical thinking and he was accused of pandering to the needs of the railway companies, which would have been hard hit by quarantine measures and, at a higher level, the needs of Britain's free-trade policies, as foreign governments would be reluctant to take goods from India. As Ritika Prasad concludes, 'questions about how quarantine would affect free trade were a staple in discussions about how transport technologies disseminated disease',[21] and, indeed, it was around the time the report was compiled in the mid-1870s that a substantial increase in railway mileage was taking place. Despite Cunningham's report, by the 1890s the notion that increased train travel was, at least partly, responsible for spreading disease had taken hold. In fact, it is now known that cholera spread by contaminated water and food, and the mortality of local people is greatly increased in areas of famine as undernourished people do not have resistance to the disease. In reality, it is rare for the disease to be transmitted from person to person and therefore Cunningham was largely correct, even if he did not know why.

Plague was a different matter. The Bombay plague epidemic, which began in 1896, resulted in the setting up of inspection areas at many railway stations on several different railways across the nation. Although it was not until after the First World War that the precise nature of the transmission of plague through rat fleas was fully understood, there were suspicions that the railways facilitated its spread. Indeed, railways carried several possible transmitters, including sick passengers, rats, and merchandise or belongings with infected secretions. The authorities realized that a total land quarantine, cutting off Bombay from the rest of the country, was impossible and therefore focused their attention on the railways, or rather, specifically, on the passengers travelling in and out of the city.

The examinations carried out at these inspection areas were in many respects humiliating as they were often performed in an insensitive manner by heavy-handed European sanitary inspectors with little medical training. Essentially, once passengers got on their trains, they became prisoners of the railway and sanitary authorities. Complex rules setting out the process for inspection were issued and resulted in a degrading procedure, frequently involving long waits – and consequently delays – while examinations were carried out, sometimes in public. The carriage doors of trains were locked from the outside between inspection stations to prevent uncon-trolled exits. On arrival, all passengers had to disembark onto the platform, with police watching for any attempts to leave the train on the trackside. Men and women were separated, with the latter being taken behind screens for privacy, where they were examined by female medical staff, some of whom were seconded from the Salvation Army. Particular attention was paid at the inspections to people who looked poor or were wearing dirty clothes. The medical staff had wide discretion in selecting those whose belongings they thought needed disinfection. Passengers refusing to be screened were considered 'contumacious' and were at risk of being locked in the carriage that was sent to a siding as a form of punitive quarantine.

The examinations offended the cultural and religious sensibilities of local people. The standard procedure consisted of checking people's glands near the ear as well as the inside thigh, the armpit and the groin, all parts of the body which could reveal the swellings that are a telltale sign of plague infection. Even being touched by a white person or someone of a different caste would be seen as defiling, and such intimate contact was clearly deeply objectionable to many. Any passengers with signs of fever were detained and sent to be quarantined for seven days, while their goods were disinfected, with no compensation being offered for any damage or loss. Trains were only allowed to proceed once the medical officer had signed off the paperwork. Any coaches that had carried infected passengers were taken out of commission for ten days after being disinfected with a mixture of carbolic acid and water.

Not surprisingly, many passengers resented this intrusive examination and did everything possible to avoid it, such as hiding in carriages or trying to leave stations without being checked. The examinations were perceived by many as part of the British attempt to control the population. The railway companies, some still in the private sector, suffered during this period because not only did these indignities put people off travelling, but also the government discouraged unnecessary travel and tried to restrict the use of the railways. Passengers arriving from stations in areas listed as being at risk of plague were asked to provide detailed information about themselves, such as names and addresses and reason for travelling. This information could be followed up by local-authority officials and village headmen, and therefore large parts of India were effectively turned into a police state, with the railways as the main instrument of surveillance. The native population understandably felt that there was a punitive aspect to the whole process.

The quarantine hospitals were racially segregated, and different classes of Indians were also separated, with better accommodation offered to the more 'respectable' natives. Hospitalization and segregation often led to those selected for further examination losing their job and livelihoods, and, in order to avoid the searches, victims were frequently smuggled out and hidden in their own houses. Moreover, false rumours about the medical process spread rapidly through the population, such as claims that Western doctors killed Indians for experimental purposes, and that inoculation, which was developed by Waldemar Haffkine, a pioneering medical scientist, at the instigation of the Government of India, would lead to death or impotence (interestingly, similar rumours about vaccines are still prevalent today in polio and smallpox campaigns). There were even suggestions that the needles used were a yard long.

There was, too, opposition within government circles, both in India and in the UK. Partly, the objections were motivated by economic considerations, given the damaging effect on a key industry, but there were also complaints from pressure groups in the UK and from more affluent sections of Indian society (those travelling in first and second class were often – but by no means always – exempted from screening), aghast at the treatment of their poorer countrymen. Harrison notes that: 'The desire to sanitise the Indian population, most evident among the military and certain officers of the IMS [Indian Medical Service], was held in check by financial considerations, logistical difficulties, and by opposition from British humanitarians and Indian elites.'[22]

None of these harsh measures proved very effective in countering disease. In the event, very few passengers were detained, and of those only a small percentage developed the disease. Government officials claimed the low number of infections discovered among railway passengers was the result of lack of cooperation, but in reality the very nature of the campaign was ill-conceived from the outset. The railways were not the main agents of dissemination and the plague continued to spread throughout the country. The railway companies were often reluctant to follow the stringent and detailed regulations concerning the spread of disease that had been set out in the Railways Act 1890 and resisted the imposition of inspection areas. The Great Indian Peninsula Railway, in particular, fought a long rearguard action against the government over being required to burn upholstery in any first- or second-class accommodation that had carried infected passengers.

The railways could, however, be held partly responsible for epidemics of cholera and plague that spread through groups of pilgrims in the early twentieth century. In this case, the terrible practice, mentioned above, of using goods wagons to carry pilgrims undoubtedly contributed, given their unsanitary condition, to the spread of disease.

While it was third-class passengers who bore the brunt of the discriminatory practices of the rail companies, elite Indians were not immune to suffering other types of railway-induced humiliation. And occasionally they got their revenge. An amusing but significant anecdote is the story of a journey in a first-class sleeper by Sir Asutosh Mukherjee, who, arriving before the other occupant, bagged the bottom bunk, which most people favour, and went to sleep. Later, when a British passenger who had booked into the same compartment arrived, he objected to sharing the cabin with an Indian, let alone having to use the top bunk. Spying Mukherjee's sandals, which looked well-used, he threw them out of the window of the train and went up to his bed. Mukherjee, however, clearly noticed what had happened, because when the Englishman awoke, he found his jacket missing. After being questioned by his fellow passenger, Mukherjee replied, 'your coat has gone to fetch my slippers'.[23] The Englishman had failed to realize that Mukherjee was particularly distinguished – he was the first Indian to serve as chief justice at the Calcutta High Court and as vice-chancellor of Calcutta University. There were many such examples of British passengers objecting to sharing accommodation with Indians, even when they had paid the fare to travel in premium classes.

Given all the indignities suffered by Indian rail passengers, it was not surprising that the most skilled politician of the nationalist movement, Gandhi, exploited the widespread antagonism towards the railways. Early in his career, he had expressed criticism of the very existence of the railways. His influential book *Hind Swaraj* (Indian Home Rule), published in 1909, was an attack on modernism and he considered railways to be a particularly malign influence. The book is written as an interrogation between 'The Editor' and 'The Reader'. The Reader is the ordinary Indian, curious about various aspects of the country's history and politics, while the Editor is Gandhi himself, setting out his views and vision. The discussion soon turns to the railways after the Editor warns that 'Railways, lawyers and doctors have impoverished the country so much so that, if we do not wake up in time, we shall be ruined', a deliberately ironic comment, given that Gandhi himself was a lawyer.[24] In a long section Gandhi cites all the objections to the railways mentioned in this chapter. He suggests that the railways spread the bubonic plague, and increased the incidence of famines, as people were able to sell excess grain on the open market rather than locally. As mentioned above, Gandhi averred that the railways had cheapened the notion of pilgrimage and accentuated the evil nature of man because bad men were enabled to fulfil their nefarious designs with greater rapidity: 'The holy places of India have become unholy. Formerly, people went to these places with very great difficulty. Generally, therefore, only the real devotees visited such places. Nowadays rogues visit them in order to practice their roguery.'[25] This was part of a wider denunciation of modern society in which Gandhi felt the role of the railways was to propagate evil. Questioned by his interlocutor as to why they did not spread 'good' as well, he replied that 'Good travels at a snail's pace – it can, therefore, have little to do with the railways. Those who want to do good are not selfish, they are not in a hurry, they know that to impregnate people with good requires a long time.'[26] Above all, the railways were the reason for the continued occupation of India by the British: 'but for the railways, the English could not have such a hold on India as they have'.[27]

More pertinent was Gandhi's famous letter to the railway authorities, written in 1917, two years after his return from twenty years in South Africa, in which he sets out, with some wit, his criticisms of the railways. Gandhi made a point of travelling with the people, in third class, although, as a lawyer, he could well have afforded better accommodation. Remarkably, he claimed to have spent a quarter of his time since his return travelling on the railways, an insight into their importance as a means of transport but also to their slowness. In the letter, addressed to the editor of *The Leader*, and later issued as a pamphlet, he took the railway companies to task over the way they breached the rules on passenger numbers and cleanliness.

He describes the discomfort and overcrowding during a trip of 750 miles from Bombay to Madras that required two overnight stays. It showed how the conditions in which people had to travel had changed little since the nineteenth century. Indeed, because there was a massive increase in passenger numbers in the period running up to the First World War, conditions, if anything, were worse. He describes how, initially, until Poona, 120 miles from Bombay, there were not more than the specified limit of twenty-two passengers in his carriage, but, after that, despite the efforts of his travelling companions to keep people out, there were thirty-five or more during most of the trip. At night, 'some lay on the floor in the midst of dirt and some had to keep standing. A free fight was at one time avoided only by the intervention of some of the older passengers who did not want to add to the discomfort by an exhibition of temper.'[28] Dirt was his other chief complaint:

Not during the whole of the journey was the compartment once swept or cleaned. The result was every time you walked on the floor or rather cut your way through the passengers seated on the floor, you waded through dirt. The closet was also not cleaned during the journey and there was no water in the water tank. Refreshments sold to the passengers were dirty-looking, handed by dirtier hands, coming out of filthy receptacles and weighed in equally unattractive scales.[29]

He went through all the familiar grievances. He pointed out that first class was five times the cost of a third-class ticket but the passenger in third class did not enjoy one tenth, let alone one fifth, of the facilities. He reiterated the argument that it was the third-class passengers who paid for the luxuries of those travelling in the better accommodation. While he recognized it was wartime, he argued that the service should be either stopped entirely or run properly, as war was no excuse for the terrible conditions imposed on the passengers. He pointed out that smoking took place everywhere, even in areas where it was not permitted. The toilets were particularly disgusting and 'defied description' as the army of flies around them were a warning against their use: 'I have not the power to adequately describe them without committing a breach of the laws of decent speech,' he wrote, and asked rhetorically that, given the unhygienic conditions: 'Is it any wonder that plague has become endemic in India?'[30]

In a typically populist move, Gandhi suggested that the rajahs, the imperial councillors and even the Viceroy himself should travel in third class and that would ensure rapid change. Gandhi's continued dislike of the railways was exacerbated by a later incident when his youngest son, Devdas, was asked to leave his compartment after two European women complained he was inappropriately dressed. Devdas was wearing what had become standard for nationalists, a *dhoti* (a long piece of cloth worn round the legs and tucked into itself), a vest and a cap. An argument ensued and Devdas only avoided arrest because his identity became known.

As Gandhi intimated, the war had taken its toll on the railways. As in the UK, the railways had been used extensively to export goods and material needed by the troops and suffered from under-investment and a neglect of maintenance and renewal. Given the poor state of the railways, and the growing anger among the population about their performance, immediately after the war the Government of India set up yet another committee to investigate their operation. Chaired by Sir (inevitably) William Acworth, it was to prove the most influential of this string of investigations and resulted in major changes, and indeed considerable improvements, for India's railways.

ESTABLISHMENT
OF THE RAILWAY

THE DISCONNECTION BETWEEN the experience of the European users of the railway and that of the average Indian was quite remarkable. It was as if the conditions endured by Indian travellers took place on a completely different system to the one used by passengers in the premium classes. The disparity was far greater even than between air travellers today. That is well illustrated by a lengthy analysis in the British-based *Railway Gazette*, which produced several special issues on Indian railways in the period before and after the First World War.

The anonymous reporters, who looked in depth at the operation of Indian railways, could not hide their enthusiasm for the system. The first impression was striking:

On an Indian railway, one is at once struck by the smart appearance of the guards and stationmasters in their white uniforms. The price of 'ducks' [cotton canvas trousers and jackets] and of washing being so much less than at home, clean suits are often donned daily ... the permanent way on

many of the lines is magnificently kept but there are exceptions to this remark as to that on cleanliness of the carriages
… all station names and most notices are in English … and
in many places given in four languages.[1]

It all seemed rather like back home, or, indeed, rather better:
'The European waiting rooms are often, in smaller stations,
arranged for the use of passengers by night (bringing of course
their own bedding) with baths, and in most cases good meals …
Good station gardens are sometimes to be found in the south
and as a rule even the smaller stations offer successful examples.'[2]
Even the equivalent of W. H. Smith was available: 'Book stalls
are found at all the larger stations and refreshment rooms … the
food is as good as that in the hotels (more cannot be honestly
said) and reasonable in price.'[3] The only complaint from the
reporter who travelled on the North Western Railway for a later
edition of the *Gazette* was that the menu on the train offered a
bit too much choice:

> *Soup Italian*
> *Boiled fish and butter sauce*
> *Mutton cutlets*
> *Teal salmi [strongly flavoured game duck]*
> *Roast sirloin of beef*
> *Cheese boondia [sweet little garam flour balls]*
> *Albert pudding [a kind of bread pudding]*
> *Strawberry cream and peaches*
> *Cheese biscuit*
> *Dessert and coffee*

The reason for the wide choice, he surmised, was to cater for 'hot weather appetites' and 'customers with livers [who] always complain unless there is ample choice of dishes'.[4] This was clearly very expensive to provide and the *Gazette* admitted that it was not always economic, since on many long-distance trains 'there are only a few upper class passengers who are desirous of taking meals en route but the catering staff has to be prepared to meet emergencies as they arise' – emergencies being, of course, a sudden influx of European passengers. There was also a constant supply of water provided in a reserved compartment with an attendant always on duty to supply ice and 'aerated waters' at any time of the night or day. The *Gazette* saw this as a life saver: 'How essential this is only those can realise who know that too often in India there is death lurking in an unconsidered drink of water, and the same grim visitor has more than once stalked into a compartment on the long journey across the stony wilds of the Deccan or the Scinde desert in pitiless hot weather and claimed a victim that some ice would have saved.'[5]

It was, again, the third-class passengers who were subsidizing the teal and the roast sirloin of beef (the latter, of course, would have been deeply offensive to Hindus had they known how the profits from their fares were being used): 'Despite high first class fares, it is doubtful whether first-class passenger travel was ever remunerative for the railways.'[6] First class was not even the most luxurious form of transport on the railways: 'The private coaches of the agents and government officials are exceedingly well designed and tastefully decorated, but those of the native princes are naturally the more gorgeous.'[7] The *Gazette* did belatedly notice the Indian passengers, reporting that 'the platforms offer a picturesque site with the crowds of natives squatting on the platforms or in the waiting rooms and while the train is in, with the crowds of sellers of sweetmeats, native food, curios (small stuffed alligators, for instance) etc.',[8] but mentioned little about their conditions of travel, other than that they seemed to enjoy being packed in: 'Third and intermediate class had four rows of parallel, longitudinally placed seats ... but the natives appear to enjoy plenty of company.'[9]

However, the *Gazette* realized that all was not well on the railways. There was insufficient investment and consequently India was short of railway track in relation to its size. Much more money was needed. The *Gazette* placed the blame firmly on the fact that the budget for the railways was part of the overall government accounts and was, therefore, dependent on vagaries, such as 'the success or failure of crops, visitations of plague, political or military disturbances, and other things ...'[10] In an argument redolent of that used by supporters of privatization in the John Major government of the mid-1990s, the *Gazette* strongly opposed greater government involvement, suggesting instead that the private sector should fill the investment gap. The author seemed to demonstrate wilful ignorance of the history of Indian railways and their struggle to attract capital which led to the controversial government guarantees, by insisting that there were plenty of potential funders in Britain willing to come forward. Even though, as previously mentioned, since 1900 the railways had turned the corner and begun, taken as a whole, to be profitable, the need to provide security for British investors remained paramount, and without renewed guarantees, which had become politically unpalatable, there was little appetite among private investors to build new lines. Although all the major towns and cities were connected to the network before the outbreak of the First World War, many sizeable and growing urban areas remained off the railway map as India had a far less dense railway system, in terms of track per square mile of land mass, than most European countries or the US. Reaching those places off the railway track was not easy. In these cases, the *Gazette* noted, 'The government provides a tonga – two wheeled covered cart – service to many places where there are no railways … tonga travelling is fatiguing for long distances as the speed averages 9–10 mph and the horses which are frequently changed often gallop or canter for the whole stage.'

In keeping with the political zeitgeist in the UK, the *Gazette* had ideological objections to the involvement of government in the railways: 'The chief objections to state-worked railways in any democratic country are firstly, the danger of the employees putting pressure, by means of the ballot or otherwise, on the government and of the government making the railways part of the political machine – and secondly the loss of efficiency and stifling of enterprise and initiative.'[11]

Ignoring the fact that India was hardly a democracy whilst under British rule, the argument about the public sector has been used by opponents of nationalization, ever since the first lines were built, in debates across the world and was, as we see below, considered in depth by the Acworth Committee. Indeed, these words could well have appeared in John Major's Tory manifesto of 1992, which resulted in Britain's railways being privatized.

The *Gazette*, an influential voice at the time, however, indulged its prejudices. The magazine argued that the 'pressure of native opinion, usually noisy, caused more natives to be employed as officials on the state lines than would be the case were efficiency the sole consideration, or than the companies find desirable'. In fact, the move towards Indianization was well underway by the early years of the twentieth century, stimulated, as we have seen, both by government policy and by the expense and difficulty of recruiting sufficient Europeans and Eurasians.

There was, however, another problem with state-owned railways. They were too nice to their passengers as, according to the *Gazette*, 'for safety sake, all third-class passengers were formerly locked in waiting rooms, as on the Continent, to prevent their attempting to board trains before coming to rest. Now certain of the state lines have been compelled to discontinue this practice as "humiliating to the native".' In fact, locking the passengers who had arrived early for their trains into waiting rooms had not been a widespread practice as it was simply impractical and there were many stations where the passengers could not be prevented from entering the platform before the arrival of the train, as witnessed by the *Gazette* itself, with its description of the numerous sellers quoted above.

The *Gazette* had failed to recognize or reflect the depth of antagonism from the native population towards the railways and their British owners. The tide was flowing in the opposite direction to the *Gazette*'s imperial view. The Indian public, or, more specifically, the Indian elite, took the opposite stance about ownership of the railways. Nationalization would enable more investment and greater control, and fewer remittances to British shareholders.

As we have seen, the Government of India's policy in the early years of the twentieth century was rather confusing since it was assuming ownership of most of the network as the old guarantee contracts ran out, while handing the operations back to the previous owners. By 1908, all the major lines had been purchased or reclaimed by the government and most had been leased out to private companies, creating what was, in modern parlance, a Public–Private Partnership. The involvement of these British companies, which were still run from the UK with a European 'agent' – effectively the Chief Executive Officer – managing the company in India, was hugely unpopular. The Indian public was alert to the contradictions of this policy, and a controversy in 1910 over returning the operation of the South India Railway to its previous owners when the previous contract ran out was to prove instrumental in putting pressure on the Government of India to increase the role of the state in the running of the railways. The matter was raised that year in the Imperial Legislative Council, which despite its name was merely an advisory body, but had recently, following the Indian Councils Act of 1909, seen its predominantly Indian membership greatly increased and had become partly elected for the first time.

Gopal Krishna Gokhale, one of the leaders of the Indian National Congress, made a widely reported speech to the Imperial Legislative Council criticizing the failure of the railways to become sufficiently Indianized, and arguing for their nationalization. He was particularly incensed by the fact that Indians were still being discriminated against in terms of employment:

> Whereas in the Public Works Department, a considerable portion consists of Indians, in the railway service it is only here and there that you find an Indian. Now if all the railways were managed by the Government, the Government would in the first place be more sympathetic to our aspirations than the board sitting in London, and, secondly, the Government would be more responsive to any pressure of opinion put on it.[12]

It was precisely the opposite of what the *Gazette* was advocating. Yet, Gokhale was on the moderate wing of the Indian National Congress, opposed to overthrowing the British and a key influence on Gandhi. His speech, therefore, had all the more impact, and the issue of nationalization was raised on numerous occasions by the Legislative Council in the following decade. Several resolutions passed by the Council urged the appointment of a committee of inquiry into the future ownership and management of the railways. Supporters of greater government involvement stressed that the state could save money as it would no longer have to pay profits to the companies – an argument frequently espoused these days by the Labour Party in Britain – and that a nationalized railway would benefit Indian interests, as it would be informed by local public opinion, rather than by members of a board of directors sitting thousands of miles away in London. There were complaints, too, from nationalists that the railway network was simply not up to its role as the mainstay of the subcontinent's transport infrastructure. They pointed to how the Delhi Durbar, the huge ceremony in December 1911 marking the coronation of King George V, had caused a virtual paralysis in the network for several days because the railways could not cope with the huge crowds seeking to attend. There were, too, permanent bottlenecks in the system, notably the routes to and from the ports of Bombay and Calcutta, which, despite expansion such as quadrupling of sections of track, were unable to cater to the growing demand from both freight and local commuters.

The war only made matters worse. As part of the British Empire, India was immediately placed on a war footing as soon as Germany opened hostilities in August 1914. Inevitably, the railways were crucial to the war effort, but their long-term viability was sacrificed for the short-term benefit of helping the cause. Routine spending on maintenance was cut back and work on major capital projects ground to a halt. Not only was there a strain from the extra services used to send material and men to the front, via the main ports of Bombay and Karachi, but large quantities of railway equipment were exported to France, including locomotives and carriages (despite the need to change the gauge), as well as rails and sleepers. Therefore, repairs could often not be attended to and the condition of the whole system deteriorated markedly. All the equipment on little-used branch lines was removed and exported. Other material such as tools and spare parts was requisitioned for military purposes in East Africa and Mesopotamia (now Iraq), and many Indian railway workshops were transformed into factories for the production of shells, hospital coaches and other war equipment. The railways were also used to transport the thousands of Indian men who were enlisted in far greater numbers than from any other British overseas territory and fought for the British in Europe as well as the Middle East.

After a couple of years of the conflict, the system was at breaking point. As Kerr notes, 'By December 1916, the railroads could no longer handle all the traffic requiring railed transportation, so passenger traffic was curtailed, fares increased, pilgrim traffic prohibited and a Central Priority Committee set up to control goods traffic.'[3] Not surprisingly, these drastic measures had an immediate impact, reducing the number of passengers and the tonnage of goods being carried. Just over 400 million passengers were carried in the year to the end of March 1918, a drop of 50 million, or 13 per cent, from the previous year.

According to Sahni, the official historian of Indian railways, the system 'emerged from the war in a battered and dilapidated condition. Rolling stock was in a state of disrepair and shortage of equipment was made worse by the fact that many locomotives and carriages had long passed the age of superannuation.'[4] The war had left the network in dire straits, much like the railway system in the UK, which had also been greatly overused and neglected in those four years. The inevitable delays and cancellations added to the Indians' antagonism towards the railway companies. Even the official history recognized that the system was near collapse by the end of the conflict: 'Speeds were reduced owing to the worn-out track and ageing locomotives. All this naturally led to the restriction of passenger services, congestion in trains, serious curtailment in the carrying of goods and commodities, [and] unjustifiable economies in maintenance, repair and amenities, leading to wider and deeper public discontent and dissatisfaction.'[5] The railways were the transport lifeline of the nation as the roads were remarkably primitive – and were to remain so until the end of the twentieth century – and therefore there was no alternative but the incredibly slow bullock carts when a railway line was out of commission.

There was no lack of examples of the system's shortcomings: 'Because of the absence of competition, but largely because shortage of capacity in relation to demand enabled railway managers to adopt a take-it-or-leave it attitude, freight consignors did not receive the best possible service.'[6] That was an understatement. Freight train speeds were remarkably slow, averaging at times as little as 4 mph and showing little improvement in the early decades of the twentieth century. Freight was, in fact, the mainstay of the Indian railway, earning at the time around two thirds of its total revenue, and an even higher proportion in some companies. Yet, it was not always profitable because freight rates were determined by government, which was subject to conflicting demands, meaning that throughout the period of company ownership, and, indeed, for the most part right up to Independence, there was an underlying conflict between the railways and government over tariffs, as Westwood explains: 'The government preferred low freight and passenger tariffs, regarding the railways as a means to economic development, while the railways preferred the opposite, having profit as the prime, though not sole, consideration.'[17] By and large, rates remained low, sometimes unprofitably so, although occasionally the railway companies did manage to push up tariffs against the wishes of the Government of India.

The inadequacy of the rail freight service damaged the economy. The coal mines, and consequently the iron and steel industry, suffered greatly from the lack of proper transportation to shift minerals because of the poor state of the East Indian Railway, which had a virtual monopoly of coal transport. After grain, coal was the largest item of freight transport, and the service offered by the East Indian was widely criticized.

The company exploited its monopoly position by imposing high tariffs for the short journeys to Calcutta from the main Bengal coalfields, 150 miles from the port, but charged much higher rates per mile for longer trips. This proved counterproductive; because of the cost of the long rail journey across India, it was cheaper for the mining companies to send Bengal coal to Bombay via Calcutta rather than direct by rail. Instead of a 1,150-mile rail journey, with no transshipment required, the coal was carried on rail for the short trip to the port and then taken more than 2,000 miles by ship through the Palk Strait separating India and Ceylon (now Sri Lanka) to reach Bombay. Although this journey required three transshipments, it remained cheaper than the single long rail journey. The higher rates imposed for long journeys meant, too, that some railway companies whose routes were far from the eastern coalfields actually found it economic to use British coal transported halfway around the world rather than the locally mined mineral.

Merchants and traders were also deterred from using the railways by the considerable rate of loss, partly from pilferage and partly from coal simply falling off overloaded wagons while running on poor track. Consignments were at times completely lost, their valuable cargo purloined by railway staff and local people, and yet the railway company refused to pay compensation or even weigh the wagons when they arrived to assess losses. The war greatly worsened the freight situation. By the end of the conflict, Nagpur (in Maharashtra), a key textile producer, was receiving supplies of cotton up to six months late. The railways were not only paying the price of the wartime effort, but also bearing the costs of the long period of under-investment which preceded the conflict.

The freight rates became a cause célèbre for the nationalists, who argued that the railway tariff policy held back India's development. They complained that, despite the example above relating to coal, by and large freight rates to and from ports were kept down to lower the price of imports from Britain and to reduce the cost of exporting raw materials to the mother country. In 1924, in response to these criticisms, which came largely from Indian business people, a tribunal was established to set and regulate tariff rates across the rail network. Minimum and maximum freight rates were established, restricting exploitation while giving the companies some leeway over charges. Special rates were introduced as well to protect the domestic economy from imports of iron, steel and cement.

Despite all these complaints about the railways from both passengers and freight users, support for nationalization was by no means universal. The provincial councils set up as part of the 1909 reforms were divided in their views. Those in Bombay and Madras favoured state management, while the council in Bengal took the opposite stance. This was because the latter was dominated by European commercial interests and the split in opinion was reflected among the wider business community. The various European chambers of commerce generally favoured the continuation of the status quo, which was hardly surprising given that the railway companies themselves were part of this community, while their Indian equivalents, who had no personal stake in these companies, wanted state management.

The government equivocated throughout the 1910s over its role in the running of the railways but could do so no longer as the contract for the huge East Indian Railway was due to expire in 1919. The government hesitated over whether to continue as before, by handing over the management to a private company, or taking over operations itself. Its response, when faced with having to make a choice, was, in the traditionally British way, to appoint the East Indian Railway Committee,[18] headed by Sir William Acworth, a barrister. He was far more suited to the role than his two predecessors, Robertson and Mackie, as he was also a renowned international railway economist and had written a seminal work on Britain's railway network, *Railways of England* (and a similar tome on Scotland), as well as a textbook, *The Elements of Railway Economics*, based on lectures he gave at the London School of Economics.

Although Acworth was supposed to report solely on the question of public ownership and operation, inevitably he touched on the general state of Indian railways, whose condition had deteriorated in the war and which were owned and managed in a complex structure by diverse public and private bodies. This time, neither the chairman nor the committee members were the type of hapless amateur mentioned in relation to the Robertson Committee. The ten members of the committee, which included three Indians, were each an expert in their field and included major industrialists as well as people with great knowledge of railway systems. As Sahni reported, 'according to witnesses who appeared before the Committee, except in the case of America, where even railways set up originally by the State were transferred to the control of private ownership, the experience of virtually every other country had shown that State ownership and State management was by far the best method of running and developing the railway system'.[19] At the time, in Germany, Japan and Russia, railways had come fully under government control, while France was considering legislation for nationalization (and soon afterwards created the government-owned Société Nationale des Chemins de Fer Français). Similarly, in other parts of the British Empire, such as Australia and Canada, railways were run by the state.

Acworth, a former Tory councillor on the London County Council, was no radical but his report certainly was. He was firmly of the view that the Indian railways should be run by the state as it was simply impossible to justify the involvement of the British companies. At the time he started his enquiry, in 1920, the government owned 27,000 route miles but only managed two thirds of those itself. There were also a further 4,400 miles owned by the princely states and 5,750 in private hands. Not surprisingly, as a result, the system, which by then was the fifth-largest in the world, lacked coherence and consistency.

In a crucial minute written by Acworth on publication of the report in 1921 (which, interestingly, was supported by only four of the nine other committee members, including two of the three Indians), he argued that the very fact that public opinion was so strongly against the management of railways by British companies was a key factor in his thinking. The minute pointed out that the railways had not been built with British money, since investors were only shareholders earning a good rate of return, but rather 'it is by money secured from the Indian taxpayer that the Indian Railways have been almost entirely built. It is the Indian public that uses the railways and pays the railway rates and fares.'[20] The conclusion was unequivocal and one that the Government of India could not ignore, given the eminence of Acworth and his committee: 'We have failed to find any solution of the problem submitted to us consistent with the retention of company management.' Simply put, this meant that when contracts for the management of the railways ran out, they should all be taken over by the state. Indeed, although Acworth revealed that most of the committee members had a 'strong prepossession in favour of private enterprise', he argued that there was no other option than to allow the state to manage the railways.

There were two other main issues to resolve: the structure of the new organization – and in particular whether there should be one central organization or several smaller ones – and the control of finances. Again, Acworth was unequivocal. There was a widespread view that 37,000 miles of railway spread over such a vast country could not be run from one authority in Delhi, but Acworth disagreed. He pointed to France, where nationalization was to be under a single centralized organization, and to Germany, where both mileage and the amount of traffic were greater than in India, which was also run in that way. Moreover, the organization needed to have considerable autonomy in order to ensure it would not be constrained by rules and procedures that would hamper its ability to make commercial decisions free of political influence. Its budget, therefore, had to be separated out from other government finances.

The financial situation of the state-owned railways, whose accounts were merely a line on the government's books and therefore did not have a clear budget, had been a familiar story, and one from which British Rail perennially suffered. When money was plentiful, government was ready to meet its prior promises for railway spending. However, when finances went awry – and in India this was not an infrequent occurrence, especially in relation to bad harvests, which both reduced government income and required expenditure on famine relief – the railways suffered, and making long-term plans for investment proved impossible.

Although the Mackay Committee in 1907 had specifically recommended that the railways be allocated a separate amount of capital expenditure annually in order to be able to plan ahead, in practice this had not happened. Schemes would be cut at a late stage and even routine maintenance might be delayed for want of money. Even the construction of new railways would be halted temporarily in the bad times and the committee quoted the example of the Itarsi–Nagpur Railway, linking present-day Maharashtra and Madhya Pradesh, which was started in 1908, but because of financial difficulties was not completed until seventeen years later, despite facing no particular engineering challenges.

Acworth was convinced that the under-investment in the railways was not the result of the excessive demands placed on the system during the war but, rather, the consequence of the government failing to prioritize their development. Given that the railways had been profitable since 1900, the committee found that had the railway budget been separate from government, 'there would have been no difficulty in providing all the money

Indian State Railways, the nationalized railway system between the wars, produced stunning posters to advertise services, including, remarkably, for the little-used Khyber Pass Railway.

Indian Railways, created after Independence, brought together virtually all the nation's lines and remains a nationalized concern today.

These evocative pictures, taken by the late Chris Gammell, show typical scenes from rural India in the 1980s and are part of a far larger unpublished collection.

The 461-mile-long Konkan railway, completed in 1993, opened a new route south from Mumbai to Maharastra and Goa and was built at a time when many other nations were closing lines rather than expanding their networks.

The Nilgiri Mountain Railway from Mettupalayam to Ooty was one of the last mountain railways to be built because of the difficulties of constructing it on a steep incline. It consequently uses a rack and pinion system, developed initially for a railway in Switzerland, on the lower section.

Thousands of people are killed every year on Indian railways as they are used by pedestrians as walking routes, such as this commuter line in Mumbai, and many people also live on railway land by the side of the tracks.

The accident rate on Indian railways has reduced enormously since Independence, though there are still occasional spectacular crashes, often caused by poor weather. This picture shows a crash at Kasara near Mumbai in September 2012, resulting in one death, caused by a local train derailing and being hit by an express.

Much freight is still manhandled on and off trains in India, though modern containers are beginning to be used. Here we see cement bags being transported in 2011.

Most travellers on Indian railways are dependent on hawkers at stations to obtain food and drink, such as those pictured here at Agra in February 2008.

Crowding, as this scene from a train in New Delhi in 2013 shows, is endemic on Indian railways because they remain the key part of the nation's transport system and are cheap to use.

Passenger numbers are so great at commuter stations in the major cities that any disruption can cause chaos, as seen here at Borivli station in the outskirts of Mumbai when protesters occupied the track following a cancellation of a peak service.

Commuters at Chennai station in March 2013.

The daily chaotic scenes at rush hour outside Sealdah station in Kolkata.

Pictures of the author's trip round India in February 2016. Top row, from left: the author checking his ticket at Kolkata station; a typical second-class carriage at Chennai. Middle row: the author in front of a steam locomotive of the Nigiri Mountain Railway; riding high on the Nigiri. Bottom row: the sole platform at Lakshmipur Road station in Odisha, which means passengers heading north have to climb up from the ballast (*right*).

the railways needed to keep up their programme of growth and development'.[21] The new central organization must, therefore, have its own budget.

This was a momentous change and was effectively the genesis of the Indian Railways that exists today. The government accepted most of Acworth's recommendations and the whole structure of the industry began to change, in what was a creeping gradual nationalization. Over the next three years, the Railway Board was reconstituted with extra powers and far greater independence, and railway finances were separated from government. Oddly, fearful that the finances could go awry, the government soon appointed what it called a 'Retrenchment Committee' – in modern parlance a 'star chamber' to make cuts – to look at ways for the railways to reduce what it perceived as high expenses. The chairman was none other than Sir James Mackay, now elevated to the House of Lords as Lord Inchcape. He was no expert, unlike Acworth, and recommended that the working expenses of the railways should be drastically cut. There were undoubted inefficiencies, but it seemed odd to focus on this aspect when the real problem of the railways was a long period of under-investment and even neglect. Inchcape was concerned that too much money was being invested in the system. As the Board assumed control, it did try to make savings through measures such as reducing staff, making better use of materials and preventing loss through theft and ticketless travel. In truth, however, these efforts were mostly in vain and corruption and theft remained rife, as the *Railway Gazette*, of 1923, noted: 'Not only do portable articles such as glasses, soap and towels soon disappear from the carriages, but the leather straps in the windows and even the bronze or gun metal coat hooks seldom last long … In consequence, a different method of raising windows had to be adopted while the plainest malleable iron fillings are being used in many of the newer carriages.'[22]

Freight was frequently targeted by thieves, and new methods of sealing and locking wagons were being introduced. There were even parts of the rail network where permanent encampments of thieves had been established near the line where trains slowed or stopped at signals so that they could always be ready to pounce and plunder the wagons. The Acworth Committee addressed the corruption issue and discovered that shippers were being asked to pay stationmasters to obtain an adequate supply of wagons, given that there was often a shortage – or at least an alleged one. It was just one of the routine practices of corruption that bedevilled the railway (covered in more detail in Chapter 10).

The gradual nationalization – which would not be completed until after Independence – gathered pace in line with Acworth's recommendations. The East Indian Railway had cynically moved its headquarters from London to India but could not stave off the inevitable. Along with the Great Indian Peninsula Railway, it was taken over by the government in 1925 and was merged with the Oudh & Rohilkand. This meant that the two biggest companies, which between them were responsible for more than a third of overall railway revenues, were nationalized.

Several other railways which had longer contracts were not brought into the government fold until the Second World War, including the Bombay, Baroda & Central India, the Assam–Bengal and the South Indian. However, even the railways which were not immediately nationalized and were still run from London realized that they had to change their policies and pay far greater heed to Indian public opinion.

The first half-dozen years of the new regime, up to 1930, were a boom time for the Indian railways. Passenger numbers rose steeply every year throughout this period, quickly recovering from the wartime restrictions which had seen them drop off temporarily. By 1921, passenger numbers had already reached 560 million per year, compared with just under 200 million at the turn of the century, on a network that had only grown by a few per cent in length. And this trend was to continue throughout the 1920s. It was a virtuous circle: an increase in investment led to widespread improvements which attracted more people to use trains. India was growing economically and clearly that generated quite a lot of this extra traffic.

The population was increasing, too, and commuting was becoming a regular habit in the major cities. There were some other, stranger, factors behind the continued increase. The *Gazette* reported that the Oudh & Rohilkand Railway, for example, enjoyed 'very heavy passenger traffic chiefly due to the fondness of Indians for litigation and to the large number of pilgrims attending religious fairs or "*melas*"'. The rush to seek justice or redress was such, apparently, that 'the timetables are as far as possible arranged to admit of litigants attending courts and returning to their homes every day'.[23] That was quite possibly a first in railway history. The railway reported that weddings, too, a grand occasion in India, where every conceivable relative and long-lost friend is invited, were also a profitable source of revenue. It was probably too tactful to note that funerals were also good business.

The extra income from fares and freight charges, and the guaranteed funds for investment from the government, ensured there was plenty of money available for improvements to the network. The original Mackay Committee had recommended that the optimum route mileage for the entire system was 100,000 miles, compared with the 39,000 miles built by 1924. That was clearly far too ambitious, but the Railway Board developed a plan for rapid expansion of the network. The aim, announced in 1924 as a five-year programme, was to open 1,000 miles of new railway per year. The most significant addition was a 125-mile broad-gauge link in His Exalted Highness the Nizam's Guaranteed State Railways (the official name of the railway in Hyderabad started in 1879 by the local ruler), between Ballarshah in Maharashtra and Kazipet in Telangana. This reduced the journey between Delhi and Madras, a key route connecting northern and southern India, by 200 miles.[24] In the event, more than 4,000 miles of line were built on the Indian subcontinent in the six years running up to 1930, a time when many countries around the world had stopped building new railways. The continued expansion was partly the result of the fact that the network in India was still comparatively sparse in relation to both the land area and to the population, but also because of the growing recognition that, in a country with very poor roads, the railways were the mainstay of the nation's transport infrastructure.

Sensibly, though, the investment funds were not only being spent on building new routes. A comprehensive programme of improvement for all aspects of the railway was implemented. The most notable was the electrification of suburban lines, which greatly speeded up performance. The first electric line, the ten-mile Harbour branch of the Great Indian Peninsula Railway, from Bombay's Victoria Terminus (now the Chhatrapati Shivaji Terminus but still known locally as VT) to Kurla, was opened with great ceremony in February 1925, and other suburban lines in the city soon followed.

Bombay was the natural location for electrification given its high density and its geography. The city is built on seven islands and a peninsula, and therefore access to the centre is constrained, giving railways a distinct advantage. Consequently, the city had a symbiotic relationship with its railways, the two growing in tandem with the suburban lines underpinning Bombay's rapid expansion. The city's textile industry required ever greater numbers of workers and commuting had already become a way of life for many by the turn of the century, when there were 400,000 local journeys daily on the tracks of the Great Indian Peninsula Railway and the Bombay, Baroda & Central Indian Railway, which both had a series of suburban stations. As Ian Kerr puts it, while various forms of motorized and animal transport developed in the suburbs, 'only the trains, however, historically and today, could provide the mass transportation the commuters of the ever-growing Greater Bombay needed'.[25] The two railways had to cope with carrying both vast quantities of raw cotton and manufactured textiles, as well as commuters, and consequently electrification was accompanied by the addition of tracks on many parts of the system, including even some four-tracking of particularly busy sections. The *Railway Gazette*, for once, was delighted, positively purring: 'Electrification would be the most profitable expenditure the Government could make on railways today.'[26]

Interestingly, the oldest railways in India became the early pioneers of electrification. The suburban line to Kalyan, and the main route to Poona over the ghats, soon followed. The latter was selected for conversion because the extra power of the electric locomotives increased the speed and efficiency on this very heavily trafficked line, eliminating what had long been a bottleneck for services to and from the ever-expanding city. This knocked sixty minutes off the journey time between Bombay and Poona, reducing it to just three hours. This proved a great boon to members of the Bombay elite, who enjoyed nothing more than a day at the races at Poona's Royal Western India Turf Club, the most prestigious racecourse in India, as the faster trains allowed them to get there and back easily in a day. The suburban system in Madras was also electrified by 1931, but then the Depression, with its reduction in rail traffic, stopped the programme. A plan to electrify Calcutta's urban network was shelved, and not restarted till 1957, and no other lines were converted under the Raj.

There were plenty of other improvements in what was truly a golden period for the railways, and the system received something of a total makeover: the track bed, signals, workshops, locomotives, coaches and goods wagons were all modernized, and much new equipment was purchased. There was innovation, too, with the first colour-light automatic signals being introduced, along with larger freight wagons and new heavier locomotives, which allowed for bigger loads and shorter journey times. Some services were speeded up, though the railways remained, by international standards, rather slow. On the largest railway, the Bombay, Baroda & Central India Railway (3,850 route miles), the fastest service was the Frontier Mail, which covered the 865 miles between Bombay and Delhi in 23 hours 35 minutes, an average of 37 mph.

The quickest trains were those connecting with the P&O sailings to Bombay. In the early 1920s, the Great Indian Peninsula Railway operated express boat trains from the port to Madras, Delhi and Calcutta. These were seen as the most important services because they were part of the fastest connection between the UK and the major Indian cities, which it was now possible to reach in two weeks. Every Friday evening, in the early years of the twentieth century, a train left Cannon Street station in London for the coast, carrying passengers bound for India. After the short Channel crossing to Calais, they proceeded by rail to Brindisi on the Italian Adriatic Coast. From there, a small P&O steamer would take the passengers – and the mail bound for India which had travelled in a second train – to Port Said in Egypt, where a larger liner would convey them through the Suez Canal and on to Bombay. The Indian boat train services would meet this train precisely two weeks after the passengers had left London and transport them and the mail through to India's other major cities at average speeds of around 36 mph. In comparison, in the UK during the interwar period the best trains routinely ran at an average speed of between 50 and 60 mph. Given the requirements of stops to allow people to eat and to take on water for the locomotives, and the maximum speed limit of 60 mph, such average speeds could never be achieved in India. Metre-gauge trains were even slower. For example, the relatively fast service connecting Madras with Tuticorin, connecting with the boat to Ceylon, took nearly twenty-two hours to cover the 443 miles, an average of a mere 20 mph. Those metre-gauge trains, which ran on little-used, single-track lines, often shared with freight trains, were even more sluggish, struggling to reach an average of 15 mph, which meant that even a run of a couple of hundred miles would normally require an overnight stay on the train.

Many stations were rebuilt in this period. There had long been a move away from the notion that stations should be built as fortresses which would provide a redoubt and protection for Europeans in the case of a repeat of the 1857 Rebellion. In the last quarter of the nineteenth century, there had been a return to building stations in city centres rather than outside them, which had been justified on the basis that they would be easier to protect in the event of a riot. (There was a counter-argument, too, in that city-centre stations would allow troops to arrive rapidly by train to where the riot was likely to be taking place, such was the convoluted thinking indulged in by India's colonial masters.)

Several magnificent stations were built in the belief that their aesthetic value would be appreciated by the local population, demonstrating that the railways were an elegant instrument of peaceful development rather than an ugly colonial imposition. The most impressive was undoubtedly the Victoria Terminus in Bombay, built in a Gothic Revival style, partly redolent of St Pancras, over a ten-year period, ending in 1888. Designed by Frederick William Stevens, it was the headquarters of the Great Indian Peninsula Railway and was extended in 1929 to accommodate more long-distance trains. The station's revamp was celebrated with the launch of the fastest main-line train in India, the *Deccan Queen*, which replaced the slower *Poona Mail*, and became the continent's first luxury train, offering accommodation solely to first- and second-class passengers and running just at weekends to serve Bombay's mainly European spectators for the races at Poona. It halved the journey time of the old *Poona Mail* and for a time, hauling only a few elegant carriages, managed the 120-mile trip in just 2 hours 45 minutes, an average of 43 mph. The Great Indian Peninsula thought it unprofitable to run the train during the week, and, according to the history of the Victoria Terminus, only in 1943 'when Indians were allowed to travel on the train did traffic increase sufficiently to allow a daily service'.[27] It was not until 1966, however, that third-class travellers were allowed to travel on the train.

Several other major stations were reconstructed at the time, notably in Lucknow, Howrah and Kanpur. At times of heightened tension, however, they could still be turned into fortresses, with armed soldiers at every corner housed in military posts and sentry boxes. As an obvious site of protest, and also being the key entry points to the country's main form of transport, the protection of stations was forever uppermost in the minds of the colonial rulers.

Despite the widespread improvements for rail passengers, there remained considerable discontent with the railways. A good measure of the level of dissatisfaction was the disproportionate time spent in the Legislative Assembly on railway matters. A remarkable 30 per cent of questions[28] raised in the Assembly in the year 1927/8 concerned the railways, covering a wide variety of topics, such as the Indianization of the railway service, new projects and even the purchase of coal. Passenger grievances remained high on the agenda, not least because, despite quasi-nationalization and considerable investment, little had been done to improve the lot of the third-class passenger, while the cosseted first-class travellers enjoyed ever greater luxury, such as the baths in every compartment of first class introduced during this period by the East Indian Railway.

In spite of such complaints, the implementation of Acworth's recommendations resulted in a much improved railway in the interwar period. The editor of the *Railway Gazette*, writing at the end of the decade, was positively lyrical, noting that thanks to Acworth:

the railway administration for the first time were able to frame development programmes with the assurance that funds would be made available and as a result the past five years has been a period of ceaseless activity in the provision of facilities essential to meet the needs of the growing traffic. Remarkable improvements have been made and these have naturally been reflected in the financial position which, in the whole of Indian railways, has never been better.[29]

The editor went on to quote Sir Clement Hindley, the Chief Commissioner, Indian Railways, who reported how during the 1920s the railways had made 'a remarkable recovery from a condition of insolvency and inefficiency amounting almost to a breakdown to undoubted financial prosperity and a state of efficiency as measured by public service which will bear comparison with the standard of any other railway system in the world'.[30]

It was not, though, all plain sailing for the railways. Even with the availability of a steady flow of funds and a far better structure to allow the railways to flourish, massive waste in spending that money and poor industrial relations were flies in the ointment. As is usual with organizations that suddenly find themselves flush with cash, there were issues of overspending, as Sir Charles Innes, the member of Legislative Council responsible for the railways, pointed out: 'The principal difficulty with which we are now confronted is that of spending the money, that is, of executing rapidly sanctioned projects.'[31] Schemes were costing as much as twice the original budget and local officials were given carte blanche to spend without adequate checks and with no recognition of the need to get value for money. To be fair, Indian railways were by no means the only ones guilty of gold-plating projects, particularly in the interwar period when railways across the world were beginning to face the full-on competition of cars and planes and were desperate to improve their technology.

Labour disputes, as we have seen, began to spread in the early years of the twentieth century, but it was after the war that they became far more prevalent. This was part of the interwar worldwide phenomenon of worker unrest, which led to revolutions in several countries, and to increased unionization almost everywhere else. The Indian railway unions grew rapidly in this period: the All India

Trade Union Congress was formed in 1920 and, four years later, an All India Railwaymen's Federation was created, with a dozen smaller unions as affiliates with a combined membership of around 200,000. The railway unions remained highly fragmented, with many small ones representing a particular trade, but also, just to add further complication, others based on caste or region. White-collar unions emerged during the same period, even though the workers undoubtedly had an easier time. More-educated Indians favoured clerical tasks, but the *Railway Gazette* complained how many were eager for an easy life: 'far too many clerks willing to sit on their stools for 20 rupees per month and too few who would earn up to 100 rupees per month as a clerk in the shops', where the work was harder and more intense.[32] The *Gazette*, ever close to overt racism, put this down to the failure of the Indian 'character'.

During the First World War, the shortage of labour and the rise in inflation that routinely accompanies conflict forced the railways to increase wages and allowances quite substantially, and some companies provided subsidized food grains as the war had caused prices to rise sharply. The rising trend of employment in the industry had continued apace and by 1921 there were 725,000 workers in the rail industry, mostly low-paid. The variety of tasks was immense, ranging from porters at stations and gangers on the permanent way to train examiners and even ferrymen, since the railways owned and operated numerous ships to navigate unbridged rivers. As the state took on more railways, Indian Railways became, by far, the biggest civil employer in India and, indeed, across the world, although it has now been overtaken by Wal-Mart.

There were inevitably many sources of dispute. Basic wages and conditions were, of course, often the issue, as well as the desire for job security. There was an inherent tension in the industry as most managers and foremen were still European or Eurasian, despite the various attempts at Indianization. The railways retained many petty rules and regulations, which frequently led to arbitrary fines being imposed, and there were numerous other disciplinary measures that demeaned the Indian workforce. The unions were strongest in the 145 major workshops dotted across India, but firemen, who were virtually all Indian, were also well-organized. Collective bargaining, almost unknown before the war, began to be the norm and in 1929 the government reluctantly recognized the All India Railwaymen's Federation, setting up regular meetings with the union representatives.

There was the added radicalizing effect of the nationalist movement, which stimulated further discontent. The movement tried to exploit industrial disputes, sending in their agitators to liaise with the strikers. However, the relationship between the unions and nationalists was by no means a simple matter of mutual support. There was an expectation that the two groups always had common cause, but this was not necessarily the case, and, in fact, as we shall see, after Independence the Congress Party formed its own railway union in competition with the Federation. Nevertheless, the railway workers were a considerable force in society and many became active in the nationalist movement. There was undoubtedly a political undertone to the growing militancy of the workforce, as Khosla explains in his official history of Indian railways: 'Workers resorted to these strikes not purely from the motive of forcing railway management to give them higher wages and better working conditions, but also to give expression to the national upsurge against a system, which has been largely exploited to serve the political ends of a foreign power.'[33] Indians, in other words, were getting their own back.

According to Sahni, there were no fewer than forty-eight strikes in the financial year 1921/2, 'lasting from a day or two to three months'.[34] The East Indian Railway was particularly badly hit by a variety of disputes. In December 1921, for example, 7,000 workers, almost the whole workforce of the Lillooah works near Calcutta, walked out over a pay settlement. The disruption continued for a couple of months and led to riots at Howrah station the following February. Numerous other railways, such as the Oudh & Rohilkand, the Madras & Southern Mahratta and the Great Indian Peninsula, suffered from major industrial action in this period. The most bitterly fought strike was on the South Indian Railway in June to August 1928, when thousands of workers, angered over proposals for 3,200 redundancies and widespread pay cuts, walked out of their workshops and staged Gandhi-style sit-ins along the tracks. They managed to close down much of the rail network, and some 75,000 workers were then promptly locked out by the management. The Government of India was anxious that the unrest should not spread to other railways, which were also under pressure to reduce costs, and took a very hard line, sending in the police to break up demonstrations. The government was particularly concerned that the strike would become a cause célèbre for the nationalists and therefore tried to nip the protests in the bud. Armed escorts were provided on train services that were still operating, but several trains were derailed and there were numerous outbreaks of violence between the police and the workers. With the police making repeated *lathi* attacks (baton charges) and even using bayonets at times, the strikers' resolve was broken and they went back to work after a few days, although incidents and protests continued until the beginning of August.

The readiness of the government to take such strong action showed how the railways were viewed as an important symbol of the rule of the Raj: 'The South Indian Railway strike illustrated the lengths to which the colonial government would go to protect the smooth running of the railway system against any and all perceived threats ... They realized that a successful strike by the mammoth railway labour force could easily have had a cascading effect on other sectors of industrial production.'[35] While the more confrontational managers tried to have strikes made illegal, others sought conciliation, and there was even a suggestion for workers' representatives to be appointed onto railway companies' boards, an idea well before its time that was summarily rejected. However, as we see in the next chapter, towards the end of the decade trade unions did become recognized.

The 1920s also saw the last splutterings of the policy of using the railways as a form of defence, with the renewal of the construction of military railways. The most ambitious railway built during this period was the famous line up the Khyber Pass. Russia was, again, the main potential *casus belli*, despite the fact that its ignominious defeat in the Russo-Japanese War of 1904–5 demonstrated all too obviously that the notion of waging a distant war using a very long single-track railway line was a non-starter. The inadequacy of the recently built Transsiberian in that conflict, which left the Russians short of troops and materiel, should have put an end to British concerns over the potential invasion of India from the north-west.

The doves, who made precisely that point, did prevail for a while. The government refused to accede to demands for continued construction of railways in the North-West Frontier by the Viceroy, Lord Minto, a hawkish supporter of military expansion (his most famous quote was 'The *Raj* will not disappear in India as long as the

British race remains what it is, because we shall fight for the *Raj* as hard as we have ever fought'), who replaced the more measured Curzon in 1905. In its reply, the government dismissed the notion of aggression from Russia, as quoted in Stuart Sweeney's book on Indian military railways: 'Afghanistan was now "as undesirable from the Russian point of view as from our own" since it would tie down resources while yielding little. If railways no longer deterred Russian aggression in Afghanistan, nor improved internal security with hostile Afghan tribesmen on the Indian border, [the report] suggested that the external defence rationale for Indian railways was dead by 1906.'[36]

Not so. The hawks eventually prevailed thanks to yet another conflict with Afghanistan, straight after the First World War, which gave the more bellicose members of the government the chance to resurrect their pet project. There were in fact 300 passes through the mountains of the North-West Frontier, and some particularly combative generals had wanted railways constructed up all of them. The most obvious gap in the potential defences against a hostile Afghanistan was the Khyber Pass, which was the most direct trade route between India and central Asia via Kabul, and was in fact part of the old Silk Road.

As we saw in Chapter 5, several railways ran up to the Indo-Afghani border and the hope among the more optimistic hawks was that, this time, a railway could be built right into Afghanistan. A survey of the Khyber Pass in 1890 had concluded that it was impassable, but in 1901 the North Western Railway, which was a state-owned company created in 1886 by merging the various railways that were mostly in what is now Pakistan, built a line to Jamrud, the entrance to the Pass. Construction actually started in 1905, but progress was slow and an alliance with Russia meant there was no longer a political imperative to continue the work. Consequently, in 1909, the whole scheme was abandoned and the twenty miles which had been laid were torn up in order for the material to be recycled.

However, the Third Afghan War, which started in 1919, and the fear of expansionary policies by the Bolshevik government which came to power in 1917 renewed interest in the line. A military surveyor, Colonel (later Sir) Gordon Hearn, was despatched to examine the best potential alignment for a railway and, despite previous doubts about the impossibility of the task, he found a route suitable for a single-track broad-gauge railway. It was to be built entirely through tribal territory, officially designated as the Khyber Agency, 'under the care of the Political Agent of the Khyber where there was in those days no law but tribal custom, and where human life and property were lightly esteemed'.[37] Not only was the terrain difficult, but it was, too, a period when the local tribes were likely to be particularly hostile given the war.

The risk of attack was largely allayed by the clever ploy of hiring local people to build the line and they proved to be highly efficient and effective workers. As a result, many enriched themselves from the high wages paid to persuade them to work, and apart from the occasional dispute, often the result of historic inter-tribal conflicts, there was little trouble. Construction of the line, though, was a heroic enterprise involving the laying of tracks through inhospitable country with few local resources, except, bizarrely, flows of water in sufficient number to ensure workers had enough to assuage their thirst and, later, refill locomotive tanks. Construction was given continued impetus by the further bellicose propaganda back home. A reporter for a noted illustrated paper warned of the 'Russian menace' and the stealthy advance of the Bolsheviks, who were allegedly secretly building a railway in Afghanistan. There were even photographs, but the only problem was that they were, in fact, pictures of the Khyber Railway, itself under construction.

The sheer statistics of the legendary railway hardly do justice to the scale of the achievement. The thirty-two-mile line required thirty-four tunnels with a total length of three miles, as well as ninety-two bridges, and there were four reversing stations, where, as on the line through the ghats built nearly three quarters of a century previously, trains had to be driven along a track hewn out of the mountain towards a precipice protected only by a flimsy buffer stop, and then reversed up to continue climbing (or descending). The average gradient was 2 per cent – a rise of nearly 2,000 feet in twenty-one miles, enough to tax the strength of the locomotives and the skill of the drivers. The line included six sections of double track where trains could pass each other, as well as extensive sidings and modern signalling to ensure its viability as a troop carrier.

The railway was completed to Landi Kotal, the top of the pass, in November 1925, when a lavish ceremony was held, marred only by the absence of the Viceroy as a result of illness, and the following year the railway was continued a couple of kilometres down to Landi Khana. However, it is unclear whether tracks were ever laid right up to the customs post at Torkham, possibly due to opposition from the local Afghani ruler. The importance of the enterprise can be judged by the fact that the heir to the throne, the Prince of Wales (the future King Edward VIII), visited the region during construction of the line.

The reason for this massive deployment of resources remained unclear. Even P. S. A. Berridge, the engineer in charge, who later wrote a book on the railways of the North-West Frontier, was pretty gloomy, admitting that he had probably wasted his time and the government's money, though that, rightly, made him no less proud of the achievement: 'The Khyber Railway was the last of the great railway constructions undertaken on the frontier during the British Raj. Whether the enormous cost was justified no one can ever tell, but it brought wealth to the tribesmen who helped to build it and proved that a railway could be constructed through the "most impossible" country.'[38]

It wasn't his fault that the Khyber Railway was a misguided enterprise. Despite the huge cost of £1.6m (about £90m in today's money) – which worked out at £50,000 per mile, ten times the average per mile spent on the Russian lines on the other side of Afghanistan, making it the most expensive railway ever built in India – it proved to be largely useless, and was pretty much a white elephant from the start. It was never used militarily and when opened never exceeded two trains per week, which were mainly patronized by the local tribespeople who had been appeased by a promise they would be able to use it for free. (Indeed when, in the 1990s, a private service, the Khyber Train Safari, was launched aimed at affluent adventurous tourists, the tribespeople had not forgotten this offer and many availed themselves of free journeys. The presence of these armed locals in traditional garb did not go down too well with the posh punters who had paid top dollar to ride on the famous Khyber Pass and were reported to be rather taken aback by their presence.)

The line closed in 1932 when a section of track was washed away, but was reopened by Pakistan in 1947, largely on military grounds. However, it shut again in 1982 because it was so uneconomic, given the high cost of maintaining the track and the paucity of passengers. An enterprising travel company began operating tourist trains in the mid-1990s, which ran till 2006 when damage to the line by floods, and the series of conflicts in the region which deterred even the hardiest of tourists, led to the line's permanent closure. However, in 2015 the Pakistan government expressed interest in reviving the railway and commissioned a survey into its viability, but nothing is likely to come of this initiative while the political instability in the region continues.

The Khyber Pass may have been the most expensive of these military railways on the North-West Frontier, but the accolade of the least used goes to the Nushki Extension Railway, a 450-mile branch of the Sibi–Quetta line running westwards to Zahidan, fifty miles over the border into Persia (now Iran). The purpose of what became known as 'The Lonely Line', which started to be constructed during the First World War, was, like the other railways in the region, strategic, linking India with Persia in order to protect the eastern border of Persia, alongside the Russians, who were still allies at that point. The idea was that the troops based in Quetta would be transported rapidly westwards on the railway to ward off any invasion of Afghanistan by the Germans or Turks, and they would also be able to link up with British forces based in eastern Persia. There was also the suggestion that the line might carry oil from the Persian wells to India. It could have been the first railway to link the subcontinent with Europe, except for the fact that its terminus, Zahidan, was not connected to the rest of the Persian rail network (it was eventually linked in 2009, though through trains remain impossible because of the change in gauge).

The cost of its construction fell on the Government of India, though the British did pay for the section running into Iran. Around 100 miles of the line, between Quetta and Nushki, had been completed in the nineteenth century and work on the extension towards Persia was started by the British army in late 1916. Running in the desert south of the Afghan mountains, the terrain was flat, making tracklaying relatively easy, but the incessant sandstorms and the lack of water held up construction. Conditions in the treeless, parched desert were among the most difficult faced by any railway builders across the world. For eight months of the year, the temperature reaches 40°C or more every day and the workers on the line had to endure what the locals call the 120-day wind – which Berridge says 'actually blows unceasingly for five months of the year [and] lashes the coarse sand so that it cuts the skin like a sand-blast'. He added: 'The whole country is coated with sulphur dust, and water when it is obtainable is a concentrated solution of mixed common and Epsom salts.'[39]

The completion of the Nushki Extension Railway was delayed by a shortage of water and lack of equipment, and construction was eventually halted as a result of the end of the First World War and the Russian October 1917 revolution, which, in fact, changed the strategic objectives. Consequently, the line only reached Zahidan, its terminus in Persia, six years later, by which time not only was the war long over, but the Russians were no longer allies since the new Bolshevik regime had sued for peace with the Germans after the revolution. There was now a Soviet threat which the military used to justify building this remote railway despite the change in the global situation and their strategic objectives. Presumably, the hawks in the military argued that the line might be useful in a further conflict, given the fluidity of regional alliances, but, nevertheless, that seemed a thin excuse to justify the high cost and the operational difficulties.

There were only fourteen stations or, rather, halts, on the whole line and virtually no inhabitants to use them, apart from nomadic tribes. 'The Lonely Line' certainly deserved its moniker given that it traversed a region so remote that the railway company had to ensure it had a well-stocked buffet car in order to feed and water the passengers during the not infrequent occasions when the train broke down and had to await rescue.

The trains and their few passengers faced two main risks from the terrain and the climate. When there was rain, the whole year's fall might occur in a few hours, which caused flash flooding sufficient to douse and extinguish a steam engine's fire. Drivers had to carefully judge whether they would be able to plough through the pools of water with sufficient momentum or wait for them to recede. A slower but potentially worse risk was caused by the 'marching sandhills', known locally as *do-reg*. This is not a matter of a few small mounds of sand but rather 'crescent shaped sandhills formed by the wind [which are] constantly on the move'.[40] They move at up to 600 metres per year and consequently, at times, new tracks had to be laid to avoid the new mountains of sand covering the rails. The old tracks were left in situ so that the trains could return to them if the *do-reg* moved again. Occasionally, the marching sandhills covered the track so quickly that the train would have to stop and all the male passengers would be required to help dig it out or even relay the track. With remarkable foresight, the railway company left spare lengths of rails, shoes and sleepers alongside the line in readiness for such an emergency, probably making it the only railway in the world where paying passengers were required to help build the railway on which they were travelling.

The heroic effort of the Nushki's construction was pretty much in vain. There was just one weekly train in each direction, which took forty hours, an average of 12 mph, for the journey, but the service only survived for a decade. A 140-mile section between Nok Kundi and Zahidan was dismantled in the 1930s because there seemed little point in keeping the train running given the paucity of passengers. However, this section was hastily relaid in 1940, as a result of the outbreak of the Second World War, and for a while during the conflict the Nushki Extension Railway was used for transporting tea and sulphur. It was also reopened because it was envisaged that the line might help transport supplies for the USSR via a back route through Persia, but in fact the materiel never arrived for transport on the railway and it was not used for this purpose. Taken over by Pakistan at Partition, the line, now called the Trans-Baluchistan, has survived and operates a service once a fortnight.

A rather more useful construction during the interwar period was the Kalabagh Bridge over the Indus, in what is now Pakistan, which took four years to build because of the width of the river and its rapid flow during the spring. Berridge was in no doubt about the value of what was the longest railway bridge built before Partition, which 'affording permanent rail access to the fertile irrigated lands beyond the Indus and bringing better trading conditions to the men of the frontier, has played its part in harnessing the resource of nature to the benefits of mankind'. While a barrage had tamed the Indus downriver from the bridge, Berridge wrote that it was the railway which was 'the agent of civilisation', and enabled the conversion of 'arid desert to rich fertile land under the vast irrigation schemes', with the result that 'No longer does the tribesman of the wild north-west have to go marauding to survive starvation.'[41]

However, the rapid growth and financial success of the railways during the 1920s was soon to be brought to an abrupt end by the Wall Street Crash of October 1929 and the ensuing worldwide depression. While there would be no more crazy projects built for spurious military objectives, the downturn also spelled the end for the continuation of the greatly needed expansion programme that had seen many useful additions to the network in the interwar period. The economic crisis that lasted for much of the following decade hit India hard because of its reliance on exports and its lack of domestic industry.

NINE

TOWARDS INDEPENDENCE

THE GOOD TIMES came to an end quickly. Within a year of the Wall Street Crash, passenger numbers started falling and, more significantly, freight tonnages plummeted. The worldwide economic crisis had an immediate impact on India as it was highly dependent on its exports of raw materials. The introduction of protectionist policies by the United States, which imposed extra tariffs on many imports, proved deeply damaging both to the Indian railways and to the wider economy, sparking off a decline in railway revenues that lasted until 1937, by which time a third of the railways' income had been lost.

The railways did not only suffer a downturn in traffic. They were also failing to become more efficient, which meant less money was available for investment in new lines, equipment and maintenance. The successes of the 1920s, when passenger numbers rose steadily, meant that little attention had been paid to the economic performance of the railways. However, when passenger numbers stopped rising and costs remained high, their relative inefficiency caused consternation in government circles.

Until the First World War, productivity had been on an ever upward curve, as would be expected in an industry with a rapidly improving technology, but the conflict had left the railways in a parlous state, requiring massive amounts of capital investment to renew the infrastructure and the rolling stock. However, the new investment, far from making the railways more productive in relation to each pound invested, had the opposite effect. Many extra workers were employed because of a tendency of the rail companies to take on extra staff along with the introduction of new equipment. The tradition of overstaffing in the railways dates from this period but the underlying reasons for it remain unclear, though at root it is undoubtedly down to the weak management of the network. Interestingly, Britain's railways, too, experienced a similar level of inefficiency during the interwar period and in both nations there seems to have been a failure to exploit the potential of modern technology to reduce the need for labour.

John Hurd, an economist who has written extensively on India, suggests that managerial 'arteriosclerosis' might have played a role: 'Many of the directors of management companies were old India hands, chosen for their connections but not necessarily for their knowledge of running complex organisations that were designed, in theory, to serve the public.' While many directors were engineers, this did not mean they were good at making long-term decisions over investment in proposed projects. Others, however, were barely *compos mentis* as, according to Hurd, 'some directors were so aged, in their 90s, that they had to be carried into the meetings'.[1] The minutes of these meetings, invariably held in London, reveal that the focus was not always on the most urgent matters. It was not unusual, for example, that these illustrious men – and, of course, they were all men – would indulge in lengthy discussions as to whether the wife of a particular British engine driver should be allowed to accompany her husband for free on the boat journey to India and how much that would set the company back, while ignoring far more weighty matters, such as overall staffing levels or where best to target investment.

There were, in fairness to these geriatric directors, numerous other reasons for the overall inefficiency of the network. The various government committees and commissions, such as Acworth's, which recommended modernization were not always consistent with one another and led to the sort of regular administrative reorganizations that today bedevil large establishments such as the UK's National Health Service. As we have seen, while Acworth suggested expansion and investment, the purpose of several subsequent reports, with words like 'retrenchment' and 'efficiency' in their titles, was all too obviously the opposite.

Furthermore, there was a growing fear among railway managers of unrest, given that the unions gained considerable strength in the immediate postwar period and managements were far more reluctant to take them on after the spate of strikes in the early 1920s. The right of labour to organize was now largely accepted by both the railway companies and the Government of India. Union rights became entrenched in law through the passing of the Trade Unions Act of 1926, which allowed groups of seven or more workers to form a trade union and register it with a government agency to ensure recognition from the employer. Crucially, too, the new legislation gave trade union leaders immunity from prosecution in some circumstances. An amendment to the 1890 Indian Railways Act, passed in 1930, limited the maximum time staff were allowed to work to sixty hours per week, in line with international conventions, which resulted in more staff having to be taken on.

While providing these improved conditions for workers, the Government of India missed an opportunity to raise productivity by refusing to sanction several planned mergers between the major railway companies because it did not want to pay compensation to their British owners for ending contracts prematurely. Moreover, there was too much government enthusiasm for the construction of new lines when the available money would have been better targeted on renewing worn-out equipment. Many of these new routes were branch lines, built to satisfy local political interests rather than to serve profitable local markets, and consequently were little used but still required considerable extra staff.

Increasing concerns of the Government of India about the poor economic performance of the railways led, in 1936, to the establishment of yet another committee, this time to 'examine the position of Indian state-owned railways' (which by then were the majority), in order to suggest ways of improving profits and 'at a reasonable and early date place railway finances on a sound and remunerative basis'.[2] This was the type of enquiry that, incidentally, was paralleled across the world as railways everywhere faced increasing competition from road transport, which was wrecking the economic viability of many networks and placing ever-increasing financial burdens on the governments which owned them. The search for a 'profitable' or 'economic' railway was akin to seeking the Holy Grail, and discovered almost as rarely. India, in fact, was rather ahead of the game in that work on the infamous Beeching Report, which had a very similar remit in the UK, did not start until a quarter of a century later.

The Indian Railway Enquiry Committee was chaired by Sir – of course – Ralph Wedgwood, who, reporting in 1937, found that the tendency to spend lavishly on new projects had surprisingly survived the Depression. The railways, in other words, had got in the habit of spending above their means, which had been fine in the highly profitable 1920s but was now a serious problem. Sir Ralph mused: 'We cannot help feeling that in the past 15 years stations, workshops and marshalling yards have often been built to be the last word in railway technique rather than on a careful calculation of probable requirements, and that prestige has perhaps counted far more than prudence.'[3] Such excesses were made more costly by the rise in interest rates following the Depression, which further worsened overall railway finances.

Thanks to Wedgwood's experience as the chief officer of the London & North Eastern Railway, a job he retained while he investigated India's railways, his report was far more incisive and positive than many others in this endless series of government investigations into the state of India's railways. Wedgwood travelled extensively around the country on the railways accompanied by his wife, Iris, who, as mentioned previously, was a novelist and travel writer, and she has left us with a delightful account of her travels for the *Railway Gazette*. She clearly relished the whole experience of learning about India and its iron road, and her descriptions give us a rather better insight into the realities of rail travel in the 1930s than the articles in the *Gazette*, which were mostly written by the companies' bosses or public relations officers.

Unlike most visitors from Britain, Mrs Wedgwood actually enjoyed the climate, commenting that the tropical heat 'was a joyful change after the English summer and it made the electric fans welcome enough'. However, the nights, in the north, were cold and she was grateful she had brought her fur coat, which doubled as an extra blanket. Noting that the temperature change from day to night could be as much as forty degrees, she wrote: 'To the Europeans living in India, it is their one chance of being cool; to me it was my one chance of being hot.' Her description of the relationship between the railway and the countryside is wonderfully evocative: 'At times the train seemed so terribly small, a little ridiculous toy running through eternity, an absurd thing that no one wanted, that would get lost and never be found and then I used to be just frankly afraid because India looked so immense from the carriage window.'[4]

The by-product of the railways' poor productivity was an increase in fares and freight rates. Although these still remained low in international terms, they reduced the number of passengers and the amount of freight carried. Moreover, they went some way to breaking the implicit pact between the railways and the Indian people which had been established since the first line opened more than three quarters of a century previously. While the British determined the routes and the services in line with the requirements of their economic interests, the people at least benefited from cheap travel in return. As fares rose, so did levels of resentment, especially as the increases had a wider effect on the economy and on the nation's growth prospects, as John Hurd emphasizes: 'India may have paid a terrible price for the ineptitude. Costs for railway production rose in crucial years. Real rates and fares charged on customers rose at key points. This could have been a factor in the stagnation of the economy.'[5] The lack of money available for investment had the effect of slowing down the modernization of the network, such as electrification, which, as we have seen, ground to a halt in 1936 and was not restored until after Independence more than a decade later.

Nevertheless, the railways were by no means the financial basket case they had been until the turn of the century. Despite the low level of productivity, they were profitable and, in international terms, gave a decent rate of return on capital. By the mid-1930s, invested capital on Indian railways was earning 3.4 per cent annually, compared with 3.1 per cent back in the UK and just 2.6 per cent in the US, which was already beginning to suffer more intensely from road and air competition. The relatively high profitability of the Indian system remained the result of the heavy patronage by third-class travellers, who still made up 90 per cent or more of passengers.

The railways, of course, are not just about money collected through the fare box. Their value also comes in the form of what economists call the 'externalities', which are the positive aspects, such as the benefits to industry, to job creation and to economic development generally. Because these benefits are less easy to quantify, they are often omitted, but in India they were clearly enormous. Without the railways, Indians would not have been able to move faster than those wretchedly slow bullock carts.

As a result of the Wedgwood report, the government appointed for the first time a minister for transport and communications, who had the power to intervene in any decisions made by the Railway Board. The minister, though, was a senior civil servant and it was not until after Independence that the role became the preserve of a politician. There was, too, a change in emphasis to a more commercial approach by the railways, as recommended by Wedgwood. Already, in the early 1930s, there had been some effort on the part of the railway companies to attract new passengers and retain existing ones. Air-conditioned carriages made their first appearance around this time, but only for first-class passengers on services between Calcutta and Bombay, operated jointly by the East Indian and Great Indian Peninsula railways. In overall terms, the few thousand travellers who benefited from the cool air were a tiny proportion, fewer than 0.1 per cent, of annual passengers carried on the network, but 'AC', as it is always known in India, had a symbolic importance, demonstrating the subcontinent was embracing modernity. For freight carriers, there was a series of targeted rate reductions and efforts to develop new markets, and there was considerable success with boosting the transport of sugar cane. Parcel traffic was also encouraged and the mail services, a traditional part of railway transport in India, were expanded.

The exotically named His Exalted Highness, the Nizam's Guaranteed State Railway – known more prosaically as the Nizam's State Railway – was an innovator in trying to increase passenger traffic. The railway, whose rate of return was guaranteed by Hyderabad state, rather than the Government of India, introduced a series of connecting buses to feed into its rail network. This not only boosted the number of passengers, but the buses themselves made a profit, and eventually a network operated by sixty-five vehicles was developed. Wedgwood recommended that rail companies should be running their own road services, as they did in the UK, but the chaotic conditions resulting from an almost complete absence of any rules for road traffic and the failure to implement even the most basic safety regulations made this difficult elsewhere. Hyderabad had the advantage of having a state government that had imposed some controls over its road traffic, and consequently its buses were able to operate reasonably efficiently and without unfair competition.

This was a growing issue for the railways. As in many countries in the world, the interwar years were the period when road competition started to have an impact on the railways, and the Wedgwood Committee's report emphasized the need to impose regulations on the use of roads by motor vehicles as otherwise they represented unfair competition. In the first of many criticisms that would be heard from railway managers in the following years, J. A. Bell, the agent (general manager) of the East Indian Railway, complained about the chaotic unregulated conditions on the roads and the widely used subterfuge to avoid paying taxes: 'Conditions in regard to the regulation and control of road motor transport are generally far from satisfactory. The overloading of buses and lorries, and the registration of goods lorries as private vehicles in order to avoid payment of higher taxation, registration and licence fees, are commonly resorted to.'[6] Bell stressed that unrestricted bus and lorry competition was the major problem of the day. Despite the Wedgwood Committee's recommendation for new laws on stricter control of road traffic, legislation was slow to be passed, and even then enforcement of rules was non-existent, as it largely remains today, despite recent government attempts to fine or even jail bad drivers.

By forcing the railways out of their complacency, born of having long enjoyed an effective monopoly on medium- and long-distance travel, the competition did have beneficial effects. The general manager of the North Western Railway, for example, realized the need for the railways to combat the threat from other modes of transport: 'Competition from road transport has awakened the railway to the necessity of providing greater facilities to the public and they are now showing a belated but nonetheless welcome regard for the convenience of both passengers and merchants.'[7] In particular, freight for shorter journeys was being lost to the roads while, for the most part, long-distance freight stayed on the tracks because the condition of the roads and the reliability of the lorries were so poor.

Bell, in common with many other senior rail managers, was in no doubt that the railway companies had to respond. He suggested a range of measures, such as increasing the frequency of services and making them faster, having greater flexibility in rates for freight, introducing road services to take goods to and from their final destination, and greater marketing of services for both passengers and freight. On the South Indian, the reduction of fares for third-class passengers and the introduction of cheap return tickets resulted in some journeys costing as little as 2 pies per mile (a mere 0.19 of an old penny). The manager of the South Indian reported that these measures had met with success and had the effect of forcing bus companies to serve as feeders to the trains, a move which the railway encouraged through the issuing of joint bus/rail tickets, a very early example of integrated transport. Another innovation by the South Indian was the abolition of first class on the Madras electric network, which boosted the space available to the other two classes. The number of trains was increased as well, to a train every seven minutes, allowing for 140 trains per day rather than ninety. Most other railways, aware of the threat of competition, introduced similar measures of cutting fares, increasing frequencies and offering an improved service for freight users.

As well as providing more trains, the railway companies responded to Wedgwood's injunction to be more commercial by seeking to attract extra passengers. One imaginative innovation was the introduction of the bazaar train. The huge distance between Indian cities meant many rural dwellers had little access to the range of goods offered in larger conurbations. The solution was for the companies to run long-distance tours by a bazaar train, which was fitted out as a travelling shop offering a huge range of goods that could not be obtained locally. It would be hauled overnight to relatively remote stations and then opened up to local shoppers during the day. The Eastern Bengal Railway was the first to adopt this idea, running a train which stopped at thirty stations round its network, and that initiative was so successful the service became an annual event. The Bombay, Baroda & Central India Railway responded in 1934 with a far more ambitious tour, covering 5,000 miles from Ahmedabad to within 300 miles of Calcutta in a journey that took 112 days. The new service was welcomed by the Viceroy, the Marquess of Willingdon, who saw it as a way of not only providing a profit for the railways but also of promoting the sale of locally produced goods. The Marquess was so impressed that he, and his wife, the Countess, met the train personally when it arrived in Delhi.

The railways started to recover after the low point of 1933, which was when the total of passenger numbers annually dipped below 500 million for the first time in a decade, and carryings returned to their pre-Depression levels in 1937/8, helped by the efforts of the railway companies to boost traffic. This would be the beginning of a remarkable decade of growth for the railways, despite it also being a time of political turmoil and conflict when the British government began to recognize it could not hold on to India indefinitely.

The Government of India Act 1935 had mandated elections to the provincial (state) governments for the first time, albeit on a limited male franchise, and these were held in 1937, despite the Congress Party not yet having decided whether it would agree to form administrations if elected. Nevertheless, the Congress leader and future Prime Minister, Jawaharlal Nehru, crisscrossed the country electioneering by train and was mobbed at every station he visited. He was not averse to commenting on the relative merits of the railway lines on which he travelled, and complained, in his autobiography, about the incomprehensible fares structure: 'I think I gave first place to the East Indian Railway, the North Western was fair; but the Great Indian Peninsula was bad and shook one thoroughly. Why this was so I do not know, nor do I know why fares should differ so greatly between the different railway companies all under state control.'[8] The Great Indian Peninsula, he complained, was far more expensive and did not even issue ordinary return tickets.

The railways were subject, too, to rather less peaceful politically motivated interventions. The rise of nationalism in the interwar period inevitably affected the railways, not least because of their symbolic importance for both the British and the Indians. As the historian David A. Campion puts it, 'For the British, the railways remained the most visible symbol (with the possible exception of the army) of their technical superiority and the physical conquest of the land as well as their political control over its people.'[9] For Indians, the railways were an all too obvious target. As we have seen, the humiliations imposed on third-class passengers were a radical-izing force experienced by millions of Indians, and the railway companies, many still controlled from London, easily became the subject of their resentment. Moreover, taking action was easy. Ticketless travel, already the bane of the railway companies, was perceived by many as a political act as it deprived British share-holders or the British-controlled Government of India of revenue. With a bit of encouragement from nationalist leaders, fare dodging became more widespread and reached levels where it was impos-sible for the overworked rail staff to cope, even though at times they travelled with a magistrate able to impose immediate fines on miscreants: 'The ultimate goal was to wrest control of India's railways from the state and return it to the people who paid for its operation.'[10]

The other simple trick to disrupt services was to pull the communication cord, which was supposed only to be used in an emergency. Unlike on most modern trains, the device on Indian trains activated the brakes directly, rather than simply communicating a warning to the driver, and therefore could be used to stop the train in order to disrupt services. Heavy fines were imposed on those misusing the system, but these were hardly a deterrent since finding the culprits, particularly if all the passengers around them were fellow political activists, was nigh on impossible. Cleverly, the nationalists were using the great iron road against the very people that had introduced it in India, as Ritika Prasad notes: 'Railway lines, which had been imagined as conduits that allowed India's rulers to travel to hill stations to recuperate and replicate a sense of home, instead became the means through which the message of *satyagraha* [Gandhi's concept of 'search for the truth', which underpinned his non-violent philosophy] was transmitted.'[11]

At times, inevitably, more concerted and violent action against the railways was undertaken by nationalist forces. Relatively peaceful periods were interspersed with others when there were numerous and prolonged attempts to disrupt the working of the network because: 'Trains never lost their appeal as the object of anti-government fury. To disrupt the smooth running of the rail system remained the easiest and most dramatic way to strike at the heart of the colonial regime and cripple its military and economic power.'[12] Just as in the years running up to the First World War mentioned in Chapter 7, attacks on the railway intensified. One notable incident was the unsuccessful attempt near Delhi to blow up the train carrying the Viceroy, Lord Irwin, by Punjabi revolutionaries in December 1929, which caused only minor injuries and little damage because the bomb failed to detonate properly. This was part of a series of assassination attempts by radical nationalist elements during a particularly violent but fortunately brief period.

Another series of coordinated attacks on the railways was launched a decade later in the run-up to the Second World War. Normally, the rail companies and the Government of India were reluctant to mention the existence of attacks, but in its summary of 'recent events' published in the 1939 overseas edition of the *Railway Gazette* the East Indian Railway company revealed that it had been the subject of numerous attacks in the previous year: '1938/9 was marked by regular outbreaks of sabotage on the system. In three instances, there were derailments attended by loss of life. In two subsequent cases, serious disaster was averted by the timely discovery of damage to the track. The Government of India viewed the frequency of these incidents with grave concern and ordered a thorough inquiry by a tribunal headed by a high court judge.'[13]

The inquiry revealed that these attacks had, indeed, been caused by terrorists who were probably responsible for a series of other derailments. Extra police were taken on to patrol lines at night, but the railways are incredibly difficult to defend against such acts of sabotage. For example, in Uttar Pradesh, *dacoits* (bandits) stopped trains and robbed mail vans to raise funds for the nationalist movement.

The entry of India into the war, without any reference to local politicians, was extremely controversial as it was opposed by the Congress Party, which, in the summer of 1942, launched the Quit India movement with the aim of ending the British Raj. Although both Gandhi and Nehru were sympathetic to the Allies, neither, for different reasons – one was a pacifist, the other a socialist – supported India's involvement in the war. The methods of the independence campaign, however, were the subject of fierce debate within the Congress Party. Gandhi was always opposed to any violent action, but elements within Quit India were not so restrained. After the arrest on 9 August 1942 of Gandhi, Nehru and all the other Congress leaders, who would spend the rest of the war in jail without facing trial, there were widespread protests, many of them violent, with the railways as the principal target. The crucial north-eastern corner, where the railways were needed as the principal line of communication for the war against Japan, suffered the worst. Within a couple of days of the arrests, large parts of the East Indian Railway and almost the entire Bengal & North Western were put out of action. For much of the next few weeks, Bengal was virtually cut off from northern India, but there were also attacks as far south as Madras. The railways in Bihar, too, suffered greatly, with many of the Bengal & North Western's stations in the state being destroyed by arsonists. The damage was carefully directed, with control centres and communications equipment being targeted. Many stations and signal boxes were set on fire and several trains were derailed as sections of track were removed, with, on at least three occasions, fatal consequences. There were many peaceful protests, too. In Bihar, one of the most active states, students hijacked trains and used them to travel to the countryside, telling local people that the Raj had gone and that India was free. The engines of the trains were draped with the national flag and Quit India slogans were daubed on the carriages. According to one report, 'students also wiped out class distinctions by asking villagers to board the first class compartments. Passengers wearing western clothes were not allowed to board the train.'[14]

The British responded very forcefully, jailing tens of thousands of activists, imposing fines on countless others and violently breaking up crowds of protestors, causing hundreds of deaths.

There were even public floggings and the antagonism raised by the British actions made independence inevitable. The ferocity of the British response was born of the fear that the whole war effort could be undermined by the Quit India activists. Repression rather than conciliation was the order of the day. The military men saw it as a life-or-death struggle, and viewed the Quit India activists as being a kind of fifth column of the German–Japanese Axis tactics. Commenting on the destruction of a crucial section of line in Bihar, one officer later wrote: 'If the attacks had been coordinated from Tokyo the wreckers could not have chosen a more vital length of track for their attentions. The only direct route from western India to the front line areas was rendered useless.'[15] He was convinced that 'the attacks were not spontaneous expressions of anti-Government feeling. They were planned moves in a deliberate scheme to impede the war effort.'[16]

There is no doubt that the war effort was hampered and that much of the damage was strategically inflicted, but, by and large, the aim of most of those involved was not to help the Japanese win the war but rather to show the British that they could no longer hold on to their most prized colonial possession. Although clearly there was much local planning of the protests, which were often well-organized and targeted, there was little national coordination because the leadership had been incarcerated. In particular, the Congress Party, which as a result of the entire top level in the organization's hierarchy being jailed was run by a group of inexperienced young activists, was divided on the issue of how far the protests should go. While Gandhi abjured any violence, it was not exactly clear what was permissible to those organizing protests. K. G. Mashruwala, one of the editors of Gandhi's *Harijan* newspaper, argued that disrupting transport communications was acceptable, provided precautions were taken to safeguard life, as was cutting wires, removing rails and destroying small bridges. Although he stressed this was his personal opinion, the official report into the role of Congress in railway sabotage published in 1943 concluded that Gandhi must have sanctioned this policy, given that the editors of his newspaper were unlikely to depart radically from his ideas.

The violence continued into the autumn but largely abated by the end of the year because of the strength of the response from the British and the lack of coordination among the few remaining Congress activists who had not been detained. Order was eventually restored but only at the cost of many lives and hundreds of thousands of people being thrown into jail without trial. The driving force behind the repression was to ensure that the trains had to be kept running. The 1857 Rebellion had demonstrated the importance of the railways in keeping order and had led to their expansion. The Quit India campaign had shown how easy it was to disrupt services and how much repression was needed to ensure their continued functioning. However, the campaign had shown that the railways were a double-edged sword. They were still the mainstay of transport for the police and troops and without them it was impossible to keep hold of the country. On the other hand, they were also used by militants to travel around India rapidly and their very ubiquity meant that there was invariably a local line or station that could be made the focus of an attack by a group of activists. The events of just a few years later, during the Partition, would show the disastrous consequences of the authorities totally losing control of the railways.

As in the First World War, the railways were the cornerstone of transport for the war effort because they were vital in moving troops and supplies across the country. By the outbreak of the war in 1939, the network had 41,000 miles, of which just over half were broad gauge, with the rest divided between 15,700 miles of one-metre gauge and a surprisingly significant 4,200 miles of narrow gauge, split between 2ft and 2ft 6in. It was, in truth, still not a very extensive network for such a big country. The US, by contrast, had six times the number of route miles for an area that was only double that of India. Just under 10 per cent of India's total mileage was both run and owned by private companies, however, a further 14,000 miles were still in the hands of private companies but run by public organizations. However, the government, through ownership and its control and regulation of train operations, was able to decide which trains should run once conflict broke out as the rail network became the engine room of the war effort.

This time the conflict, which, thanks to the Japanese attack on Pearl Harbor in December 1941, included Asia, was far closer to home for Indians and consequently the railways played an even greater role than during the First World War. The railways were, again, worked into the ground while routine maintenance was neglected and investment postponed. The east–west routes across northern India were the most heavily used, playing a key role both in helping evacuate troops fleeing, with large amounts of equipment, from the Japanese, who had quickly conquered Singapore, Malaya and Burma, and in supporting the build-up of the counter-offensive.

In the first part of the war, before Pearl Harbor, India's network not only had to accommodate the transport needs of the huge Indian army, whose numbers increased more than tenfold during the conflict to a staggering 2.5 million, but also was forced to close several lines and despatch the dismantled equipment to build and expand railways in the Middle East. It was mostly the metre-gauge lines, which were less well-used, that were closed, and provided 4,000 miles of rail, hundreds of locomotives and several thousand wagons, all of which were shipped westwards from Bombay. Overall, twenty-six branch lines were closed and services on many others curtailed. The timetable on main-line railways was also greatly reduced, with ordinary passenger traffic being officially 'discouraged' and at times reduced to a skeleton service. War traffic was prioritized. This included massive quantities of coal from the Bengal and Bihar mines alone, which formerly had been transported via Calcutta. A large number of daily trains were now rerouted through Bombay because of the lack of coastal shipping, necessitating the operation of thousands of additional special services, which clogged up the network.

After Japan had overrun much of south-east Asia, the priorities changed. Some branch and minor lines that had been neglected suddenly became vital links in the logistical exercise of defending India's eastern border. Burma, which had been a province of India until 1937, was overrun in 1942 by Japan, which attempted to use it as a staging post for the invasion of India, constructing the infamous Death Railway between Thailand and Burma as a way of keeping its troops supplied.

The Allies were conscious of the need to protect eastern Bengal and Assam from Japanese attack and began to strengthen the railway line of communication. There was an irony here. All that effort to build up the railways on the North-West Frontier, from where an attack on India had been expected, proved to have been wasted. On the other hand, the railways in the north-east had been neglected and were a mess, with three different gauges, many single-track lines and a historic lack of investment. The most immediate

threat was to the line which runs on the west bank of the massive
Brahmaputra River and was, at times, very close to the Japanese
front lines. The route to Assam from Calcutta initially headed
north on a broad-gauge line on the west side of the Brahmaputra
River towards Siliguri, at the foothills of the Himalayas, but at
Parbatipur, 233 miles from Calcutta, all passengers and freight had
to be transshipped to a metre-gauge railway which terminated
at Amingaon, on the river bank, where a small ferry was the sole
route across the massive waterway. From Pandu, on the other bank,
the metre-gauge single line wound on through the Brahmaputra
valley to Tinkusia in the north-east corner of Assam. A plan to
ford the river with a bridge was considered but eventually ruled out
as impractical during the war, which meant that the manhandling
of goods three times between the various forms of transport had to
be maintained throughout the conflict.

This route was not only important for resisting the Japanese
invasion, but also because the Allied forces in China were supplied
by an airlift over the Himalayas from a series of landing strips
dotted along the railway in Assam. The metre-gauge line had
originally been built to serve the tea plantations in Assam but was
utterly inadequate for the war effort. As John Thomas, an officer
who wrote an account of the way the line assumed such importance during the war, put it, with possibly just a hint of hyperbole:
'The fate of India, and to a degree, the British Empire, depended
on this slender line of communication.'[7]

The transport difficulties were compounded by the fact that this
railway suffered from a chronic shortage of locomotives and, as
mentioned above, was repeatedly the subject of acts of sabotage
by Quit India activists. There were also floods to contend with,
which swept away major bridges, and a famine in 1943 that not

only killed an estimated 3 million people but weakened many railway workers who operated the trains or shifted goods. Thanks to the arrival of 4,000 American and 400 British troops to oversee work on the line, huge improvements were made rapidly which increased capacity more than tenfold, from 600 to 7,000 tons per day, through the construction of passing loops, the doubling of all the broad-gauge as well as sections of the metre-gauge tracks, and other improvements to speed up services, such as running trains on single-track sections in 'fleets' in the same direction for several hours and then in the other direction for a similar period.

It was not only a matter of overcoming the physical obstacles, but also, according to Thomas, of instilling a sense of urgency among the Indian staff, whose work practices were, at times, singularly inefficient. While Thomas was rather too ready to recount stories of Indian railway workers that fitted in with his prejudices, there is enough that rings true to suggest these are genuine accounts. He recalls how a train carrying an urgent military load was due to leave a yard when the guard noticed one of the wagons had a door open. It was only two cars away, but instead of shutting the door himself, he walked the length of the train to find the train examiner whose job it was to close it and consequently delayed the departure by twenty minutes. This insistence on refusing to carry out a task that was another man's job was deeply ingrained: 'This was not an isolated example. Such incidents occurred frequently and the combined result of the efficiency of the system can be well imagined.'[18]

The most intractable problem was convincing signallers to stop prioritizing the old 'Mail' and 'Express' services, which previously had always been given precedence over other traffic: 'The Indians could not get out their heads that the Mails must not be delayed a minute and Indian controllers, horror-stricken by the thought that they might commit the supreme sacrilege of causing a mighty Mail to meet an adverse distant [a yellow signal warning of a red one ahead] often put vital military trains into loops out of the way.'[19] Meanwhile, the Mail would thunder through on the main track.

Despite his criticisms, Thomas repeatedly expressed his deep respect for the Indian railway workers, who kept the system going in very difficult circumstances and consequently played a key role in the war effort. Moreover, he did not confine his criticism to the locals, as he was also scathing about some of his American counterparts, such as the fellow who pulled the communication cord upon discovering that no toilet paper had been provided on his train and the officers who habitually took over the most comfortable carriages as offices, leaving the railway short of rolling stock.

The Americans, who arrived in large numbers from late 1943 to assure the integrity of the line of communication, ran the railway by their rules, cannibalizing anything available to provide the equipment they needed, such as ripping out fans from carriages to provide ventilation for their offices and recycling components from lesser-used railways. They ignored the safety rules that had been built up over the years, with the result that while services were, indeed, speeded up, there was a spate of accidents that left a trail of broken wagons and derailed locomotives by the side of the tracks. While the American intervention was successful, it caused widespread resentment among both Indians and even the British.

After the invasion of Singapore and Burma in 1942, the British had expected the Japanese to attack Dinapur, 600 miles north-east of Calcutta, which would have given them a new supply route for invading India via the port of Chittagong. In the event, hampered by the lack of supplies, the Japanese hesitated and the attack was delayed, by which time the defences had been strengthened thanks to the improved line of communication. As a result, the Allies won the crucial battle of Imphal in the spring and summer of 1944, averting the Japanese threat. Thomas has no doubts about the importance of this little-known part of the conflict: 'The Bengal–Assam line of communication was an epic in the history of railway transport.'[20]

The war left the railways in an exhausted and overused state. One side effect was that many of the British railway managers and, indeed, the senior engineers and locomotive drivers left India to fight, never to return, because they foresaw that the end of the Raj would soon see them displaced by locals. The conflict consequently speeded up the Indianization of the senior railway staff, which turned out to be fortuitous since they would soon be required to take over the whole service. To add to the difficulties, passenger numbers were increasing rapidly thanks to the growth in the economy and the effects of war. Between 1938/9, the last year before the war, and 1947/8, the year of Independence, the numbers using the railways (excluding the lines affected by Partition) went up from 355 million to 902 million, an increase of 154 per cent. Yet, the train mileage remained broadly the same, as little money was available for investment, resulting, not surprisingly, in serious overcrowding, delays to passenger services and widespread, lengthy hold-ups in the movement of freight.

The railways would soon become subsumed into one national concern, Indian Railways, which would recognize the need for massive investment through a series of Five-Year Plans, but first there was the rush to Independence and the consequent disastrous and hurried partition of India and Pakistan in which the railways played a crucial and, at times, tragic role. Although the British had begun to realize that Independence could no longer be avoided, due mainly to the widespread actions of the Quit India campaign, together with the growing strength of the Congress Party, India was to be the first major non-white decolonization and they had little idea of how to go about it. The very forces which the British had encouraged with their divide-and-rule policies that were intended to emphasise, rather than dissipate, religious difference were to be the major obstacle to a peaceful transfer of power. Given Britain's depleted economy at the end of the war, the imperial power was hardly worthy of that term. Britain simply did not have the resources or the desire to control its greatest colonial asset, but the mistakes of the Labour government elected in 1945 and the haste to get out contributed to the unrest and the massacres in which an estimated 2 million people died.

At the end of the war, Independence was widely recognized as inevitable, but there was still a whiff of hope that partition would not be necessary. That last bit of optimism was soon snuffed out when Lord Mountbatten came to India as its last Viceroy in February 1947. Within a few days of arriving, talks with the main politicians led him to decide he had no chance of keeping a united India, given the antagonism between the two Hindu leaders, Gandhi and Nehru, and Muhammad Ali Jinnah, the head of the Muslim League. Mountbatten, eager that Britain should not oversee what he thought looked like becoming a civil war and bloodbath, brought forward the date of Independence, announcing on 3 June 1947 that the handover would be on 15 August, a mere ten weeks away.

Mountbatten brought in a British lawyer, Sir Cyril Radcliffe, who had no knowledge of south Asia, had never even been there and would never return, to head two boundary commissions (one for the east, one for the west), which would determine the territory of the two states, and gave him just five weeks to carry out this momentous task. Radcliffe, whose odd nickname at public school had been 'Squit', spent most of that time sweating over Ordnance Survey maps in a bungalow in the Viceroy's grounds and admitted later that it would have taken years to establish proper boundaries recognizing the communal preferences. He could not, however, be blamed for the chaos that ensued. The key decision, to accede to the Muslim League's demand for a separate state, was effectively made by default. The new nation, Pakistan, was to have two separate parts, East Pakistan and West Pakistan, separated by 1,000 miles of Indian territory. It was not a sustainable solution, as the secession of East Pakistan and its transformation into the new nation of Bangladesh a mere twenty-four years later showed.

The unseemly haste with which Mountbatten implemented the process of independence undoubtedly contributed to the orgy of violence and killing. The British failed to anticipate the huge numbers who would want to move to the state where their religion was dominant or the violence that this would engender. Around 15 million people moved between India and Pakistan during the period of Partition, the largest such migration in world history. The railways were to be the main mass transport mode, carrying around 4 million refugees during this period, and therefore its passengers, travelling en masse in confined spaces with greatly overcrowded conditions, were sitting ducks. The year 1947 would be the bleakest in the near century of Indian railway history, and the violence would at times bring parts of the system to a complete halt, forcing refugees onto the roads, where they faced even greater danger.

The prospect of independence had already triggered, in the summer and autumn of 1946, sporadic communal violence between

Muslims and Hindus, and, occassionally, Sikhs, who also formed a separate religious group that was at times hostile to Islam and indeed participated strongly in many attacks. In particular, a bloody riot and massacre of Hindus in Calcutta in August 1946 led to tit-for-tat reprisals later in the year in Bihar, the start of the series of killings that would ultimately take 1–2 million lives – the very vagueness of the estimate shows the extent of the loss of control by the authorities. In the days running up to Independence, services began to be disrupted as railway staff stayed at home to protect their families. Lahore, which became the capital of the new Pakistan state of Punjab, was in chaos as, according to Khosla, the historian of the Indian railways, 'there seemed to be no authority in command and it was surprising how a few trains moved in and out'.[21]

Even before the formal separation of the countries, there were attacks on the railway traffic between India and the soon-to-be-created Pakistan. The first special train carrying the secretariat personnel and records of the new government of Pakistan was blown up on its way from Delhi to Karachi on the night of 9 August, near Girddarbaha in the Punjab. After independence was declared on 15 August, the situation deteriorated rapidly. Inevitably, the Punjab, which was split by the boundary line established by Radcliffe between India and West Pakistan, was the worst affected. Trains across the new frontier were soon halted, and the carnage began. William Dalrymple, the historian and writer, describes how events worsened on the very day of Independence:

Outside the well-guarded enclaves of New Delhi the horror was well under way. That same evening [15 August 1947], as the remaining British officials in Lahore set off for the railway station, they had to pick their way through streets littered with dead bodies. On the platforms, they found the railway staff hosing down pools of blood. Hours earlier, a group of Hindus fleeing the city had been murdered by a Muslim mob as they sat waiting for a train. As the Bombay Express pulled out of Lahore and began its journey south, the officials could see that Punjab was ablaze, with flames rising from village after village.[22]

In his award-winning book, *Midnight's Furies*, Nisid Hajari wrote:

> Foot caravans of destitute refugees fleeing the violence stretched for 50 miles and more. As the peasants trudged along wearily, mounted guerrillas burst out of the tall crops that lined the road and culled them like sheep. Special refugee trains, filled to bursting when they set out, suffered repeated ambushes along the way. All too often they crossed the border in funereal silence, blood seeping from under their carriage doors.[23]

As he puts it, 'the image of the "corpse train" arriving full of dead and mutilated bodies remains perhaps the most enduring icon of Partition'.[24] The worst period for the railway massacres was September, when several '"corpse trains" rolled into Lahore station dripping blood, their carriages filled with hacked-off limbs, women without breasts or noses, disembowelled children'. The arrival of these trains was used by 'provocateurs [who] made sure that even those who did not witness these atrocities heard about them in graphic, often exaggerated detail' in order to encourage their co-religionists to carry out revenge attacks.[25]

One of the first railway massacres occurred on 24 August on the southbound Frontier Mail, which ran from Peshawar on the North-West Frontier, which had just become part of Pakistan. It arrived, a day late, in Bombay having been held up by several hundred armed men who murdered many passengers and looted their baggage. The arrival of trains at their destination littered with corpses began to be a regular phenomenon. By simply pulling the communication cord, trains could be stopped in places where gangs were waiting in lineside ambushes to massacre the passengers. As is often the case in such periods of civil strife, routine criminal activity increased greatly, as thieves and rapists took advantage of the lack of authority from the British, who had simply decamped, to join in the mayhem. There was less violence in the east, possibly because Gandhi was in Calcutta and announced he would fast until peace was restored, which had the effect of greatly reducing the killings.

The railways quickly became overburdened. In the first month after Partition, 700,000 refugees were carried, far more than the railways could cope with. Special refugee trains, which were supposed to take people over the border in safety, were introduced, but often people had to wait days or even weeks in terrible conditions at the stations before they were able to leave. For a time, both main termini in Bombay were so clogged up with refugees hoping to be taken to Pakistan that few other services operated. Similarly, both Sealdah and Howrah stations in Calcutta were packed with refugees arriving from East Pakistan with nowhere to go. In Delhi, the huge groups of Muslims awaiting transportation were attacked several times, and at one point all services were suspended for a week.

One woman's experience is typical. Shrimati Laj Wanti, a Hindu woman, was just twenty-three when she and the rest of the family were advised to flee Khewra in the Punjab, where her husband worked in a chemical factory. In early September, they left Khewra by train but it was stopped at Kamoke station en route to India and then, without explanation, stayed there all night. The following morning all the men's weapons, even penknives, were taken away and then the killing began. As the train was about to start, a large group of Muslims, armed with axes, rifles and knives, surrounded the carriages and started murdering the male passengers. The Pakistan military did not intervene and soon actually joined the mob in shooting passengers. As she said in her statement:

> Those of the passengers who tried to run towards the platform out of the compartments were shot dead by the police and the military and those who went out of the compartments towards the *maidan* [the public open space] were butchered by the Muslim mob. In this way, most of the passengers were either butchered or shot dead. A few who were taken as dead after having been injured were later rescued.[26]

Her uncle, aunt and husband were all killed at the station and she never discovered the fate of her son or the daughter of her aunt. Her story would be repeated millions of times over.

Stations were, indeed, not safe havens and there were numerous attacks on refugees by armed vigilante groups in several major towns and cities. Corpses would be left unattended for days because of the breakdown of law and order, and basic toilet facilities were not available, leading to the spread of disease.

The need to prioritize refugee trains paralysed large parts of the network, and at times other services ceased entirely. On occasion, trains carrying refugees in opposite directions would be stopped next to each other, resulting in a murderous pitched battle. Due to the frequency of attacks, the railways temporarily stopped carrying refugees until protection arrangements were agreed with the military. Each refugee train, which normally carried 5,000 people, with as many as a third of these travelling on the carriage roofs, was given an escort of sixty soldiers travelling at the rear in a sandbagged flat wagon, but this was often not sufficient as the front of the train remained largely unprotected and could still be attacked. Moreover, soldiers tended to side with their co-religionists, though this improved when emergency legislation introduced the death penalty for those who failed to make sufficient effort to protect the lives of civilians.

In a cruel twist of fate, as if to compound the misery of the refugees and the difficulty for the railways, the monsoons in September that year were particularly strong, causing widespread flooding and the breach of numerous embankments. Several bridges on the key Ghaziabad–Delhi–Amritsar line were swept away or damaged by floods and had to be hastily rebuilt.

The reciprocal nature of the violence suggested it was well-organized. In September, a train near Amritsar was attacked and 3,000 Muslim refugees trying to reach Pakistan were murdered. As a reprisal, a few days later, a train containing Hindus and Sikhs was set upon in Lahore, resulting in a death toll of around 1,500. Overall, a total of 673 refugee trains were run up to the first week of November 1947, by which time the worst of the violence was over, and while they probably saved thousands of lives, the image of the death trains remains seared in India's history. The massacres would leave a legacy of antagonism between India and Pakistan which lasts to this day. It was a time, as Ian J. Kerr puts it eloquently, when 'Hindus and Moslems – and other communities

– as the politics of identity intensified, lost sight of their shared humanity'.[27]

The violence abated in the late autumn, though sporadic attacks erupted again in early 1948. The killings finally stopped later that year when the civil and military authorities at last managed to impose control. A few thousand refugees were still carried on the railways between the two countries in 1948, but the main task within India shifted to transporting hundreds of thousands of refugees stuck in major cities, where they had arrived from Pakistan, to new homes around the country. The railways were left to their own devices in their struggle to restore a normal service. Given the damage caused during the strife, together with the obvious problems of splitting up a rail network into three sections, it would not be an easy task.

TEN

INDIAN AT LAST

G IVEN THE AWFUL context, the administrative difficulties posed by Partition for the railways may seem trivial, but they were nevertheless deeply damaging and required considerable investment to remedy. There was the obvious difficulty of separating out services and control systems between two countries, but also the challenge of dealing with thousands of displaced workers and setting up new structures to run the railways. They were still suffering from the effects of the overuse and underinvestment in the war, as well as damage caused during the civil strife of Partition. It was not an auspicious start for India's control of its railways and the rapid creation of a single nationalized body, Indian Railways, in 1951.

The war had coincided with the takeover by the state of the remaining privately managed and owned railways in 1944, although a few harbour lines and small narrow-gauge branches stayed in private hands. Initially, the structure was the same, with the old companies retaining their identity but becoming part of the state apparatus. The incorporation of the hitherto autonomous princely states into independent India meant that their railways, too, became part of the nationalized network in 1947.

The immediate issue arising out of Partition was to sort out the sections of railway that had lost huge chunks of their mileage to Pakistan. Two major systems, the Bengal Assam Railway in the east and the North Western in the west, were split, and a few other minor companies also saw sections of their routes cut off by the new border. The North Western was the worst affected, losing 5,000 of its 6,900 route miles, which included all those difficult-to-build but little-used frontier lines, while the Bengal Assam was more fortunate, retaining 2,600 miles (60 per cent) of its former 3,550 route miles.

However, Assam became disconnected from India, as the tracks linking Calcutta with the north-east ran through what was now East Pakistani territory, and, consequently, an alternative route had to be devised to maintain a connection with the rest of India. The new 143-mile-long metre-gauge Assam Rail Link was completed with the urgency that nationalism can inspire. Work started in January 1948 and ended a mere two years later. Just under half the route involved conversion of an existing narrow-gauge railway from Siliguri, while the rest required construction of a new line through a mountainous and deeply forested region that suffered from heavy rainfall. Twenty-two bridges had to be built over turbulent rivers, with deep foundations required to protect them against the annual spring snow melt. However, given the importance to India of retaining the railway connection with Assam, money was made available to carry out the work quickly. More controversially, a line was also hastily built to give India a better connection with the territory of Jammu and Kashmir, which was – and remains – the subject of a dispute between India and Pakistan. A new twenty-six-mile railway, another remarkable engineering feat, reduced the distance between Pathankot, the gateway to the Kashmir and Kulu valleys, by forty-five miles, through the construction of more than 100 bridges over the mountainous terrain.

The government also moved quickly to sort out the administrative chaos of the railways. At Independence, there were forty-two different railway systems varying greatly in size and technical standards. The government decided to incorporate them all into regional zones large enough to be self-standing but still reckoned to be a manageable size. Railways around the world are always struggling with how best to structure themselves and India was no different. Long before Independence, the British colonial power and the numerous committees it had set up periodically grappled with this issue, but had never bitten the bullet to reorganize the structure that was effectively based on company boundaries. Now, though, with the ownership all in government hands, reorganization was both necessary and easier to achieve.

The initial scheme, implemented by 1952, was for six zones, each of around 6,000 route miles, and despite the obvious difficulties of setting standards for such vast new organizations and merging in staff with different work practices, the reorganization was relatively successful. However, with greatly increasing numbers of passengers, the Eastern Zone soon split into two, as later did the North-Eastern and the Southern. These zones, which were further divided into operating divisions, have a measure of independence and there is rivalry between them, as the different customs and practices of their former companies live on, very much as in the UK where even today some the peculiarities of the former private companies, nationalized in 1948, survive. One only has to read a hagiographic book, such as *Western Railway: A Glorious Saga*, published by the railway in 2008, to see the pride with which railway managers view their own particular railway and the importance of the traditions of the component companies, which in the case of the Western was principally the old Bombay, Baroda & Central India Railway, with the addition of a few minor railways, both metre and narrow gauge. Over time, more and more zones have been split, with the result that by 2016 there were seventeen.

It was not only the physical railway which had to be carved up between the two nations but also many railway workers, who suddenly found themselves living in a nation where they were members of a minority religion and consequently sought to move. The biggest displaced group were Hindi and Sikh staff of the North Western who had been based in Karachi in Sindh Province. They had been advised by Gandhi to stay put, but the massacre of twenty-five non-Muslims at the Lahore workshop two days before Independence ensured their determination to leave. However, they were understandably wary of taking any special trains, as the long journey from Karachi to Amritsar via Lahore would have involved 1,000 miles travelling through Pakistani territory. Therefore, ironically, special flights had to be organized between Karachi and Delhi to transport the railway workers.

Services in the border regions were disrupted for a long time. Very few trains crossed the new border and consequently what had been the North Western Railway's busiest route, between Lahore and Delhi, was in a shambles. The difficulties for the railways were compounded by the fact that, as mentioned previously, many tasks had been performed by specific religious or caste groups. Muslims, for example, had predominated in driving and firing locomotives and in workshop trades, whereas Hindus dominated the traffic (operations) and clerical tasks. This meant that at Partition in India there was an overall shortage of almost 20 per cent among engine crew and, given that the railways in the south were little affected, the impact was disproportionate on railways such as the East Indian, which lost up to 45 per cent of its enginemen.

The number of railway workers had continued to rise throughout the troubled period of war and Partition. The railways remaining in India after Partition – including the few surviving private concerns – employed just over a million workers, of which just 1,345 were British, who included 100 senior managers with most of the rest being locomotive drivers, and 12,300 Eurasians. While the majority of the British decamped quickly, the Anglo Indians often had nowhere else to go and stayed on, although, statistically, they disappeared as they were no longer counted separately in official reports.

There were immediate measures to 'Indianize' and standardize the rail system. The distinction between first and second class refreshment rooms was abolished, and those which previously only served Western food now had to provide Indian fare. The separation of water stations for different religions was scrapped, so that no longer was there 'Hindu *Pani*' and 'Mohamadan *Pani*'. The Railway Board, which to this day continues to run the railways, was expanded and oversaw the reorganization of the whole system. The Board came under the control of the Railway Ministry, which was, for the first time, overseen by a politician rather than, as previously, a civil servant. By and large, this structure remained the same until 1985, when a Ministry of Transport was created, which absorbed the Railway Ministry.

The tasks carried out by this huge workforce needed to be categorized given the disparities between the conditions in the various companies and the maintenance of numerous colonial practices. In particular, there was still widespread use of the rather feudal system of fining employees for transgressions, even very minor ones, and punishing people by demoting them, which created a general atmosphere of fear and instability among the workforce. Impatient to see changes, the unions pushed for action even before Independence and the interim government only narrowly averted a strike by agreeing to create a Central Pay Commission to consider the rates of pay for the post-colonial period of all government employees, including railway workers.

The various disputes brewing among staff were referred to an adjudicator. Nehru's government, which had a strong socialist hue, accepted the recommendations of the Commission and the adjudicator, with the result that the maximum hours of most permanent staff were reduced from sixty to fifty-four and pay rates were raised considerably, almost doubling the overall wages bill between 1946 and 1951. Moreover, the number of staff increased, too, rising steadily until it reached its peak of 1.7 million in the early 1990s (and now stands at about 1.3 million). Indeed, the first few years following Independence saw a particularly sharp rise as casual workers were given permanent contracts and new workers were taken on to cover the reduction in maximum hours.

The new zonal structure led to the simplification of an unfathomably complex bureaucracy and hierarchy, with the establishment of four main categories of staff ranging from the top managers in group A, of which there were around 8,000, and the engineers and middle managers in B, to the hundreds of thousands of manual staff in D. The lower two categories, C (formerly known as 'subordinate services') and D (previously called 'inferior servants'), comprised no fewer than 700 different occupational categories. Although the new structure was still bureaucratic and complex, it represented considerable progress by rationalizing hundreds of different scales of pay left over from the former rail companies, as well as simplifying the process to grant various benefits, such as rent and family allowances.

As well as sorting out the structure, the government moved quickly away from the old colonial appointments system, which favoured Europeans and Eurasians, adopting new procedures that were an attempt to preclude nepotism and favouritism, as well as corruption. A job on the railways was regarded as desirable and competition was intense. While unskilled workers were recruited locally, the higher grades were taken on through competitive exams and even locomotive staff had to sit papers set, strangely, by Cambridge University. The most senior offices, called 'gazetted staff', were selected by a government commission, but despite all these safeguards, which undoubtedly made the system fairer, there were still ways to get jobs through corruption and nepotism. The desirability of the jobs was not so much the pay, which remained relatively modest, but the permanency of the position and the generous extra benefits.

The fact that the railways not only held together in this time of turmoil following Independence, but actually flourished in the post-Partition period, was the most powerful possible rebuke to the British, who had so long resisted the Indianization of the railways. All the more so, because their failure to bring forward Indian senior staff seemingly left a vacuum, which, remarkably, was quickly filled by locals who were eager to make a success of Independence. The British left hastily and with little effort to ensure the continuation of the service, and yet continue it did. There was a tremendous spirit of 'we will show them' that helped bring about this success, which was also a fantastic tribute to both politicians and railway managers, who had the confidence to maintain a high level of investment in the network and the ability to carry out improvements in the face of what must have seemed like insuperable difficulties.

The increase in usage in the immediate postwar period was staggering. For example, passengers on the Bombay suburban network rose from 47 million in the last year before war to 135 million in 1948/9. Similarly, the numbers travelling on Great Indian Peninsula's tracks more than trebled in that period. In the conclusion to a humorous account of Indian Railways written in the 1990s, the author Bill Aitken drops the acerbic tone of the rest of the volume, as he has nothing but praise for the way that the Indians coped with the sudden departure of the British, most of whom expected the system to collapse: 'No amount of petty criticism of the system can shake the astounding unlikelihood of India having overcome the odds to allow her railways to flourish after the British departed. As well as manage its own rail destiny, IR has won laurels abroad for the professional way in which it set up railway lines in several disparate situations.'[1]

It is difficult to exaggerate the importance of the creation of Indian Railways for both the politicians and the government and the desperate need for it to be successful. The company was the biggest in India and a crucial part of government, with its own minister. It had become even more of a state within a state, given its huge number of workers, and its political importance, as a symbol of India's ability to be self-sustaining. Nehru personally invested considerable political capital in ensuring that the railways were a success. In a lengthy speech in April 1952, at the inaugural ceremony for three of the new railway divisions, he recalled:

> I remember five years ago or about that time when the question of the then state of the Indian Railways came up repeatedly before us – before the Government, before the Cabinet. It was an obnoxious state, after the war, with our

resources depleted ... it was a painful experience not only
to travel but to see other people travelling ... it was hardly
conceivable ... how many people were jammed into our
third class compartments ... trains were late by hours and
hours and nobody knew when they would arrive.[2]

Turning to the present situation, Nehru said the railways were
now 'functioning with a large measure of efficiency and punctuality
... we should not only take note of that change, and I hope even our
worst critics will note that change – but also of how that change
has been brought about ... we as a Government have every reason
to be proud of this work and to congratulate all those connected
with our railways for what they have done'. In a later inauguration
he went even further: 'The railways are and will continue to be our
greatest national undertaking.'[3]

The importance of the railways to the government and to the
efficient functioning of India's economy led to considerable efforts
to create a stable and competent workforce. There was a 'cradle to
grave' approach from Indian Railways, which provided its workforce
with a huge range of benefits and facilities. While there had already
been similar provision by many of the railway companies, the
socialist ethos of the government and its keenness to improve the
railways resulted in much more attention being paid to the welfare
of workers. Consequently, Indian Railways was one of the nation's
biggest providers of housing. Nearly all staff with jobs at sites where
accommodation was not easily available, such as remote stations
and distant workshops, were given housing, as were many of the
staff working in major cities because of the lack of suitably priced
accommodation. By 1988, no fewer than 40 per cent of staff lived in
Indian Railways accommodation, which comprised 630,000 flats

and houses, and there was an active building programme to expand that number with new settlements. Schools, too, were available to many of the children of employees. Again, the scale was enormous, making Indian Railways a vast educational authority, with, by 1989, a degree college, seven intermediate colleges, nineteen central schools (called Kendriya Vidalayas, specially catering for army personnel and civil servants), twenty-nine middle schools and no fewer than 562 primary schools. This number was being expanded and many other employees received an educational allowance to help send their children to school where no Indian Railways facility was available.

Then there were the medical facilities, where again the sheer numbers are mindboggling. By 1993, there were 670 health units and 122 central hospitals on the Indian Railways. This had grown rapidly since Independence, with the number of beds increasing sixfold to 13,800 during the period from 1951 to 1994. Every zone of the railway was provided with a fully fledged medical department, including a central hospital, and there were minor medical centres at most major stations. The facilities available to staff were – and still are – leading edge, with several railway hospitals being at the forefront of medical practice on the subcontinent. As a historian of the system, writing in the mid-1990s, recounts, 'Super specialist facilities in the field of orthopaedic surgery, plastic surgery, gastro-enterology, micro vascular surgery and cancer have been provided at the central hospitals of some of the zonal railways. The Indian Railways Cancer Institute at Varanasi has become a premier institute of the North East area ...'[4] and so on. Add in forty training centres, 267 canteens, countless sports facilities, retirement homes and a huge Staff Benefit Fund, and it can be seen that Indian Railways is rather more than a mere transport facility.

All these facilities did not prevent industrial strife. Despite the relatively good working conditions, there have been several instances of unrest in the post-colonial period, often as a result of political machination rather than industrial grievance. That was because two large federated union structures emerged after Independence when the Congress Party established the Indian National Railway Workers Federation – now called the National Federation of Indian Railwaymen (NFIR) – as a rival to the long-established All India Railwaymen's Federation (AIRF). This was an attempt to bring the unions, which were dominated by socialists and Communists, to heel with Congress Party discipline, but the survival of the original Federation resulted in continued rivalry between the two groups. The Congress-dominated NFIR specifically aimed to reduce the influence of Communists on the trade unions but was unable to do so. Over time, the NFIR got the reputation of failing to defend its members because its leaders were unwilling to challenge the management of an organization owned by a government controlled by the Congress Party.

There was a series of disputes in the first couple of years which, in retrospect, can be seen as building up to the general railway strike of 1974, by far the biggest-ever strike on the Indian railways. The first serious industrial action after Independence was a walkout at the Kharagpur workshop in West Bengal, which nearly paralysed the entire South-Eastern Railway network in 1956. The dispute had started in the mechanical workshops but spread through sympathy action and continued for a fortnight. Trains were held up by workers squatting on the tracks outside Howrah station, a tactic that would be copied in future disputes.

A more widespread strike on the railways broke out in 1960 as part of a wider protest by central government employees demanding higher wages. The dispute, which was supported by around 200,000 workers, ended after five days when Nehru threatened widespread arrests and refused to buckle to any demands. In the aftermath, recognition of the All India Railwaymen's Federation was withdrawn, only to be reinstated fifteen months later. There was a further extensive strike in 1968, although this encompassed fewer than half the numbers involved in the previous action and ended swiftly.

The 1974 strike was seminal both because of the widespread support, which saw, for the first time, many railway workers across the country leaving their posts, and because of its far-reaching long-term impact. Because of dissatisfaction with the two major federations – controlled respectively by the Congress and Socialist parties – several smaller and more militant unions emerged in this period, mostly affiliated to particular smaller political parties. The large federations were seen as complicit in acquiescing to management decisions and unwilling to confront them.

The grievances had been mounting for several years. After the 1947 Pay Commission, which had been successful from the workers' point of view, two subsequent commissions had reported and neither resulted in an increase in real wages (i.e. after being discounted for inflation) for railway workers. The Federation calculated, for instance, that engine drivers' pay had declined by 22 per cent in real terms between 1960 and 1972, and was falling further behind given that inflation had reached 30 per cent by the time the Commission reported. There were other grievances, notably on the working hours of enginemen, who were paid partly by the mileage they covered, with the result that they had to work extended hours to earn a reasonable wage.

By 1974, anger over continued declining wages – in real terms

– boiled over and a general railway strike was started on 8 May, organized by George Fernandes, the recently elected leader of the All India Railwaymen's Federation. In terms of action, the strike was amazingly successful. Most of the network ground to a halt, stations were empty, goods trains held up for lengthy periods and few passenger services operated. However, the reaction of the government was uncompromising. Nehru's daughter, the Prime Minister, Indira Gandhi (she had taken the name of her husband, Feroze Gandhi, born Gandhy, who was not related to Mahatma Gandhi), reacted strongly, arresting 30,000 railway workers under emergency preventative detention laws, and at least four protesting railway workers were killed during battles with the police.

The strike was undermined by the use of strikebreakers from the Railway Territorial Army. This was an organization that had been created out of the Railway Volunteers, the not-so voluntary force of Europeans and Eurasians which, as mentioned in Chapter 6, Kipling had seen being trained. The Railway Territorial Army (which changed its name after the strike to the less militaristic-sounding Railway Engineers Regiment) was made up of railway staff boosted by a few military personnel and was trained to ensure the continuation of services in the event of war. However, in the 1974 strike, the 'volunteers' were used to drive trains and operate signal boxes, which ensured that at least some trains ran, though many suffered lengthy delays.

After twenty days, Fernandes called off the action in the face of Indira Gandhi's strongarm tactics as her refusal to negotiate meant that there was no chance of gaining any concessions. Although the strike was a defeat, it served to strengthen future union activity and conditions for workers improved in subsequent years. Industrial relations also got better and there has been relatively little conflict, given the sheer size and geographical spread of Indian Railways since that dispute. As Ian Kerr, writing in the mid-2000s, put it, 'given the size and complexity of the Indian Railways workforce one can say, that, on the whole, industrial relations within independent India's railroad industry have been reasonably, but not entirely, calm since the later 1970s'.[5] Interestingly, the firebrand Fernandes profited from Indira Gandhi's defeat, becoming railways minister in the administration that succeeded hers and later defence minister from 1998 to 2004.

There is no doubt that the failure of the strike had consequences well beyond the railways. Emboldened by the success of her hardline tactics in the dispute, the following year Indira Gandhi responded to widespread unrest at her rule by imposing a state of emergency for nearly two years, which suspended democratic processes and gave her the power to rule by decree, effectively turning India into a dictatorship. It was independent India's darkest hour and ultimately led to her demise, and assassination.

Following the reorganization of the railways into six zones in 1951, the government announced the first Five-Year Plan for the railways, rather like the similar plans that determined Soviet Russia's economic policy. The first of these plans, which started in April 1951, aimed to repair much of the damage and decay caused by the chaotic years of war and Partition, as well as making up for the lack of investment which stretched back to the Depression of the 1930s. This was a rather modest aim, given that India desperately needed more railways and a modernized network. Rather more ambitiously, the Plan sought to set India on the path of making its railways largely self-sufficient, breaking its longstanding dependency on imports of equipment from the UK. This was one of the early aims of Independence. The site for the first factory to build steam locomotives domestically had been chosen in 1947 at Asansol in West Bengal, where the Chittaranjan Locomotive Works, named after a freedom fighter, opened three years later. It was sited in a rural area and a sizeable railway community soon built up around the works, much like those that emerged under British rule. The works remain the sole employer in the area, which is today a vast township, with a population of 80,000, with all the facilities being provided by Indian Railways. The first steam locomotive was delivered in November 1950, built largely on designs and with machine tools supplied by British manufacturers.

The works were a key part of making India's railway self-sufficient, but this could not be done overnight. The Chittaranjan works concentrated on manufacturing freight locomotives, and by the time the 100th was driven out of the factory by the future Prime Minister, Lal Bahadur Shastri, in January 1954, around 90 per cent of its components were manufactured locally. Until 1957, however, locomotives were still being imported, but their provenance ranged from Japan and Australia to Belgium and Germany, as well as Britain. Initially, the home-produced locomotives were subsidized by the government, with Indian Railways only having to pay the price of an imported engine, but by the late 1950s costs had been reduced to match those of foreign locomotives. This showed that had the British allowed a domestic industry to develop, as it would have done in an independent country, the Indian economy would have been able to benefit far more from the growth of the railways.

Coaches, too, had been imported but it took rather longer to establish the first significant works, the oddly named Integral Coach Factory at Perambur, near Madras. Like Chittaranjan, this too quickly grew into a vast complex, which today employs 13,000 workers and produces 1,500 coaches annually. It was for a long time the only major coach works, but two more were subsequently built – at Kapurthala in the Punjab, opened in 1986, and, more recently, at Raebareli in Uttar Pradesh, which began production in 2012. In a further move towards self-sufficiency, a special plant dedicated to manufacturing wheels and axles was opened in 1984 near Bangalore, in order to reduce India's import bill. There is also both a diesel locomotive works in Benares in Uttar Pradesh and a diesel maintenance facility at Patiala in the Punjab. The locomotives built in India were developed with the help of various international companies, such as Hitachi, who were prepared to allow the Indians to use their technology to produce the vehicles domestically. This technology transfer in the rail industry was an important catalyst for the industrialization process that took off in India during the postwar years.

The First Plan's lack of ambition, however, in the face of a rapidly growing population and an even faster increase in demand for travel meant that there was a great shortage of capacity on the railways, particularly for carrying goods. The Second Plan, from 1956 to 1961, therefore, attempted to increase the number of services available, in particular to freight carriers, with new and expanded marshalling yards, quadrupling of key sections of track, the revival of the electrification programme and the introduction of more diesel trains. By the time of the Third Plan, which started in 1961, the railway had begun to catch up with the growing demand, though for passengers it was still difficult to get tickets on many services. Subsequent plans focused on increasing capacity and modernization, with the electrification programme being revived and speeded up.

Unusually of nations around the world, India was still building new lines throughout the postwar period, and has added around

100 miles per year annually on average since Independence. This was partly because, relative to its size, the nation's network was rather sparse, but it was also part of the overall transport policy. The government wanted railways to provide the main method of long-distance travel, both for passengers and for freight, while its roads policy for the first few decades after the war was based on the target of connecting every village in the country to the network rather than on improving inter-urban routes. The first motorway was not built until the late 1990s, and even today many are little used because of high tolls. While there has been an expansion of flights in recent years, including the arrival of low-cost airlines, there is still a lack of capacity, and travelling by train remains by far the cheapest option. Several of the new railway lines were built for specific freight traffic, principally carrying minerals to ports, but there were also some remarkable additions of passenger routes.

The most startling achievement was the construction of the Konkan line along the west coast south of Bombay, which had long been a missing link in the network. The new 460-mile line, running south to connect with an existing railway to the port of Mangalore in Karnataka, reduced the distance between Goa and Bombay by 120 miles. It was an ambitious project as the line runs through the mountainous terrain of the ghats along the west coast and, consequently, is considered, with justification, to be the most difficult railway route ever built in India. The project had been mooted for almost a century but the scale and expense of the undertaking delayed the start of work until a scheme was finally accepted in the late 1980s and then started in 1990. Indian Railways did not have sufficient finance and therefore a special company, the Konkan Railway Corporation, was created to build the line with funding from central government and the states through which it passes, and bonds sold to the public. That marked a key departure from previous practice, although nearly all the money still came from the public sector.

Even though the railway was built using modern equipment, which made its construction far more capital intensive than on older lines, it was still delayed by construction difficulties caused by the challenging conditions. The weather was a frequent problem, with flash floods and landslides in the monsoon period, and even though construction took place in the final years of the twentieth century, the thickly forested sections were plagued by wild animals, which resulted in some casualties. It was rather like the construction of the hill railways like the Nilgiri but on a far larger scale, requiring more than 2,000 bridges and ninety-two tunnels. The longest of these was four miles, but it was the tunnelling through soft soil that caused the worst problems. While a large section of the line was opened by 1995, the through connection could not be made because of continued collapses of a mile-long tunnel near Pernem in Goa. The whole project was delayed by the failure to complete the tunnel and it was only when a solution was finally found that the whole route opened to traffic in January 1998. One of the collapses at the tunnel had cost nine lives and the overall death toll of seventy-four workers during the entire construction process may not have been high when compared with the thousands who died on the original assault on the ghats, but was excessive for a modern project.

The line was built to modern standards, allowing for 100 mph running by diesel rather than electric trains, the first such railway in India, and as well as being fast it was also a short cut as it obviated the need to go inland. The distance between the two ports of Bombay and Mangalore had been reduced by half, from a very circuitous route of 1,265 miles to just 614. Moreover, because the roads are still bad through the ghats and take a heavy toll on the underpowered lorries, the railway provides flat-bed wagons which can carry lorries with their cabs, enabling the drivers to simply drive on and off, like a ro-ro cross-Channel ferry. This has not only proved popular but has also provided much of the income for a project that was by far the most expensive ever in India: the total cost was eventually 3,500 crore rupees (that is 350 billion rupees, or around £4bn). The heavy use, with 25 million passengers as well as 25,000 lorries and other freight per year, means there is already talk of doubling the track, but the staggering estimated cost of 15,000 crore rupees, more than four times that of the original construction cost, probably makes that unlikely, especially given that the Konkan Railway still has a debt of around 3,000 crore.

The line may have been an astonishing engineering achievement but it has had a poor safety record, with two major train accidents in its short history. They occurred within a year of each other, both caused by debris fouling the tracks in the monsoon period. The first was in June 2003, when a major landslide derailed an express train, causing fifty-one deaths, while the second, almost precisely a year later, killed twenty people. As a result, safety improvements, such as netting to prevent rocks falling on the track and better patrols, have been introduced.

Safety on the Indian railways has, in fact, improved considerably throughout the postwar period. The spectacular nature of some of the crashes, which often have a high death toll because of the overcrowded trains, gives a rather unbalanced perception of the overall safety record. Railways are a very safe form of transport in India, especially when compared with the roads, where the death toll was a terrible 146,000 in 2015 – 400 every day. However, there is no doubt that safety was a neglected area for much of Indian railway history, with a far higher rate of incidents than on most other systems across the world. Statistics are not available for the early days of the railways and accounts of accidents are therefore largely anecdotal. Before the First World War, major accidents were comparatively rare, partly because trains were slow, but also because the tracks were not heavily used, reducing the chances of collision. The tight supervision of the large workforce, in particular the permanent-way staff, also helped ensure there were few disasters.

There were exceptions and strange mishaps. For example, in January 1869, a brake failure led to a runaway train which tumbled over an embankment on the Bhor Ghat and fifteen people were killed. Twenty people died in a particularly spectacular head-on collision near Ludhiana in the Punjab, in December 1907. This resulted in the two locomotives rising into the air in a deadly clinch which was captured by a photographer. Probably the most bizarre of early accidents was on the East Indian Railway when a train ran through a herd of elephants and collided with one, causing its derailment and killing the driver, as well as the unfortunate animal.

As with many aspects of India under the Raj, even in the aftermath of a tragedy the native population suffered discrimination in relation to the Europeans. According to J. N. Westwood: 'While European victims of Indian railway accidents could hope to receive just compensation, native passengers were less fortunate. Railway officers, it was alleged, did all they could to minimise the injuries received by passengers, so that any compensation would at least be small.'[6] There was, too, some evidence of under-reporting of deaths. In a pamphlet, *Secret Doings on Indian Railways*, written in 1911, the author, O. Lloyd, alleged that the railway authorities deliberately underestimated the number of fatalities and were culpable of gross neglect in relation to safety. For instance, Lloyd claimed that a crash at Ghaziabad in Uttar Pradesh in 1907 had killed 400 people, rather than the official death toll of seventy-two. Indeed, even in recent times, the casualty figures are often vague, particularly for incidents involving trains plunging into rivers, due to the large numbers of people travelling on trains without tickets.

As lines became busier, maintenance standards were, at times, inadequate due to the heavy use of the tracks. Several serious accidents occurred in the interwar period, most notably at Bihta in Bihar in 1937, when a train from Calcutta fell down an embankment because it was going too fast in monsoon conditions, killing 119 people – the single greatest loss of life on the Indian railway up to that point.

However, it was in the immediate aftermath of the war and Partition that the rate of accidents was at its highest, and the 1950s were marked by a series of particularly deadly disasters with at least 100 killed in three separate crashes involving trains plunging into rivers. While the number of major accidents declined in subsequent decades, the worst-ever disaster on the Indian rail network also involved a train falling into a river. On 6 June 1981, a train running between Mansi and Saharsa in Bihar, 250 miles from Calcutta, derailed on a bridge and plummeted into the Bagmati River. As it occurred in a remote area, its cause has never been properly ascertained. There were at least 1,000 people officially on the train, as well as an unknown number of ticketless passengers, so the final death toll is not known, but with best estimates suggesting it was 600–800, this was undoubtedly the worst accident in India's railway history. While originally thought to have been the result of a cyclone, investigations suggest that the disaster may have been caused by the driver trying to avoid hitting a cow (or possibly a buffalo according to other reports) on the tracks and braking too hard, which made the carriages derail and crash into the river. This is a plausible explanation as severe braking can cause derailment. Two other very serious accidents occurred in the late twentieth century. The first, in the early hours of 20 August 1995, at Firozabad in Uttar Pradesh, involved a train on its way to Delhi smashing into the rear of another one that had struck a cow and stopped on the tracks. The death toll was given officially as 358 but was probably around 400. The second, at Gaisal in West Bengal, in August 1999, was the result of signallers mistakenly allowing two trains to collide head on (which has some resonance with Britain's worst ever accident, at Quintinshill in 1915, especially as it also involved soldiers). One of the trains, the Brahmaputra Mail, was packed with soldiers and security police heading for Assam, and consequently the official death toll of 285 is thought to have been greatly underestimated, especially as the wrecked trains were ravaged by fire in the aftermath, possibly as a result of explosives being carried on board by the military, which incinerated many of the victims. More recently, there have been fewer casualties with, in 2016, only one fatal rail accident, but that was particularly severe, with at least 150 killed when the Indore–Patna express derailed on 20 November, and, as I was compiling this section, forty-one people were killed on a train derailed in Andhra Pradesh in January 2017.

As mentioned in the previous chapter, sabotage and terrorism have been an ever-present risk in a vast system that extends, unprotected, into wild country occupied by bandits and terrorists. In his wonderful chronicle of life as a police officer, S. T. Hollins, who was in charge of the Railway Police Force in United Provinces (now Uttar Pradesh) in the late 1920s, recalls an attack by *dacoits* (bandits), who had deliberately removed a section of track in order to derail a train climbing an incline. It was travelling slowly and stayed upright, but the *dacoits* 'rushed down from behind the bushes on either side of the track, seized the engine-driver and guard, and plundered the train, finally making off on foot at high speed'.[7] This was the normal modus operandi of the *dacoits* and was, Hollins notes, a relatively frequent occurrence.

In the 1950s, there were about 100 train-wrecking attempts per year but, according to Westwood, 'to cope with an increased incidence of tampering with the track, rail welding was speeded up on the main lines' in order to make sections of rails too long to move without machinery, and consequently 'only 3 per cent were successful'.[8]

The vulnerability of railways to attacks by terrorists was highlighted in the spring of 1966, when three bombings on trains over the space of a couple of months in north-east India by separatists fighting for an independent Nagaland killed 135 people. There have, over the years, been other such attacks on trains by, for example, Maoists in Odisha and notably by Muslim terrorists on seven trains in the Mumbai suburban network, killing 209 people on 11 July 2006. A high proportion of the most serious accidents, such as the two on the Konkan Railway, have been caused by weather-related issues, either because bridges have been washed away or landslips have resulted in debris on the track causing derailment.

Crucially, however, the perception that the railways have become more dangerous in recent years is mistaken. Although four of the world's thirty worst-ever train disasters, those claiming more than 200 lives, have occurred in India (as well as two in Pakistan and one in Sri Lanka), India's record is not as bad as that may suggest. The statistics compiled by Indian Railways since its creation in

1951 show a steady and impressive reduction in the rate of 'consequential accident' (i.e. those that put lives at risk or cause extensive damage to equipment) per million miles travelled by train services. From nearly 2,000 incidents in the first year of Indian Railways' existence, the number fell to 501 in 1994/5 and then dropped to just 117 in 2013/14, although there was a slight rise to 131 the following year. This has been achieved by a far greater attention to safety, with the appointment of safety officers responsible for checking all aspects of the system, and staff safety training camps. Nevertheless, around two thirds of accidents are still caused by human error.

These figures showed continuous improvement since the war with one exception, the period during and immediately after Indira Gandhi's state of emergency, when the numbers rose quite substantially. This was because during this brief time, when India was effectively a dictatorship, there was an increase in acts of sabotage by dissenters on the railway. Moreover, rather like the myth of Mussolini making the trains run on time, Gandhi wanted to make the service more efficient and consequently managers cut corners, sacrificing safety for speed.

However, for the most part, the statistics show a reduction in accidents and already, before the Emergency, the rate was lower than in the USA and Canada, though slightly worse than the average in Western Europe. The number of incidents started falling again in 1982, when the impact of the Emergency receded, but it is still not good enough, as testified by comparisons with most of the rest of the world, where major disasters are now a rarity. As we have seen, many accidents occur as a result of weather conditions during the summer monsoon period, a sign that not enough attention is paid to the specific difficulties of operating in those conditions.

Moreover, in India, there is daily carnage on the tracks that does not involve rail passengers in accidents, such as those that are the subject of the statistics just quoted. Compared with the ninety-nine fatalities caused by collisions and the fifty-nine by derailments in 2014, the most recent year for which there are up-to-date figures, the number of people killed *on* the tracks is on a completely different scale. That year, across India, 27,581 people died in railway-related accidents – seventy-five per day – and while that represents a fall of 9 per cent on the previous year, it is the highest number of such deaths in the world. This must be seen, too, in the context of a country in which the annual road death toll is, as mentioned previously, around six times greater than on the railways. A small proportion of the deaths on the railways is the result of passengers falling out of carriages, but the vast majority are people walking along the tracks or killed at level crossings.

The reason for this enormous death toll is that many Indians still use the tracks, which are not fenced in, to walk along as they are often the shortest route between two places. The most horrific image I have ever seen in my life was a poster in Mumbai's CST station of 100 headshots of people about whom the authorities are seeking information because their mutilated bodies have been found on the tracks (described more fully in Chapter 11). Undoubtedly, some were likely to have been suicides but, more sinisterly, others may have been murder victims. What better way, after all, of disposing of a body than putting it on the easily accessible railway? This has caused much additional work for the hard-pressed railway police, as David Campion notes: 'It was not unusual for the body of a murder victim to be placed on the tracks to appear as a suicide, thus all bodies found on the tracks had to be initially treated as a potential homicide until an autopsy could determine otherwise.'9

It was such a well-recognized method of disposing of bodies that Laurence Fernandes, the brother of George, the union leader turned politician, was arrested during the 1974 strike and tortured by the police seeking the whereabouts of his brother, who had gone into hiding. He reported later in a High Court affidavit that 'the police threatened to throw him on the railway track in front of a moving goods train'.[10]

While safety undoubtedly improved radically after the departure of the British, an irony given their scepticism about the Indians' ability to run the railways without risking passengers' lives, corruption was the other issue that has been an endemic and damaging part of the culture of Indian Railways. It had long pervaded every aspect of the railway system, and the difficulties of the freight users mentioned in Chapter 8 were only a tiny part of the petty malpractices which plagued the network. At the most mundane level, revenue inspectors turned a blind eye, for the sake of a small consideration, to those travelling without a ticket. Sometimes it was more serious, for example, when railway personnel took payments to ignore criminal activity, such as theft of goods, or became more directly involved themselves by facilitating robberies.

There was, of course, already bribery and corruption in matters involving the state, but the opportunity for such practices grew enormously with the advent of the railways, given the vast scale of the system, the number of interfaces between people and railway officials, and the essential nature of the service they provided. Apart possibly from tax officials, people were far more likely to come into contact with the railways than with any other government agency. Therefore the potential for corruption became almost limitless.

This was recognized by a committee established by the government soon after Independence to look into corruption.

The report was published in 1955, after a two-year investigation by the committee, which was chaired by a former Congress Party politician, Acharya J. B. Kripalani. The report provided a detailed and damning account of the various forms of corruption open to railway officials and users of the network. Fleecing the freight users was, as Acworth had reported a quarter of a century previously, still the norm, except now there were more of them and new ways of extracting money. There was always a shortage of freight wagons and consequently sufficient numbers could only be found if the right railway officials were given a consideration. Similarly, wagons carrying perishables or livestock would get lost in the system and were only found when money changed hands. According to Khosla, the official historian: 'One who paid a bribe was given all possible facilities. His goods would be registered and charged at weights and values lower than merited. If he was late in bringing his goods to the station, the railway clerk would offer him an ante-dated receipt … and he would escape a penalty.'[11]

Collusion with thieves was common. A wagon with a valuable cargo could be marked with chalk and left in a siding for thieves to make off with the loot. Alternatively, trains would be stopped by signallers at isolated spots where thieves could immobilize them by cutting brake pipes, giving them time to remove all the contents. As mentioned in Chapter 8, the pilfering of coal was so widespread that it was an incentive for the railways to convert to diesel and electric power.

In the days of the Raj, the railway companies spent a considerable part of their profits on paying compensation to customers whose goods had been lost. It was such a widespread problem that their annual reports regularly boasted of reducing the number of claims and mentioned new ways of speeding up dealing with them – sixty days was not an uncommon average. New methods of sealing wagons or safeguarding depots were frequently mentioned and yet the claims kept coming in increasing numbers.

When it took over, Indian Railways also expressed concern about the issue, and after the publication of the Kripalani report, several measures to tackle the problem were introduced. The number of police engaged in anti-corruption work was greatly increased and a network of spies and informers was created to clamp down on dishonest practices. The tone of the report was evangelical, reflecting the deeply moral position of Kripalani himself, who was a socialist and follower of Gandhi (who was quoted extensively in the report). Kripalani wanted workers not to seek personal wealth by exploiting their position but rather to follow Gandhian principles of a simple life of self-sacrifice and modest habits: 'This self-sacrifice would set an austere example to their subordinates. Lower-level workers were encouraged to realise that their rights stemmed only from the performance of duties to the national organisation they served.'[12] (Kripalani was a fascinating character who left the Congress Party soon after Independence to help form a socialist party, but his wife remained loyal to Congress, becoming a senior politician and chief minister of a state, and the two frequently had arguments in public in Lok Sabha, the lower house of Parliament.)

Passengers were equally vulnerable to corrupt practices. There were simple tricks like a policeman loitering permanently in the ticket office to extract a coin from each passenger before allowing them in, or who might collude with a clerk by hustling out people who had been deliberately short-changed. Another scam was to open a booking office only shortly before the train was to depart to create chaotic conditions in which passengers, frantic to obtain their tickets, could be cheated.

The intensive period of growth in the number of passengers on the railways in the aftermath of the Second World War, without any commensurate expansion in services, resulted in far more people seeking to travel on key routes than could be accommodated. Consequently, reservations and tickets would be sold to black marketeers, who in turn offered them at greatly inflated prices to desperate travellers. Porters developed a good line of business by sitting in unoccupied seats while the train was being serviced, and selling the position to incoming passengers. Similarly, unoccupied berths could be sold by onboard staff.

Mark Tully, who was the BBC India correspondent for thirty years, recalls the vagaries of purchasing a ticket back to Delhi after visiting his family in North Bengal in the 1960s, a journey which required changing trains and gauge at Lucknow:

> We could not get a return ticket because neither the station masters at Guwahati and Lucknow would reply to the telegrams requesting berths. My uncle, a tea planter in north Bengal, had enough local clout to get us a berth as far as Lucknow but I was told there was no chance of getting the *Mail* train to Delhi. The clerk said he had never heard of us. To his embarrassment and my relief I looked at the pile of telegrams on his desk and saw that our request was there, right on top. That ended the argument and we slept comfortably to Delhi.[13]

Clearly, young Tully was too naive to realize that a bribe was needed to ensure his onward passage.

On the other side of the coin, ticketless travel remained a huge problem after Independence, despite it no longer being possible to argue it was an anti-colonial protest, and Kripalani found that most passengers who travelled without ticket did so with the collusion of the railway staff.

The other act of protest by passengers used extensively in the independence struggle, pulling the alarm cord, became an even greater problem after the takeover by Indian Railways, peaking at an astonishing thousand incidents daily by 1971. This was partly a consequence of ticketless travel as those travelling illegally would spot inspectors approaching and pull the alarm to enable them to jump off the train. It was only the draconian policing during the Indira Gandhi Emergency of the mid-1970s that reduced this phenomenon, which had soared in the postwar period, back down to a manageable number.

Unlawful activity was facilitated by the railways from the very earliest days. Since the opening of the first line in 1853, the railways had raised issues of policing. Criminals could move about the system in an unprecedented way, making it far more difficult for local police forces to keep an eye on their bad eggs. As part of its crackdown on crime and corruption generally, right at the outset Indian railway companies inevitably took on a major policing role. The colonial authorities responded to the building of the early lines by ensuring provincial (state) police forces added the oversight of the railways to the list of core duties and this inevitably took up a considerable part of their work. The cost was shared equally by the local provinces and central government, and this was the genesis of what is now the Government Railway Police run by each state and still funded in the same way.

The railway companies themselves employed *chowdikars* (watchmen) to keep an eye on railway property. Their numbers and functions grew over time, and after Independence they formed the basis of the Railway Protection Force, which is under the control of the Railway Board. Established in 1957, with just a few thousand officers, it has grown into a large organization with 75,000 members responsible mainly for the protection of property, the investigation of thefts, and the prevention of sabotage and vandalism.

The Government Railway Police, which has only half the number of staff, is the more passenger-facing organization, responsible for robberies, missing persons, the arrest of miscreants, and the investigation of injuries and deaths on the railway. Despite obvious suggestions that these two forces should merge, they remain separate to this day, adding complexity and at times confusion to the policing of the Indian railways.

In spite of the efforts of the police forces and some undoubted successes, corruption remains a major problem. In 2015, the government's anti-corruption unit, the Central Vigilance Commission, received 12,400 complaints about allegations of corruption in the railways, more than double the total of any other government organization.

For all these inherent difficulties, there is no doubt that the achievements of Indian Railways have been considerable. Ever since the full nationalization after Partition, there has been a constant process of modernization in the context of a staggering increase in usage. This was particularly steep in the early years but has continued with only the very occasional blip throughout the postwar period. This is most noticeable in freight, which throughout this period has accounted for broadly three quarters of revenue. The statistics tell the story: in 1950/51, the railways carried 73 million tons of freight, which grew to over a billion tons by 2015/16, a fourteen-fold increase, while the route miles only went up in the same period from 34,100 miles to 41,800, a rise of just over a fifth. Passenger numbers were 8.2 billion in 2015, compared with 1.3 billion in 1950/51.

As well as having to cope with this constant and rapid rise in traffic, Indian Railways faced several other daunting tasks: the complete renewal of the infrastructure, as well as the transfer from steam to diesel and electric power, and the upgrading of much of the metre-gauge network to broad gauge. It had to do all this while increasingly relying on the domestic suppliers because of a shortage of foreign currency limited imports and the emphasis by the government on self-sufficiency.

The Chittaranjan works stopped producing steam locomotives in 1973 and steam was phased out on the whole network (apart from on the odd historic line, such as the Darjeeling Himalayan Railway) by the mid-1990s. Gauge conversion started in the 1980s and got into full swing with the launch of Project Unigauge in 1991, which resulted in nearly all the network transferring to broad gauge. By the end of 2016, there were only 2,500 miles of metre gauge left, just 6 per cent of total track miles. Dalhousie would be chuffed. Two thirds of narrow gauge had also been converted, leaving just 900 miles, most of which, notably on the heritage hill railways, is likely to remain in place.

Electrification, which had stalled in the 1930s, began again in the fifties, with suburban services around Calcutta, and, in 1956, the start of the second Five-Year Plan saw the beginning of main lines being converted. The French state railway company, SNCF, was called upon to provide expertise for what was an ambitious and difficult project. This process accelerated rapidly in the 1970s and 1980s and by 2016 about a third of the whole system was electrified, including all the major suburban networks.

However, it has not all been steady progress. Since its creation,

Indian Railways has not only had to cope with a difficult series of external events, such as the aftermath of Partition, wars with neighbouring Pakistan, Indira Gandhi's State of Emergency, famines and the Mumbai terrorist attacks, but also the challenges of dealing with massive demand and having to adapt and modernize. In some respects, Indian Railways, as a state-owned enterprise, has been indulged, given its importance to politicians, and, indeed, to the nation as a whole due to the fact that it is responsible for 1 per cent of India's GDP, an unparalleled situation for any railway in the world. Its staff receive all the benefits of civil servants, along with facilities, such as schools, hospitals and housing, mentioned earlier. But being the creature of government also means being at the mercy of the whims of politicians. For example, over the past quarter of a century, some 3,000 daily long-distance trains have been added – bringing the total up to 10,000 – frequently not due to any expected passenger demand but because a powerful politician wants to be able to boast to his constituents that they now have a daily train to Delhi or Chennai, or wherever. While many invariably fill up, others remain unprofitable.

Another source of constant difficulty for Indian Railways, as a result of political interference, is raising fares, even in line with inflation. Fares are inevitably a political football and have been kept low for second-class (there is now no third class) travellers, who pay as little as 13 rupees (about 15p) per 100 kilometres. The combination of both these aspects of political involvement in the railway is to greatly reduce the commercial viability of Indian Railways. Not only do the extra trains take up paths on the network which could be used far more effectively on some routes by freight trains, but goods traffic has long subsidized passenger travel because of the low fares. It could be argued that, overall, this is the right policy, enabling people to travel more cheaply while freight carriers have to pay a bit extra to move their goods around the country. However, this has come about because of political imperative, rather than being the result of a clear policy decision.

The railways experienced an operational crisis in the early 1980s, when greatly increased traffic, particularly of slow-moving freight trains, was causing enormous delays at a time when inefficient steam engines were gradually being replaced by diesel and electric power. A new board was appointed by Indira Gandhi, chaired by a reformer, M. S. Gujral, who was also given the job of general manager of Indian Railways. He instituted a key set of reforms to make the freight operation more efficient, such as stopping ridiculous measures like the examination of freight trains every 400 km to ensure they were 'safe to run', and moving towards a system of operating whole train-loads, rather than individual wagons which need to be shunted in marshalling yards. These reforms, which had to be introduced in the face of the growing crisis on the railways in the 1980s caused by excessive demand and insufficient investment in new technology, achieved a remarkable turnaround.

Railways often require a crisis in order to make a step change in technology, and as the authors of a book which examined the modernization of Indian Railways concluded, 'the Gujral reforms resulted in a quantum jump in the Railways' operational performance. Not only did the trains roll faster, but they also increased the amount of freight transported. There was a fourfold increase in the incremental freight carried in the decade following the reforms compared to the preceding decade.'[14]

These reforms, together with modernized equipment and the phasing out of steam, staved off financial difficulties for a couple of decades, but the early 2000s saw another major crisis hit the industry. This had been brewing for some time, partly due to the dual role that railways are expected to play by government.

Ever since Indian railway finances had been separated from those of the government in 1924, as a result of the Acworth Committee's recommendations, the railway network has been treated as a commercial concern. However, it also plays a key social role, providing services that are not necessarily profitable to remote areas or on routes that are expensive to maintain. By the 1990s, Indian Railways suffered financial difficulties because India was beginning to shelve its protectionist policies and open itself up to global pressures.

Then, in 1996, the railways had to cope with increased spending due to the Fifth Pay Commission's recommendation of a substantial rise for lower-paid staff, while, at the same time, other costs were rising faster than revenue growth, which had slowed as greater competition was affecting the profitable freight market. The expenditure of widening the metre-gauge tracks was also a major drain on the railways' finances at the time, as was the politically motivated projects to build new lines.

It was politicians, too, who put the block on the closure of totally unremunerative lines, which had long been sought by the management of Indian Railways, but was politically impossible to achieve. Apart from a few light railways built in the nineteenth century, India has not closed any rail lines and has no plans to do so. While there may well be good social reasons to retain such lines in a country with few good transport alternatives, it is not such measured arguments that keep them open but rather raw political pressure from local or national politicians.

Interestingly, whereas most railways in the world were struggling to maintain levels of freight traffic, the financial difficulties of the

Indian Railways had come about largely because freight carryings were not rising as fast as they had before, a mere 1.5 per cent annually rather than the long-term postwar trend of 5 per cent. Most railway managements globally would be delighted with such an increase.

Matters came to a head in 2001, with the publication of the government-commissioned Indian Railways Report, produced by a committee of industrialists headed by a highly respected economist, Rakesh Mohan, later deputy governor of the Bank of India. The deeply critical report warned that unless radical measures were taken, Indian Railways faced the prospect of bankruptcy within a few years. The government was increasingly reluctant to fund the railways and yet political interference ensured that the railways' social role could not be reduced. The Committee therefore argued strongly for clarity between the commercial and social roles of the railways.

The report also highlighted the backlog in investment. The unigauge project was found to be attracting any spare funds to the detriment of the rest of the railway, and consequently: 'The proportion of expenditure on repairs and maintenance has been declining steadily over the years. The strain on the Railways resources has also prevented adequate investment in track renewals and other safety related areas.'[15]

The backlog of track renewals was 7,500 miles and, as a result, the accident rate was still too high, even though it was decreasing. It was a perfect storm. As the authors of *Bankruptcy to Billions*, a book which explains how the crisis was eventually resolved, concluded: 'In sum, a combination of political interference, conflicting commercial and social objectives, fiscal crunch, lack of market incentives and unproductive employees had hindered investment in track renewals and other safety measures, while the Railway was losing market share.'[16]

The report and the consequent successive appointment of a couple of railway ministers keen on reform resulted in a remarkable turnaround due to both managerial changes and better economic conditions. The number of staff was cut from the extraordinary total of 1.6 million to 1.3 million, still making it the third-largest employer in the world, after the Chinese People's Liberation Army and Wal-Mart. There were also the usual changes associated with reform, such as outsourcing ancillary services, including parcel delivery and parts of the catering provision, improving efficiency by reducing turnaround times of wagons and much more besides. Helped by favourable economic conditions, the initiative worked and, rather than a financial crisis, the railways entered a period of high profitability and booming freight carryings by the middle of the first decade of the twenty-first century.

ELEVEN

... AND TODAY

L OVE INDIA AND you have to love its railways. In no other country is the railway so indelibly connected with the image of the nation. Just as there is no nation on earth that has such a broad cultural, ethnic and racial mix as India, there is also no railway system that has played and, crucially, continues to play, such a fundamental role. There are no empty trains in India.

There are endless paradoxes about the Indian railways. They were the greatest gift left by the colonial power and yet, as we have seen, they were not built to serve the needs of local people. However, the fact that they did so was almost an accident. The companies which built them had not envisaged that people would pour en masse on to the iron road to take advantage of the immeasurably improved experience of travelling across the vast subcontinent that the train offered. Even though for the best part of the first 100 years of the railway age, they were owned and controlled by companies based 5,000 miles away, they immediately assumed an Indian identity which only became stronger over time. Nothing illustrates that better than the fact that Indian Railways adopted a rather bowdlerized version of the famous London Underground roundel on its station signs.

There is so much that is distinctively Indian about its railway network. Paul Theroux observed the uniquely symbiotic relationship with the land on which the tracks have been laid: 'In South America and in Africa, you look at the railway and see how it has been imposed on the landscape: it sticks out, it doesn't belong, it is a rusty, linear interruption of snoozing greenery, and where are the passengers?' The contrast with India could not be greater as 'once they were established, the railways of India blended with the country; they seemed as ancient and everlasting, and the stations as grand and as foolish-seeming and marvellously vain as any maharajah's palace'.[1]

The Indians took to the railways, not just physically, but emotionally. Railways and India are a good fit, an enduring one, as illustrated by the fact that not only are the Indians still building new lines, but virtually none have ever been closed. There will never, it seems, be an Indian Beeching. Moreover, the new lines are not those new-fangled high-speed jobbies being built across the world whose emphasis is 'getting there' rather than 'travelling there', but conventional ones that will have the normal mix of crowded passenger trains and meandering freight trains. There are numerous projects aimed at connecting remote regions, such as the Bilaspur–Mandi–Leh railway in Jammu and Kashmir and three new lines in Madhya Pradesh, and while these projects are inevitably subject to political whim and the vagaries of obtaining finance, few countries in the world are still considering the construction of such all-purpose railways.

India is considering a high-speed line between Mumbai and Ahmedabad, due to start in 2018, but that is also beset by uncertainty over whether it will ever be given the go-ahead for construction. Again, while having schemes delayed by politicians is hardly unique to India, the sheer length of time that it takes projects to be built is particularly characteristic of the subcontinent. Yet, they do get built, as the opening of the Konkan Railway, a century after it was first considered, shows. Interestingly, when there was an urgent need to complete a project rapidly, as with the line to connect Assam with the rest of India after Partition, the usual prevarication and delays disappeared.

The railways may have been widely criticized throughout their existence under the Raj, and they may have treated their principal source of passenger revenue, those travelling in third class, shamefully, but no one could claim they were all bad. Even Gandhi made heavy use of the railways, despite in his younger days writing a pamphlet excoriating this imperial imposition on India for breaking up its traditions and culture. The railways delivered much for India. Just as with the United States of America, they bound the country together. They allowed fast travel between one end of the country and the other, and cemented relationships between the various provinces. They enabled goods to be carried around the country far more cheaply than ever before. They allowed the development of markets in foodstuffs and other agricultural produce that increased their availability and, eventually, did make famines less likely. They created an infrastructure that in India was unprecedented in its sophistication and extent. They gave the opportunity of secure jobs to millions of Indians and enabled many of them to acquire new skills. They helped the development of the trade union movement. They laid the foundations of the large Indian middle class. They brought sophisticated technology to the subcontinent. And so much more. They were transformative in so many ways, creating the India we know today. As Theroux summarizes, 'The railway was the bloodstream of the Raj, and it affected nearly everyone. It linked the centres of population; and the cities, which until then had been identified with their temples and forts, became identified with their railway stations, Howrah with Calcutta, Victoria with Bombay, Egmore and Madras Central with Madras.'² He goes on to suggest, with some justification, that India only functions thanks to its railways.

However, as we have seen, the railways could have done so much more for India. They were, first and foremost, a colonial project designed to serve British interests, both economic and military. Sure, there were at times benign intent and a recognition of the needs of the local population, but these considerations were always secondary. The railways were an instrument of control. The stations became fortresses, the white and Eurasian staff became an auxiliary army and the tracks became lines of communication in the event of conflict. The 1857 Rebellion, coming as it did at a crucial stage in railway development, had an enormous impact on its eventual shape and the attitude of the British colonial rulers to their Indian subordinates.

This was a fantastic missed opportunity. If the British had nurtured the skills of their Indian workers and used the financial clout of the railways to stimulate the Indian economy, and if the companies had treated their third class as customers rather than as chattels, much of the antagonism towards the colonial power might have been allayed. That is not to say Independence would not have happened, as clearly decolonization was an irresistible historic force, but the horrors of Britain's rapid departure might have been avoided. And the legacy would have been so much greater.

The failure was, above all, economic. In an analysis of the impact of railways, John Hurd, concluded that India's economic development was far less than it might have been under the Raj precisely because the railways were not allowed to be the catalyst for growth that they were in so many other countries. While they undoubtedly permitted the cheaper flow of goods, stimulated increased agricultural output and created many jobs in modern industry and mining, 'these changes did not affect the basic structure of the economy. Not until Independence when economic development became a conscious and pursued policy did the railways begin to realize their potential for assisting in the transformation of the Indian economy.'3

The failure was cultural, too. Imagine if the British had allowed far greater mingling of the races on the railways; if they had consciously helped to develop a managerial class of Indians able to share the burden of running the railways with them; if they had, essentially, seen Indians as partners rather than subordinates. Who knows, there might still be a group of Europeans working on the railways today?

It is to the enormous credit of both the Indian government and its people that the railways not only survived the depredations of the postwar and post-Partition period, as well as the unseemly hasty departure of the British managers who ran the system, but quickly flourished. The railways were rightly considered a priority for the Nehru government and they have never been far from being one of the main concerns of government ever since. As Bill Aitken, an irreverent chronicler of the Indian railways, puts it, 'The genius of Indian Railways lies in its adaptation of a foreign and potentially dangerous mode of transport to suit local conditions, making a success of a vast public enterprise by fashioning it to the unique requirements of a rambling subcontinent.'4

Visitors to India are invariably shocked by what they see as a chaotic scene. The railways can give that impression, too. They are busy and crowded and seem slow. The signage in stations is random to non-existent, the ticket desks permanently assailed by desperate passengers and staffed by people for whom 'no' is the first response to any request, the staff are often indistinguishable from the masses, there is dust and dirt everywhere and more hawkers at major stations than in a Moroccan souk. The second-class coaches may look grim with their overcrowded carriages fitted with bars on every window, through which hands clutching a few rupees stretch out to the hawkers on the platforms, but they are an efficient form of mass transport no more uncomfortable than the London Underground at rush hour. In short, the system works. The seat you have reserved is available, the *dabba wallah* brings your lunch, and the train arrives on time.

It was Rajendra B. Aklekar, author and historian, who made that point most forcefully as he showed me round Mumbai's Churchgate station during the evening rush hour, while overcrowded trains departed with passengers hanging out of open doors, clutching a handle that was their only tenuous hold on staying alive: 'India functions even if it does not always look like that.' Bill Aitken, again, is right when he says, 'It is the Indianness of the Indian Railways experience that makes for its easy running and provides positive examples of the bigness of character of the Indian railwayman. Meticulous, reliable and scientific, he is everything the tourist is taught to believe the Indian is not.'[5] Precisely. European expectations are confounded every time the train leaves promptly and gets to its destination on time.

There is another unique aspect to Indian Railways. It has survived as a huge state-owned behemoth at a time when this structure for an enterprise has become unfashionable and almost wiped out by the neo-liberal onslaught, which recommends privatization, outsourcing and fragmentation. It has undoubtedly suffered from those pressures and looks to an uncertain future in the face of them. For example, its old model of manufacturing locomotives with the help of technology imported in partnership deals with foreign corporations is no longer possible, as multinational businesses are now unwilling to allow for transfer of technology. So, in future, equipment will be built in India on licence, with foreign firms retaining the knowhow, much as the British did under the Raj. Moreover, for the first time in nearly a century, the finances of Indian Railways are no longer separate, as from 2017 they have been merged into the government's overall transport budget.

The structure of Indian Railways may be old-fashioned and hark back to a different, possibly gentler, age, but it has been shown to be sufficiently resilient to have, so far, survived relatively intact. The organization has failings, but it has modernized both its infrastructure and its customer-facing functions, such as reservations and ticketing, which have been efficiently computerized. It has undergone several crises but managed to come through strengthened as a result.

This is not to be wilfully nostalgic, but merely to show that there is an alternative to the all-pervasive neoliberal model. Of course, Indian Railways is far from perfect, but then the big corporations that have built up due to globalization and marketization are hardly an example to follow universally. Corporate structures, like so much else, go in and out of fashion, and a well-run state enterprise with a public-sector ethos and a mission to serve its customers may well be an example to follow in the future.

So, in a way, a trip round India on the railways is also a journey into the past and possibly the future. This book, therefore, cannot reach its conclusion without relating some of my experiences on the railway as I travelled round the country in the winter of 2016 with my partner, Deborah Maby. It should inspire you to follow in our footsteps. It is only a taster, just the first leg between Mumbai and Kerala of a journey that took us on to Ootacamund, the hill station in Tamil Nadu, Chennai, a remote village in tribal Odisha, Kolkata and eventually Delhi.

There is only one place to start a rail tour around India: Victoria Terminus, that homage to the Victorian Gothic architecture of St Pancras, still known universally as VT even though its official name, since 1996, has been Chhatrapati Shivaji Terminus (named after a local seventeenth-century warrior king). Typically, it took Indians half a century to agree a name to replace the one originally given to the country's most famous railway station by the colonial power.

The station was the scene of a bloody and prolonged terrorist attack just eight years previously and security is maintained by a series of what look like high-tech door frames. However, no one seems to pay the slightest attention to them and, since anyone can walk in from the trackside, the whole exercise appears to be utterly pointless. It is difficult to see how it could be otherwise, as the number of security staff required to police the vast, milling crowd would be entirely impractical. On entering, the contrast with the grandeur of the outside could not be greater. We arrived at 6.30 a.m. when the station and its occupants were just beginning to wake up, but it is clear that this has been an all-nighter. We were greeted with that characteristic Indian combination of squalor and purposefulness, of haste and sluggishness, of organization and chaos. In fact, describing an Indian railway station with its hustle and bustle and seemingly endless energy is almost impossible.

There was too much to take in at such an early hour: small shops overladen with colourful displays of their wares, offices guarded by rather inattentive, corpulent uniformed men, gloomy corners and semi-abandoned areas cluttered with debris and rubbish, but, above all, people.

Carts, perilously overloaded with huge white packages, seemingly bandaged by an incompetent nurse, or with even bigger hessian sacks that seemed ready to burst, were being pushed around a huge central area to avoid running over the mass of sleeping bodies and the few early risers who were beginning to stir. They looked on impassively at the carts, the porters pushing trolleys and the bustling passengers, but most of their companions managed to continue sleeping just a few feet, or even inches, from the growing throng of those hurrying to catch trains.

It is a perfect time to observe the station; just before it gets too busy for the senses to cope. It is cool but not cold, gloomy but not dark, noisy but not loud enough to wake the countless sleepers. It is, above all, alive. Whereas travellers in the UK are generally rushing from one place to another, here time is slower and many seem content with simply waiting, perhaps because their train is not for a day or two, or perhaps because this is their refuge from the streets of the city.

While the masses of people lying under an array of multi-coloured blankets is the image that struck us most strongly when we strolled purposefully towards our train, just as the first dawn light was seeping in, that was by no means the most shocking sight. Rather, it was a seemingly banal poster stuck, oddly, at waist level on a side wall, which was probably the most gruesome vision I have ever seen in my whole life. It was a display of a series of 100 mugshots, like those for wanted criminals, but there was something odd about the images. That's because on closer examination these were close-ups of people found dead on the railway.

The pictures spared no detail. No undertakers' cosmetic skill had been employed before the harsh light of the police photographer's flash had captured the awful details of what a train, even one trundling at the slow pace that is the norm on Mumbai's busy suburban network, does when it hits a person's body. While some looked calm, even relieved, others had lost half their nose, or an eye, or even half a face, or were still covered in blood. I was told later that the poster didn't contain the worst images, as some faces are too damaged to allow for any possible identification. These unfortunate people were indeed wanted by the police, but only so that they could be identified and claimed by relatives to free up space in the overcrowded morgue.

The posters are a permanent feature of the station. There's always plenty of new faces to add to them, since the use of the railway tracks by thousands of people as thoroughfares or even living accommodation ensures a steady flow of new casualties, a staggering ten per day – or rather, even more horrendously, 3,500 per year. Only the most rookie train driver on the network will have failed to chalk up a victim, or more likely several, during their career in the cab. It is part of the routine.

In a way, those two images, the sleeping bodies and the dead ones, encapsulate the inexplicable nature of India. Superficially, that awful, almost casual, toll on the railway seems to be an illustration of everything that is wrong with this vast nation of 1.2 billion people, suggesting as it does a neglect of the fundamental tenet of civilization, cherishing human life. One could say, too, that the same applies to those people sleeping, or trying to sleep, in the middle of a busy station. But that would be wrong. In fact, they are a demonstration of the fact that the system works. They are allowed to sleep there because they cannot afford the local Ibis hotel. They will eventually wake up, board their trains and be taken to their destination safely and steadily, a tiny proportion of the 23 million people who use the railways every day. Of course, it would be better if there were ways of deterring people from walking along the tracks and reducing that awful toll, just as ideally it would be better if the station concourse were not used as a dormitory, but India simply does not work like that. The ethic is different and we Europeans have to understand that, and not judge it.

On the whole, passengers are left pretty much to their own devices. It might be expected that an organization which employs more than a million people would have a few of them at main stations solely to provide information. No chance. There are electronic displays, which are mostly reliable, but trying to find anyone official is not a simple task, made more difficult by the fact that officials do not wear uniforms – or at least ones that are clearly recognizable to inexperienced passengers.

The train information on display was confusing but fortunately we had cheated by obtaining the platform and timing from my friend Rajendra B. Aklekar, who wrote the book on the history of India's first line, which actually started from the station that stood on this spot before it was demolished to make way for the Victoria Terminus in 1878. So we didn't have to panic, as, thanks to Rajendra's information, we found our train and carriage easily. There was, in fact, only one First Class AC (air-conditioned) carriage.

Our train left on schedule at 7.10 a.m. for Madgaon Junction in Goa, where we were to take the overnight sleeper to Cochi in Kerala. It boasted the grand name of the Mandovi Express and I had expected sparkling new rolling stock, since it runs on the

Konkan Railway, a line completed as recently as 1998 and which is one of India's most scenic routes. However, our little compartment in AC designated for four was spacious but suffering badly from a lack of TLC and, in truth, really needed totally upgrading. The paintwork was shabby, the too-small windows had never seen a spot of Windolene, the light fittings were dodgy and the leather seats permanently indented by a million bums. A cockroach or two had made their home in a plastic bin in the corner. But once we had tipped up the beds, turned off the freezing AC, stowed our luggage and discovered we had the compartment to ourselves for the duration of the twelve-hour journey, it made a very cosy home and we loved it. Even though it was a day train, we got a blanket and a pillow each, as well as a towel and a little bar of soap. Deborah soon managed to make herself comfortable by turning the lower seat into a bunk-berth and wedging the pillow behind her back, so that she could read or watch the world go by. Settling into such a long journey requires a particularly relaxed state of mind. Travelling is not just about getting to the destination but about the experiences on the way. And, inevitably, on Indian trains there are lots of them.

The food and drinks were supplied by an endless stream of men – and they are all men – bustling through the train touting their wares. These are not freelances – as they were once – but employees of Indian Railways, and each one is a specialist, totally unlike his British equivalents, who are thus burdened with an almost immovable trolley. In contrast, these chaps can trot through the train only needing to carry a small tank of tea or an ice bucket with a few cans of cold drink. The first to appear was, of course, the chai *wallah*, now sadly using paper cups rather than the clay ones that used to end up as a veritable carpet over the ballast at busy stations, as they were gently and naturally recycled by the elements. The paper cups do, however, have one pleasing attribute: the lovely blue Indian Railways logo showing a stylized steam locomotive with a wisp of smoke emanating from the small chimney.

We were alerted in advance by their shouts: 'Chai-chai-chai', 'Coffee-coffee-coffee', 'sandwich-omelette-sandwich-cheese-sandwich', 'samosa-samosa'. I drank cup after cup of chai, while Deborah chose cup after cup of coffee. Both are very sweet and milky but somehow delicious and even refreshing, even though they are tiny. The *pièce de résistance* is the chap selling those round balls of syrup and sugar, *gulab jamun*, that round off every meal in India.

Settling down, the second stop was Thane, the terminus of the first railway line built in India – the twenty-mile section from central Mumbai – and now a thriving suburban station. There we were greeted by no fewer than two lots of friends: Satish, with whom I have played cricket for decades, and his delightful nephew and Rajendra, who had shown me round Mumbai's two main stations the night before. What's more, they both gave us bags of food to help us on our way and soon we were tucking into the bhajis, parathas and pooris, followed by the sweet yellow coconut delicacies that once could only be found in Euston's Drummond Street, but are now widespread in the UK. We were not going to starve on this train, unlike on the Orient Express, which we took together a decade previously in its dying days when it had no catering whatsoever.

There are no announcements or any on-train information. Therefore, without a clear idea of the intermediate stops, it can be difficult to keep track of the train's progress since they have a tendency to slip behind schedule, but often catch up in the

generous allowances made for the distance between the penul-
timate stop and the destination. Fortunately, the internet provides
detailed information of every train, but since it is not available on
most trains it is essential to print it out beforehand. We had been
forewarned. Station names are often confined to huge concrete
signs at the ends of the lengthy platforms, although bigger ones
tend to stick the names, using the purloined Underground roundel,
on any handy pillar.

The best way to experience travelling on Indian trains is sitting
in the doorway and watching the world go by. This transcends just
about every health and safety rule relating to railway practice introduced in the past 185 years, but gosh it is fun. Indian trains, on the
whole, do not go very fast – though, sadly, we found that some have
speeded up – and the doors do not have a central locking device. It
is almost expected that they are opened at will, at whatever speed
the train is running, and the rush of fresh air, even if one is in AC
class, is an immediate pleasure, not least because it dissipates the
smell of the not exactly salubrious toilets next to the gangway.

The trick, then, is to sit down, legs dangling over the steps, and
hold on tight to the handles provided to help people clamber up
and down between coach and platform. The scenery then unfolds
rather like an endless reality TV show. One minute there is the
herdsman, dressed only in a dhoti, coaxing his cows to a new
pasture, the next a group of colourfully dressed schoolchildren
waving furiously at the sight of a grey-haired Westerner sitting
precariously in the doorway above the carriage steps.

There is so much more. The countryside is varied, of course, as
it must be in a country described as a subcontinent, and there are
vistas of stunning beauty, as well as many areas where man has
wreaked havoc, but that is not the real point of interest. Rather, it

is the people, and it is rare to sit for long without seeing a few, or indeed, a few hundred. One cannot but help wonder about their lives and how they cope with what to Western eyes seems like almost impossible conditions. The little houses – huts sometimes – that border the railway may look impoverished but they are sufficient, given the benign weather conditions, to accommodate a family, because most of their time is spent outside, which allows the passing traveller to speculate on who they are and what they are doing.

There are so many questions, but no answers. Where is that old man on a rickety bicycle going? How can that fellow still ride his motorcycle when his wife is pillion, clutching a bald baby, and sitting in front of him are two children of around five and seven? Where does that red path – the dust always seems tinged with red in India – between the paddy fields lead? How does that pack of mangy dogs hanging around a dusty bit of wasteland survive? What is growing in that field where twenty women, all with scarves to protect their heads from the sun, are pulling out weeds?

There is much simply to admire. The *tuk tuks*, the auto rickshaws, which are invariably painted in black and yellow, are my favourite. These three-wheelers based on a scooter design, with a passenger seat set at right angles to the direction of travel and protected from the sun with a canvas awning, can carry three people comfortably, but I have seen six or seven squeezed in, while the driver impassively weaves his way through the traffic. They are ubiquitous as one can see them waiting at every level crossing, even in villages seemingly too impoverished to sustain a shop, and in many ways they are the lifeline of the transport system of the nation. While for Westerners the price is normally a minimum of 50 rupees (50p), the locals pay as little as 10 or 20 rupees for relatively long distances. A more accurate version of that urban myth about never being far from a rat in London is that in India there is always an auto rickshaw nearby. At the moment, there is a kind of reasonable equilibrium between the slow-running rickshaws and the potentially faster cars, whose drivers refrain from pushing them out of the way, as they know that, even if the rickshaw comes off worst, their precious paintwork will be damaged. However, more affluent Indians are contemptuous of the fragile-looking *tuk tuks*, and if cars are allowed to dominate, it will not be long before there are calls to get them off the roads. Already they are banned from posher parts of Mumbai, but, fortunately, India is a democracy and the rickshaw drivers, and their users, represent a substantial lobby.

From the steps of the train, there are other things to admire, too. This is, in many respects, a very solid, reliable and dependable system, not patched together like so much in India. There are lengthy sections of straight line, built on solid embankments, on which the trains can travel at 60 or even 80 mph with overhead electrification. (Admittedly, we were on a new line for this journey and it was relatively straight but not electrified.) The stations, too, are impressive. We stopped at twenty on our way to Madgaon, speeding through many more, and they all have platforms long enough to accommodate the twenty-five-coach trains which are standard on most main lines. There are often offices with mystifying signs, e.g. 'Electrical superintendent', and those that display homilies such as 'You can't lie to your soul', a quote from the writer Irvine Welsh.

There is, too, much to speculate on about one's fellow travellers. Most fundamentally, where are they travelling to and why? It is their fortitude that is so impressive. They do not have much, but seem not to expect much either, and tolerate the conditions with equanimity. What is the need driving them to endure these conditions and spend a considerable amount of money – the tickets may be very cheap but incomes are extremely low – to move across large swathes of the country? The trains are always full or near full, and there is a desperate need for more capacity to accommodate them, but the low fares and the costs of investing in new rolling stock prevent the easy introduction of extra services. The freight trains are the main cash cow of the railways these days.

Forget those pictures of people travelling on top and hanging out of carriages as they are not at all typical and are overused by news editors who clearly have never ventured into the subcontinent. No one travels on the roof now that there is overhead electrification and the trains are better policed for security reasons. The twenty-five coaches – most of the long-distance trains are made up of twenty-five coaches, which is the most that the platforms in many stations can accommodate – are divided into seemingly innumerable classes, stretching from First AC to Unreserved (the replacement for the old third class described in this book), with mysterious ones in between, such as Three Tier Sleeper and 'For Disabled', which looks anything but since the coach can only be reached by climbing three difficult steps. Most of the carriages are standard second class, with hard benches and only grilles instead of windows to prevent people sticking their heads out too far.

After hours of watching the scenery, which only really lived up to its reputation in the mountainous sections, we dozed, tired and jetlagged, in our cosy compartment, disturbed only by the various drink and food *wallahs*. Soon after dusk, the train arrived on time at Madgaon Junction, after a journey that had taken eleven and a half hours to cover just under 400 miles, an average of barely 35 mph. The Mandovi Express is misnamed.

Our three-hour wait on the platform was enlivened by numerous friendly locals trying to engage us in conversation, which was difficult due to the language barrier, and by the finest chai *wallahs* in India, whose little 10-rupee cups of tea were the tastiest and spiciest we drank on the whole trip. (We learnt later that Goa has the reputation of making the best chai.) We were entertained, too, by the ubiquitous dogs, who are far too scared to be threatening or even to come near people, but somehow eke out an existence from scavenging scraps, mostly on the tracks; they seem to intuitively be aware of the danger of moving trains as they shuffle slowly out of their way. We met a very cool-looking guy from Mumbai with a shaved head, a white shirt and trendy shorts, who was travelling down to Goa for a few days with his boss's son. He told us there was a direct train to Kerala and so we wondered why we had not been booked onto it. Sometimes, in India, it is not worth asking too many questions as there may, or may not, be a logical answer.

Finding the right platform for our train, without Rajendra's assistance, was not too difficult, but when the list had been stuck up outside the stationmaster's office an hour before departure, our names were not on it. We looked and looked again, and it was only when we managed to speak to a clerk, after a long wait at the ticket office, that we discovered First Class was on a different sheet, which, unaccountably, had not been displayed. Relieved, we went to find the train and our compartment. This time there were upholstered seats, but the train was grubbier and more neglected, though it proved to be more comfortable. Again, we got a blanket and a pillow each and later a man brought along two very clean starched sheets, but no soap and no towel. At the first stop, Karwar in Karnataka, a couple of silent men came into our compartment, nodded briefly at us and went straight to sleep. So did we.

When we wake up in Kerala soon after dawn, it is as if we have been transported to another land. The greenery is tropical with palm trees predominant, the people are even more numerous, but somehow seem more relaxed and less frenetic than their counterparts further north as they wait patiently at the level crossings. There are fewer cars and more *tuk tuks* and motorcycles, and little lakes and waterways are everywhere. The houses are smaller, as clearly this is a place where it never gets cold and everyone lives outside. There are different questions now: Why are some of the houses painted turquoise, pink, green or purple while other equally garish colours seem to have been eschewed? How come the people in one area are so dark, blacker than their African counterparts, and yet in the next village they are far lighter? Then there is the real unanswerable: Are the cows sufficiently grateful to the elegant egrets that sit on their backs to gorge on the parasites that they try to swat ineffectively away with their tails?

The train stops for ten minutes at Shoranur Junction, where the chai *wallah* is doing good business and his little cups are even cheaper, just 7 rupees. They are not quite as spicy as those in Goa but they do the trick, as does a doughy pastry I buy off another busy seller. The air is damp and misty with the slightest hint of a breeze, warm but not yet stifling. The new day, lit by the watery sun, seems full of potential, life and vigour. There is nowhere else I would want to be.

As we trundle towards our destination, Ernakulam Junction (there are many stations with 'Junction' or 'Road' in their names, usually because they are distant from the place after which they are named as a result of the British policy of keeping costs down and therefore not running into the centre of towns and avoiding fording rivers as much as possible), the attendant puts our blanket and pillow back on the bunks for the next passengers, so they probably weren't clean. He also says, 'My tip, please', which he hardly deserves since he has done so little, but his earnings must be pitiful compared to ours, so I slip him a few rupees. Then a guy in a suit and tie comes in bearing a clipboard. He asks whether the cleaning was good and we say yes. We sign a big green form and he bids us goodbye. We leave the train and follow the throng. There are only another ten train journeys to go. Not enough.

SELECT BIBLIOGRAPHY

THIS IS A limited bibliography of books I have used as sources or read in the course of writing this book and therefore is by no means comprehensive. It might, though, provide a few suggestions on 'what to read next'. I have confined myself to books on the railways, leaving out the wider history books I used.

As mentioned in the introduction, there are not as many books on Indian railways as the subject deserves. There is certainly plenty of scope for more. The most prolific academic writer on the topic is Ian J. Kerr, a Canadian historian, who has written or edited several excellent books on the Indian railways. His *Engines of Change: The Railroads That Made India* (Praeger, 2007) is an outstanding short account, well-described by the subtitle, and his *Building the Railways of the Raj 1850–1900* (Oxford University Press, 1995) is also aptly titled. He also edited two volumes of papers which proved very useful, the oddly named *27 Down: New Departures in Indian Railway Studies* (Orient Longman, 2007), which comes complete with a CD featuring extra material, and *Railways in Modern India* (Oxford University Press, 2001). Another compilation that had several useful articles is *Our Indian Railway: Themes in India's Railway History* (Foundation Books for the Ministry of Railways, 2006), edited by Roopa Srinivasan, Manish Tiwari and Sandeep Silas.

A rare general book, useful but dated, is *Railways of India* (David & Charles, 1974) by J. N. Westwood. *Railways of the Raj* (Scolar Press, 1980) is one of the few useful picture books which mostly contain only captioned photographs as it has a couple of chapters on history and, best of all, an elegant foreword by Paul Theroux.

There are a couple of general histories of the railways written by Indians commissioned by the Ministry of Railways. In 1953, to mark the 100th anniversary, the ministry published J. N. Sahni's *Indian Railways: One Hundred Years, 1853–1953* (Ministry of Railways, 1953), which frustratingly lacks a lot of detail and is fairly hagiographic, and thirty-five years later the much more informative and detailed *A History of Indian Railways*, by G. S. Khosla. Another rather uncritical effort is *150 Glorious Years of Indian Railways* (English Edition Publishers, 2003), by K. R. Vaidyanathan.

M. A. Rao's short account, *Indian Railways* (India Book Trust, 1999), first published in 1975 but updated in 1999, is slightly more objective, though still coloured by the fact it is written by a former general manager of the railways. Bill Aitken's *Exploring Indian Railways* (Oxford University Press, 1994) is a rather acerbic and self-indulgent account of the history and current state of the railways but has a few excellent insights and descriptions.

Two books that look at the wider impact of the railways are Laura Bear's *Lines of the Nation: Indian Railway Workers, Bureaucracy and the Intimate Historical Self* (Columbia University Press, 2007), which is somewhat academic but very well-researched, and Rikita Prasad's *Tracks of Change: Railways and Everyday Life in Colonial India* (Cambridge University Press, 2015), which details many aspects of travelling on the railways in the nineteenth and early twentieth centuries.

Again, the long subtitle of Sarah Searight's *Steaming East: The Hundred-Year Saga of the Struggle to Forge Rail and Steamship Links between Europe and India* (The Bodley Head, 1991) is an accurate description of an interesting account of how hard it was to reach

India even in the steamship age. Rajendra B. Aklekar, in *Halt Station India: The Dramatic Tale of the Nation's First Rail Lines* (Rupa Publications, 2014), describes the building of India's first railway, between Mumbai and Thane, and he brings it to life by walking along the route, finding small relics of the original line.

There are all too few books covering the history of particular lines or regions. One of the best is Sarah Hilaly's *The Railways of Assam* (Pilgrims Publishing, 2007), which sets out in context the building of the railways in that remote part of India. R. R. Bhandari's *Western Railway: A Glorious Saga* (Western Railway, 2008) is a typical PR exercise as its title implies with a few useful facts. *Couplings to the Khyber* (David & Charles, 1969) is a remarkable first-hand account of building the lines in the North-West Frontier by their chief engineer, P. S. A. Berridge.

Hill-station railways have attracted a disproportionate amount of interest and are covered in numerous books, such as Bob Cable's *Darjeeling Revisited: A Journey on the Darjeeling Himalayan Railway* (Middleton Press, 2001) and V. M. Govind Krishnan's *Nilgiri Mountain Railway: From Lifeline to Oblivion* (Star Publications, 2012), a slightly chaotic but detailed account.

Of the books covering the modern era, the best is *Bankruptcy to Billions: How the Indian Railways Transformed* (Oxford University Press, 2009) by Sudhir Kumar and Shagun Mehrotra, a rather rose-tinted view of how the economics of Indian Railways were turned around in the mid-2000s.

The best travelogue-type book I came across was Monisha Rajesh's *Around India in 80 Trains* (Nicholas Brealey Publishing, 2012), and I also enjoyed Peter Riordan's *Strangers in My Sleeper: Rail Journeys and Encounters on the Indian Subcontinent* (New Holland, 2006).

In researching a book like this, one comes across wonderful curios that are deserving of a wider audience. Two of the best are *Bengal Engineer* (Pentland Press, 1994), a series of letters by an engineer working on India railways from the mid-nineteenth century, edited by Peter Vaux, the man's great-grandson, and S. T. Hollins, *No Ten Commandments* (Arrow Books, 1958), which only has a couple of chapters on the railway but is a remarkable and well-written account of police work throughout the last forty years of the Raj. I also came across John Thomas's *Line of Communication: Railway to Victory in the East* (Locomotive Publishing Company, 1947), a pamphlet about the role of the railways in the war on India's eastern front.

I have copies of most of these books if you are unable to trace them: do email me via the website www.christianwolmar.co.uk.

REFERENCES

1. A RAILWAY FOR INDIA

1   Quoted in Rajendra B. Aklekar, *Halt Station India: The Dramatic Tale of the Nation's First Rail Lines*, Rupa Publications, 2014, p. 23.

2   Quoted in G. H. Khosla, *A History of Indian Railways*, Ministry of Railways, 1988.

3   David Thorner, 'The Pattern of Railway Development in India', in Ian J. Kerr (ed.), *Railways in Modern India*, Oxford University Press, 2001, p. 81.

4   Ibid.

5   From Lord Dalhousie's minute, quoted in W. J. Macpherson, 'Investment in Indian Railways, 1845–1875', *Economic History Review*, December 1955, p. 177.

6   Quoted in Macpherson, 'Investment in Indian Railways', p. 177.

7   John Keay, *India: From the Earliest Civilisations to the Boom of the Twenty-First Century*, Harper Press, 2010, p. 424.

8   Ian J. Kerr, *Engines of Change: The Railroads That Made India*, Praeger, 2007, p. 18.

9   Ibid.

10 Ian J. Kerr, *Building the Railways of the Raj,* Oxford University Press, 1995, p. 18.

11 Macpherson, 'Investment in Indian Railways', p. 181.

12 Aklekar, *Halt Station India*, p. 22.

13 Ibid., p. 9.

14 Quoted in Kerr, *Building the Railways of the Raj*, p. 32.

15 Ibid.

16 All quoted in S. N. Sharma, *History of the Great Indian Peninsula Railway (1853–1869)*, vol. 1, Nirav Enterprise, 1990, p. 6.

17 Aklekar, *Halt Station India*, p. 12.

18 Ibid., p. 29.

19 Ibid.

20 *Overland Telegraph and Courier*, 16 April 1853.
21 *Illustrated London News*, 4 June 1853.
22 Quoted in Sharma, *History of the Great Indian Peninsula Railway*, vol. 1, p. 10.
23 Kerr, *Building the Railways of the Raj*, p. 29.
24 J. N. Westwood, *Railways of India*, David & Charles, 1974, p. 16.

2. BUILDING FOR INDIA

1   J. N. Westwood, *Railways of India*, David & Charles, 1974, p. 25.
2   Ian J. Kerr, *Building the Railways of the Raj*, Oxford University Press, 1995, p. 21.
3   Ibid.
4   Ibid., p. 25.
5   Ian J. Kerr, 'The Building of the Bhor Ghat Railway Incline in Western India in the mid-19th Century', in *Railroads in Historical Context: Construction, Costs and Consequences*, University of Minho, 2012, p. 345.
6   Quoted in S. N. Sharma, *History of the Great Indian Peninsula Railway (1853–1869)*, vol. 1, Nirav Enterprise, 1990, p. 66.
7   Ian J. Kerr, *Engines of Change: The Railroads That Made India*, Praeger, 2007, p. 42.
8   Kerr, 'The Building of the Bhor Ghat Railway Incline', p. 353.
9   Quoted in Anthony Burton, *The Railway Empire*, John Murray, 1994, p. 152.
10 Kerr, *Engines of Change*, p. 42.
11 As described by his partner on the contract; quoted in Kerr, *Building the Railways of the Raj*, p. 56.
12 Quoted in Kerr, *Engines of Change*, p. 45.
13 Burton, *The Railway Empire*, p. 152.
14 Ibid.
15 Ibid., p. 154.
16 Edward Davidson, *The Railways of India*, 1868, reprinted by Kessinger Legacy Reprints, p. 105.
17 Burton, *The Railway Empire*, p. 155.
18 Based on the diaries of Thomas Hardinge, quoted in Kerr, *Engines of Change*, p. 53.

19 Kerr, *Engines of Change*, p. 45.
20 The speech is reproduced in full in Ian J. Kerr (ed.), *Railways in Modern India*, Oxford University Press, 2001, pp. 68–79.
21 Kerr, *Engines of Change*, p. 49.
22 G. S. Khosla, *A History of Indian Railways*, Ministry of Railways, p. 28.
23 *Civil and Military Gazette*, 2 March 1887.
24 Kerr, *Engines of Change*, p. 48.
25 Ian J. Kerr, 'The Dark Side of the Force: Mistakes, Mismanagement and Malfeasance in the Early Railways of the British Indian Empire', in Roopa Srinivasan, Manish Tiwari and Sandeep Silas (eds.), *Our Indian Railway: Themes in India's Railway History*, Foundation Books, 2006, p. 189.
26 See numerous such tales in my previous book, *The Great Railway Revolution: The Epic Story of the American Railroad*, Atlantic Books, 2013.
27 Kerr, 'The Dark Side of the Force', p. 188.
28 Westwood, *Railways of India*, p. 39.
29 Davidson, *The Railways of India*, p. 373.
30 Westwood, *Railways of India*, p. 39.
31 Burton, *The Railway Empire*, p. 144.
32 Kerr, *Building the Railways of the Raj*, p. 37.
33 Ibid.

3. CONTROLLING THE RAILWAYS

1 John Hurd, 'A huge railway system but no sustained economic development: the company perspective, 1884–1939: some hypotheses', in Ian J. Kerr (ed.), *27 Down: New Departures in Indian Railway Studies*, Orient Longman, p. 317.
2 Ibid.
3 Ian J. Kerr, *Building the Railways of the Raj*, Oxford University Press, 1995, p. 59.
4 Unnamed biographer quoted in ibid., p. 61.
5 Quoted in M. A. Rao, *Indian Railways*, National Book Trust, India, 1975, p. 23.
6 Edward Davidson, *The Railways of India*, 1868, reprinted by Kessinger Legacy Reprints, p. 102.

7   Kerr, *Building the Railways of the Raj*, p. 216.

8   Ibid., p. 107.

9   Davidson, *The Railways of India*, p. 101.

10   Daniel Thorner, 'The pattern of railway development in India', in Ian J. Kerr, *Railways in Modern India*, Oxford University Press, 2001, p. 85.

11   Ibid.

12   *Indian Railways*, p. 23.

13   G. S. Khosla, *A History of Indian Railways*, Ministry of Railways, 1988, p. 82.

14   Quoted in J. N. Westwood, *Railways of India*, David & Charles, 1974, p. 43.

15   Quoted in Ian J. Kerr, *Engines of Change: The Railroads That Made India*, Praeger, 2007, p. 75.

16   Khosla, *A History of Indian Railways*, p. 95.

17   Jim Corbett, *My India*, Oxford India Paperbacks, 1952.

4. STARVING OFF THE LINE AND FIGHTING ON IT

1   The area then known as Bengal included land that now forms parts of several other states, such as Bihar and Odisha.

2   Report of the Indian Famine Commission, 1880, cmd number 2591.

3   G. S. Khosla, *A History of Indian Railways*, Ministry of Railways, 1988, p. 116.

4   Daniel Thorner, 'The pattern of railway development in India', in Ian J. Kerr, *Railways in Modern India*, Oxford University Press, 2001, p. 86.

5   Khosla, *A History of Indian Railways*, p. 113.

6   Stuart Sweeney, 'Indian Railways and Famine, 1875–1914', *Essays in Economic & Business History*, vol. XXVI, 2008, p. 151.

7   Khosla, *A History of Indian Railways*, p. 117.

8   John Harrison, 'The Records of Indian Railways: A Neglected Resource', in Kerr, *Railways in Modern India*, p. 201.

9   Both quoted in Hareet Kumar Meena, 'Famine in Late 19th Century Natural or Man Made', *Journal of Human and Social Research*, vol. 06 (01), 2014, p. 37.

10   Sweeney, 'Indian Railways and Famine', p. 151.

11   Ibid., p. 153.

12 Sarah Hilaly, *The Railways in Assam, 1885–1947*, Pilgrims Publishing, 2007, p. 114.

13 Ibid., p. 146.

14 Ibid., p. 284.

15 Sweeney, 'Indian Railways and Famine', p. 152.

16 Laura Bear, *Lines of the Nation: Indian Railway Workers, Bureaucracy and the Intimate Historical Self'*, Columbia University Press, 2007, p. 26.

17 Ibid., p. 26.

18 J. N. Sahni, *Indian Railways: One Hundred Years, 1853–1953*, Ministry of Railways, 1953.

19 Iris Wedgwood, 'Travels in India', *Railway Gazette*, 24 November 1937, p. 12–3.

20 John Hurd, 'Railways', in Kerr, *Railways in Modern India*, p. 149.

21 J. N. Westwood, *Railways of India*, David & Charles, 1974, p. 55.

5. LIFE ON THE LINES

1 Ritika Prasad, *Tracks of Change: Railways and Everyday Life in Colonial India*, Cambridge University Press, 2015, p. 5.

2 Ibid., p. 23.

3 Ian J. Kerr, *Engines of Change: The Railroads That Made India*, Praeger, 2007, p. 89.

4 Ibid.

5 Prasad, *Tracks of Change*, p. 28.

6 Laura Bear, *Lines of the Nation: Indian Railway Workers, Bureaucracy and the Intimate Historical Self*, Columbia University Press, 2007, p. 46.

7 Mark Twain, *Following the Equator and Anti-Imperialist Essays* (1897), Oxford University Press, 1996, p. 405.

8 Ibid, p. 404.

9 Quoted in Prasad, *Tracks of Change*, p. 30.

10 Ibid.

11 Ibid., p. 32.

12 Ibid., p. 36.

13 Ibid., p. 37.

14 Quoted in ibid., p. 38.

15 Ibid., p. 39.

16 Consulting Engineer for Railways, Bombay Government, letter of 18 July 1884, quoted in Prasad, *Tracks of Change*, p. 40.

17 The following quotations are all from Curzon, Viceroy of India 1898–1905: Official Printed Material on India; copies of Official Papers 1899–1906.

18 J. N. Westwood, *Railways of India*, David & Charles, 1974, p. 79.

19 Bear, *Lines of the Nation*, pp. 47–9.

20 Quoted in Prasad, *Tracks of Change*, p. 72.

21 Bear, *Lines of the Nation*, p. 47.

22 Quotations by William Muir, Lieutenant-Governor of North-Western Provinces, minute of 17 July 1869.

23 Bear, *Lines of the Nation*, p. 50.

24 Prasad, *Tracks of Change*, p. 78.

25 From a 1918 report on the Madras & Southern Mahratta Railway by E. S. Christie, quoted in Prasad, *Tracks of Change*, p. 81.

26 From internal East Indian papers, quoted in Prasad, *Tracks of Change*, p. 79.

6. WORKING ON THE LINE

1 Laura Bear, *Lines of the Nation: Indian Railway Workers, Bureaucracy and the Intimate Historical Self*, Columbia University Press, 2007, p. 65.

2 Ibid., p. 66.

3 Ian J. Kerr, *Engines of Change: The Railroads That Made India*, Praeger, 2007, p. 82.

4 Ian Derbyshire, 'Private and State Enterprise', in *27 Down: New Departures in Indian Railway Studies*, Orient Longman, 2007, p. 302.

5 Bear, *Lines of the Nation*, p. 66.

6 Ibid., p. 67.

7 Ibid., p. 69.

8 Ibid., p. 42.

9 David A. Campion, 'Railway Policing and Security in Colonial India, c 1860–1930', in Roopa Srinivasan, Manish Tiwari and Sandeep Silas (eds.), *Our Indian Railway: Themes in India's Railway History*, Foundation Books, 2006, p. 138.

10 Ibid., p. 138.

11 'Sanitary Conditions of Railway Stations in Bengal and Punjab: Report of Committee Appointed by His Honour the Lieutenant Governor of Bengal', *India Proceedings: Public Works Department, Railways*, July 1865, nos. 49–56.

12 Quoted in Bear, *Lines of the Nation*, p. 72.

13 Rudyard Kipling, *Among the Railway Folk*, 1888, available online at https://ebooks.adelaide.edu.au/k/kipling/rudyard/railway/chapter1.html.

14 *Railway Gazette*, 28 May 1913, p. 85.

15 Colonel A. A. Phillips, 'Armoured Trains in India', *Royal United Services Institution Journal*, vol. 113, p. 254.

16 Ian J. Kerr, 'Railway Workshops and Their Labour', in *27 Down: New Departures in Indian Railway Studies*, Orient Longman, 2007, p. 249.

17 Indian Industrial Commission, 1916–18, *Inspection Notes*, quoted in Kerr, 'Railway Workshops and Their Labour', p. 237.

18 Kipling, *Among the Railway Folk*.

19 Ibid.

20 Quoted in Kerr, *Engines of Change*, p. 53.

21 Ian Derbyshire, 'The Building of India's Railways', in Ian J. Kerr, *Railways in Modern India*, Oxford University Press, 2001, p. 301.

22 Ibid., p. 301.

23 Mark Tully, 'A View of the History of Indian Railways', in Srinivasan, Tiwari and Silas (eds.), p. 235.

24 John Hurd in Dharma Kumar and Meghnad Desai (eds.), *The Cambridge Economic History of India*, vol. 2, *c.1751–c.1970*, Cambridge University Press, 1983, p. 751.

25 J. N. Sahni, *Indian Railways: One Hundred Years, 1853–1953*, Ministry of Railways, 1953, p. 102.

26 Bear, *Lines of the Nation*, p. 82.

27 Ibid.

28 Kerr, 'Railway Workshops and Their Labour', p. 261.

29 Bear, *Lines of the Nation*, p. 94.

30 Derbyshire, 'Private and State Enterprise', p. 303.

31 Bear, *Lines of the Nation*, p. 96.

7. NOT ALWAYS LOVED

1   J. N. Westwood, *Railways of India*, David & Charles, 1974, p. 57.

2   Visalakshi Menon and Sucheta Mahajan, 'Indian Nationalism and Railways', in Roopa Srinivasan, Manish Tiwari and Sandeep Silas (eds.), *Our Indian Railway: Themes in Indian Railway History*, Foundation Books, 2006, p. 155.

3   Quoted in Bipan Chandra, 'Economic Nationalism and the Railway Debate, circa 1850–1905', in Srinivasan, Tiwari and Silas (eds.), *Our Indian Railway*, p. 87.

4   Quoted in Chandra, 'Economic Nationalism and the Railway Debate', in Srinivasan, Tiwari and Silas (eds.), *Our Indian Railway*, p. 111.

5   Quoted in ibid., p. 115.

6   Ritika Prasad, *Tracks of Change: Railways and Everyday Life in Colonial India*, Cambridge University Press, 2015, p. 107.

7   Quoted in ibid., p. 109.

8   M. Saha, 'The Great Flood in Northern Bengal', *Modern Review*, vol. 32, 1922, p. 605. From *Collected Works of Meghnad Saha*, ed. Santimay Chatterjee, Orient Longman, 1987.

9   Quoted in Amitabha Bhattacharyya, 'Meghnad Saha's Paradoxical Story: Railways and the 1922 North Bengal Floods', CSSP Electronic Working Paper Series, Paper No. 6, September 2015, p. 6 (available online).

10   *Railway Gazette*, 17 September 1923, p. 6.

11   Prasad, *Tracks of Change*, p. 101.

12   Ibid., p. 48.

13   Ibid., p. 196.

14   M. C. Furnell, *From Madras to Delhi and Back to Bombay*, C. Foster and Co., 1874, p. 124, quoted in Ian J. Kerr, 'Reworking a Popular Religious Practice: The Effects of Railways on Pilgrimage in 19th and 20th Century South Asia', in Ian J. Kerr, *Railways in Modern India*, Oxford University Press, 2001, p. 317.

15   Quoted in Prasad, *Tracks of Change*, p. 66.

16   Kerr, 'Reworking a Popular Religious Practice', p. 326. Cook is rather wrongly credited with having invented the railway excursion when, in fact, there were many such excursions long before he famously first carried passengers on a temperance trip in 1841.

17 Ibid., p. 325.

18 Ibid., p. 320.

19 Mark Harrison, *Public Health in British India: Anglo-Indian Preventative medicine 1859–1914*, Cambridge University Press, 1994, p. 97.

20 *Report on Sanitary Measures in India 1875–6; with miscellaneous Information up to June 1877*, vol. IX, Eyre & Spottiswoode, 1877, p. 56.

21 Prasad, *Tracks of Change*, p. 179.

22 Harrison, *Public Health in British India*, p. 97.

23 Told in Ian J. Kerr, *Engines of Change: The Railroads That Made India*, Praeger, 2007, p. 96.

24 M. K. Gandhi, *Hind Swaraj*, Navajivan Publishing House, 1909, reprinted 1938, p. 41 (available online).

25 Ibid.

26 Ibid., p. 42.

27 Ibid., p. 41.

28 All these quotes from *Letter written by Gandhiji on third class travelling on Indian Railways*, http://mkgandhimanibhavan.blogspot.co.uk/2011/02/letter-written-by-gandhiji-on-third.html

29 Ibid.

30 Ibid.

8. ESTABLISHMENT OF THE RAILWAY

1   *Railway Gazette*, 28 May 1913, p. 4.

2   Ibid.

3   Ibid.

4   Ibid., 17 September 1923, p. 106.

5   Ibid., p. 106.

6   J. N. Westwood, *Railways of India*, David & Charles, 1974, p. 73.

7   *Railway Gazette*, 28 May 1913, p. 5.

8   Ibid.

9   Ibid, p. 4.

10 Ibid., p. 5.

11 Ibid., p. 12.

12 Quoted in J. N. Sahni, *Indian Railways: One Hundred Years, 1853–1953*, Ministry of Railways, 1953, p. 25.

13 Ian J. Kerr, *Engines of Change: The Railroads That Made India*, Praeger, 2007, p. 124.

14 Sahni, *Indian Railways*, pp. 25–6.

15 Ibid., p. 26.

16 Westwood, *Railways of India*, p. 62.

17 Ibid., p. 64.

18 Often known simply as the Indian Railway Committee.

19 Sahni, *Indian Railways*, p. 28.

20 Quotations from Minute in Sahni, *Indian Railways*, p. 28.

21 Quoted in Sahni, *Indian Railways*, p. 32.

22 *Railway Gazette*, 17 September 1923, p. 2.

23 Ibid., p. 85.

24 Interestingly, at the time of writing in summer 2016, the Indian government announced that a *third* route between these two towns would be built, as the existing two were full, at a cost of 2,000 crore rupees, about £200m.

25 Kerr, *Engines of Change*, p. 127.

26 *Railway Gazette*, 17 September 1923, p. 4.

27 Rahul Mehrotra and Sharada Dwivedi, *A City Icon: Victoria Terminus Bombay 1887 Now Chhatrapati Shivaji Terminus Mumbai 1996*, Eminence Designs, 2006, p. 250.

28 845 out of 2,765.

29 *Railway Gazette*, 11 November 1929, p. 2.

30 Ibid.

31 Quoted in Sahni, *Indian Railways*, p. 37.

32 *Railway Gazette*, 28 May 1913, p. 2.

33 G. S. Khosla, *A History of Indian Railways*, Ministry of Railways, 1988, p. 338.

34 Sahni, *Indian Railways*, p. 123.

35 David A. Campion, 'Railway Policing and Security in Colonial India', in Roopa Srinivasan, Manish Tiwari and Sandeep Silas (eds.), *Our Indian Railway: Themes in India's Railway History*, Foundation Books, 2006, p. 149.

36 Stuart Sweeney, *Financing India's Imperial Railways, 1875–1914*, Pickering and Chatto, 2011, p. 89. The direct quotation from the report is in double quotation marks.

37 P. S. A. Berridge, *Couplings to the Khyber: The Story of the North Western Railway*, David & Charles, 1969, p. 228.

38 Ibid., p. 229.

39 Ibid., p. 244.

40 Ibid.

41 Ibid., pp. 241–2.

9. TOWARDS INDEPENDENCE

1 John Hurd, 'The Company Perspective', in Ian J. Kerr (ed.), *27 Down: New Departures in Indian Railway Studies*, Orient Longman, 2007, p. 340.

2 Terms of reference quoted in J. N. Sahni, *Indian Railways: One Hundred Years, 1853–1953*, Ministry of Railways, 1953, p. 38.

3 Quoted in Sahni, *Indian Railways*, pp. 37–8.

4 Iris Wedgwood, *Railway Gazette*, 24 November 1937, pp. 12–13.

5 Hurd, 'The Company Perspective', p. 346.

6 *Railway Gazette*, 24 November 1937, p. 22.

7 Ibid., p. 15.

8 Jawaharlal Nehru, *Selected Works*, vol. 7, Oxford University Press, 1989, p. 326.

9 David A. Campion, 'Railway Policing and Security in Colonial India', in Roopa Srinivasan, Manish Tiwari and Sandeep Silas (eds.), *Our Indian Railway: Themes in India's Railway History*, Foundation Books, 2006, p. 144.

10 Ibid.

11 Ritika Prasad, *Tracks of Change: Railways and Everyday Life in Colonial India*, Cambridge University Press, 2015, p. 235.

12 Campion, 'Railway Policing and Security in Colonial India', p. 145.

13 *Railway Gazette*, 29 November 1939, p. 40.

14 Visalakshi Menon and Sacheta Mahajan, 'Indian Nationalism and Railways', in Srinivasan, Tiwari and Silas (eds.), *Our Indian Railway*, p. 168.

15 John Thomas, *Line of Communication: Railway to Victory in the East*, Locomotive Publishing Company, 1947, p. 64.

16 Ibid.

17 Ibid., p. 8.
18 Ibid., p. 15.
19 Ibid., p. 17.
20 Ibid., p. 8.
21 G. S. Khosla, *A History of Indian Railways*, Ministry of Railways, 1988, p. 192.
22 William Dalrymple, 'The Great Divide', *New Yorker*, 29 June 2015.
23 Nisid Hajari, *Midnight's Furies: The Deadly Legacy of India's Partition*, Amberley Publishing, 2015, p. xviii.
24 Ibid., p. 167.
25 Ibid., p. 141.
26 http://www.sikhiwiki.org/index.php/THE_KAMOKE_MASSACRE
27 Ian J. Kerr, *Engines of Change: The Railroads That Made India*, Praeger, 2007, p. 134.

10. INDIAN AT LAST

1   Bill Aitken, *Exploring Indian Railways*, Oxford University Press, 1994, p. 246.
2   Quoted in J. N. Sahni, *Indian Railways: One Hundred Years, 1853–1953*, Ministry of Railways, 1953, p. 160.
3   Ibid., p. 172.
4   M. A. Rao, *Indian Railways*, 3rd edn, National Book Trust, 1999, p. 183.
5   Ian J. Kerr, *Engines of Change: The Railroads That Made India*, Praeger, 2007, p. 166.
6   J. N. Westwood, *Railways of India*, David & Charles, 1974, p. 140.
7   S. T. Hollins, *No Ten Commandments*, Arrow Books, 1958 (originally published 1954), p. 207.
8   Westwood, *Railways of India*, p 141.
9   David A. Campion, 'Railway Policing and Security in Colonial India', in Roopa Srinivasan, Manish Tiwari and Sandeep Silas (eds.), *Our Indian Railway: Themes in India's Railway History*, Foundation Books, 2006, p. 151.
10 Aitken, *Exploring Indian Railways*, p. 237.
11 G. S. Khosla, *A History of Indian Railways*, Ministry of Railways, 1988, p. 361.

12 Laura Bear, *Lines of the Nation: Indian Railway Workers, Bureaucracy and the Intimate Historical Self*, Columbia University Press, 2007, p. 235.

13 Mark Tully, 'A View of the History of Indian Railways', in Srinivasan, Tiwari and Silas (eds.), *Our Indian Railway*, p. 239.

14 Sudhir Kumar and Shagun Mehrotra, *Bankruptcy to Billions: How the Indian Railways Transformed*, Oxford University Press, 2009, p. 37.

15 Expert Group on Indian Railways New Delhi, *The Indian Railways Report 2001: Policy Imperatives for Reinvention and Growth*, Volume 1: *Executive Summary*, National Council of Applied Economic Research, 2001, p. 6.

16 Kumar and Mehrotra, *Bankruptcy to Billions*, p. 41.

11 ... AND TODAY

1 Preface by Paul Theroux, in Michael Satow and Ray Desmond, *Railways of the Raj*, Scolar Press, 1980, p. 6.

2 Ibid., p. 5.

3 John Hurd, 'Railways', in Ian J. Kerr, *Railways in Modern India*, Oxford University Press, 2001, p. 172.

4 Bill Aitken, *Exploring Indian Railways*, Oxford University Press, 1994, p. 246.

5 Ibid.

INDEX